P. 137   250   258-9   724-28, 189 , 114 111 ,107-13
       93 -)   173-) , 65 -)

(Van der If ~ 155-6.)

Warelmaker -cf.   125 -)

(51)

KU-084-406

CHRIST'S COLLEGE
LIBRARY

READING FOR MEANING

*A Schools Council survey of recent research
into the reading responses of children from
the pre-reading to the post-sixth form stage,
and of the methods by which reading is 'taught'
in our infant, primary and secondary schools*

RESEARCH REPORTS FROM
THE SCHOOLS COUNCIL

Enquiry 1: Young School Leavers. A report of a survey among young people, parents and teachers carried out for the Schools Council by the Government Social Survey. (HMSO, 1968)

i.t.a.: An Independent Evaluation by F. W. Warburton and Vera Southgate. The report of a study carried out for the Schools Council on the use of the initial teaching alphabet as a medium for beginning reading with infants. (John Murray/W. & R. Chambers, 1969)

i.t.a.: What is the Evidence? by Vera Southgate. This short digest presents a selection of those findings of general interest to parents and teachers. (John Murray/W. & R. Chambers, 1970)

Schools Council Sixth Form Survey (three volumes). A report of a survey carried out for the Schools Council by the Government Social Survey. (Councils and Education Press for Books for Schools, 1970 and 1971)

The Universities and the Sixth Form Curriculum by W. A. Reid. A first report from the Schools Council Sixth Form Curriculum and Examinations Project at the University of Birmingham. (Macmillan Education, 1972)

Entry and Performance at Oxford and Cambridge, 1966–71 by Sir Desmond Lee. The report of a study carried out for the Schools Council on sixth form curricula and the academic requirements of Oxford and Cambridge. (Macmillan Education, 1972)

Paths to University: Preparation, Assessment, Selection by A. G. Hearnden. (Macmillan Education, 1973)

PAT D'ARCY

Reading for Meaning

VOLUME 1

Learning to Read

HUTCHINSON EDUCATIONAL

FOR THE SCHOOLS COUNCIL

HUTCHINSON EDUCATIONAL LTD

3 Fitzroy Square, London W 1

London Melbourne Sydney
Auckland Johannesburg Cape Town
and agencies throughout the world

First published 1973

CHRIST'S COLLEGE
LIBRARY

Access on. 39337

Class o. 372.36

Catal.

© Schools Council Publications 1973

This book has been set in Bembo type, printed in Great Britain
by Alden & Mowbray Ltd at the Alden Press, Oxford
and bound by William Brendon, Tiptree, Essex

ISBN 0 09 114930 4

Contents

Foreword

I should like to make it clear at the outset that this book was intended from its inception to be of use chiefly to practising teachers who may not have the time or the facilities to acquaint themselves at first hand with the increasingly numerous accounts of research projects concerned with the teaching of reading. *Reading for Meaning* makes no claim to be a comprehensive survey of such research—it would have taken a whole team of full-time research assistants many months to produce such a bibliography, as Roland Harris, a Senior Research Officer for the Schools Council, pointed out in an article published in the *NATE Bulletin* in March 1967. My survey is intended to be more of a sketch map than an ordnance survey—an attempt to mark out main roads and important signposts in the child's reading development during the time he spends in school.

I was invited by the Schools Council to undertake such a review because I was myself an English teacher, familiar with some of the problems that all teachers have to face inside their own classrooms (open or closed). I am certainly not an expert in the teaching of every aspect of reading to which I refer in my book, and my lack of experience may be patently obvious to those who do specialise in certain fields. If, however, any clash of opinion encourages such readers to restate or to reclarify their own beliefs about reading response, so much the better. I use the word 'beliefs' deliberately, because there is so much still that we do not know about the nature of a child's response to the written language. To assume, for instance, that the phrase 'reading age' has any kind of factual reality about it is to make a dubious and perhaps very misleading assumption.

My chief concern has been to provide some information about major research investigations (most of them conducted over the past decade) relevant to reading activities in school; to sketch in a spectrum of aims and opinions about the teaching of reading within which practising teachers might find—and possibly reconsider—their own position; and, most important of all, to raise many questions to which as yet there are no firm answers, but which we cannot ignore for that reason. Can reading skills be isolated and trained separately? Which factors are crucial in a child's experience if he is to break the code of the written language successfully at an early age? What exactly do we mean by 'reading comprehension'? And so on.

My own beliefs about what is worth preserving in our present system, and what is not, emerge quite clearly in the survey and I make no apology for this because one of those beliefs happens to be that it is essential for a teacher to commit himself to methods and materials that he personally considers to be of some value. I accept readily that many teachers, for this reason, will disagree with my preferences, but if *Reading for Meaning* helps to raise crucial questions which can be discussed by teachers across the school system with the result that they become more aware of what they actually are achieving—and what they are trying to achieve—it will, with all its defects, have been worth writing.

Acknowledgements

I should like to acknowledge with gratitude the help of my initial Steering Committee, Dr W. D. Wall, Miss Kay Burton and Miss Margaret Berry, who gave me every encouragement to find my own mode of approach, and who, when I had found it, took the trouble to read and to comment constructively about what in the end turned out to be a fairly extensive piece of work. I am also much indebted to Mrs Pauline Newton and to Mrs Margaret Barnard who coped respectively with the first and second drafts of the manuscript, to my husband, John D'Arcy, who looked after the children on many occasions so that I could work, and finally, to Professor James Britton, who persuaded me to make the attempt in the first place and who encouraged me to persist with it until the final word!

The Author, the Schools Council and Hutchinson Educational are grateful to the following for their permission to reproduce copyright material: Cassell & Co Ltd: 'Words in Colour' by Joan Dean from *The Second International Reading Symposium*; 'Are today's teachers adequately trained for the teaching of reading?' by W. Latham from *The Third International Reading Symposium*; Ginn & Co Ltd: *Children Learn to Read* by David H. Russell; The International Reading Association, USA: 'Effects of Planned Recreational Reading Programs' by Donald W. Pfau from *The Reading Teacher*; Longman Group Ltd: *The Initial Teaching of Reading and Writing* by D. Mackay and B. Thompson, *Breakthrough to Literacy* by D. Mackay, B. Thompson and P. Schaub; The Macmillan Company, New York: *The Teaching of Reading in our Schools* by Ruth Reeves; David Moseley for material on the *English Colour Code*; Methuen and Co Ltd: *Some Aspects of Educational Technology* Ed. Dunn and Holroyd; John Murray: *i.t.a. An Independent Evaluation* by F. W. Warburton and V. Southgate; National Foundation for Educational Research Publishing Company Ltd: *Standards and Progress in Reading* by J. M. Morris, *Reading in Infant Classes* by E. J. Goodacre, *Teachers and their Pupils Home Background* by E. J. Goodacre; Prentice-Hall Inc, Englewood Cliffs, New Jersey: *Teaching Disadvantaged Children in the Pre-School* © Carl Bereiter and Siegfried Engelmann 1966; Random House Inc, New York: *Children Discover Reading* by Catherine Stern and Toni Gould; University of Nottingham Institute of Education: *Progress in Reading* by J. C. Daniels and H. Diack; UNESCO: *The Teaching of Reading and Writing; An International Survey* by W. S. Gray, Monographs on Fundamental Education X, 1956.

Every effort has been made to ensure accurate acknowledgement. The Publishers would be glad to know of any corrections for subsequent reprints.

Introduction

'The views of those who see reading as a developmental process . . . suggest that three separate but closely related ideas are involved. First, reading is seen as an aspect of the sequence of related progressive changes which follow one another as the individual progresses from birth to maturity. Related closely to physical, emotional and social development, progress in reading will form an integral part of the total growth of the individual. The acquisition of reading is seen, in common with other developmental processes, to be sequential, having its roots in pre-school linguistic and life experience and proceeding through lower-order decoding skills to higher-order reading skills. Further, as the child moves through the sequential process of learning to read, the ideas acquired through his reading influence his psychological and sociological development.' *William Latham*

'Books free the child of dependence on the time, patience and availability of others and enable him to go ahead on his own and when he likes, in school and out of it.' *R. F. Dearden*

' "Is the story about me?" asked the Water Rat.
"If so I will listen to it, for I am extremely fond of fiction." '
Oscar Wilde

When I was at school a verb used to be defined as a 'doing' word: the trouble is, with some verbs like 'being' and 'thinking' and 'reading' the action itself is not self-evident. As Ruth Reeves (1966) points out in a survey of the teaching of reading in the United States, when we see children 'reading' books we are largely ignorant of the answers to any of the following questions:

Are they reading avidly, greedily, as a dog gulps food? Are they reading delicately, savouring words? Are they following carefully point by intricate point, seeking to understand a process? Are they searching for some identity for themselves—hoping that an author

I

will have put into words answers to questions that they do not know how to ask? Are they reading to find support for an argument? Are they perhaps not actually understanding the author's points at all but allowing their own fancies to cloud his meaning? Are they taking every word at face value or are they aware that an author may do strange things with words? Are they reading the concrete details with pleasure, creating mental pictures as the words call them forth and then translating them into the abstract ideas the author meant to suggest?

All these questions become relevant once a child has learnt how to read, but there are equally important questions that we can ask about how a child can be encouraged to acquire reading skills for himself. What kinds of experiences in the early years of childhood encourage the child to want to learn to read? How far do speech limitations diminish motivation to read and how far does a continuing inability to read inhibit further speech development? Is a certain 'mental age' necessary before a child can master decoding skills successfully? What kind of reading materials operate most satisfactorily for the beginner, and why, whatever the method, do some children experience far greater difficulty in learning to read than others? Not one of these questions can be answered conclusively, but the mounting number of research investigations into the nature of the reading process make it increasingly possible to be more explicit about the problems!

Like most other activities reading requires encouragement and practice if it is to give increasing pleasure to the performer. Because reading is a process it is dynamic, and if we are to examine in any kind of detail the nature of the activity which 'reading' involves, we must look for those signs of growth and change which signify that the reader's response (like the reader) is emerging from the limitations of youthful inexperience and developing towards maturity. The image of the journey with its sense of movement and exploration is in many ways applicable to the development of reading response. Initially, the young child is picked up and carried, if his parents are keen travellers, and this gives him a good start. He has stories and nursery rhymes read to him and he is provided with books of his own so that he can enjoy turning over the pages and looking at the pictures. But there comes a time when he has to learn to walk for himself, and the ease or the difficulty with which he develops this skill is going to affect his taste for travelling. If he can only crawl at a snail's pace along the road, he will soon become heartily sick of the same old scene—every day the same dreary pebbles—but if he picks up the skill of walking easily he will be round the first corner before very long and then the next—and so he will begin to have some idea of the pleasures in store. In other words, the period of pre-reading experiences and the period of learning how to read for oneself are both going to affect the final stage—indefinitely extended for some and never reached by others—of discovering how much reading has to offer at any point of human experience, exploring all areas of thought and feeling, while focusing, clarifying, stimulating and extending an awareness of inner and outer reality.

The logical pattern for this book therefore, is a chronological one. It begins with the pre-school child who is still at the stage of listening to and looking at books, then moves forward with him through the learning-to-read period to the time when he is free to enter into a private dialogue with any writer who has appeared in print. How his reading tastes and his response to what he reads (especially to literature) may develop, and how they can be analysed and assessed, will be the subject of the second volume of this survey, *The Reader's Response.*

1 The pre-reading period

THE FUNCTION OF BOOKS FOR THE PRE-SCHOOL CHILD

'As the child grows he strives to master both an outer world that is continuously expanding and an inner world of emotions that are often tumultuous. In both these realms there are many experiences to be fathomed from "Why does it rain?" to "Why do we cry?" ' *Jacquelyn Sanders*

'It seems to me that the proper satisfactions of reading even in the newly literate child—even indeed in the non-literate story-listening child— provide a robust affirmation of our common humanity, our capacity whether we are young or old to understand and to be moved by and to gather to ourselves the products of the creative imagination.' *E. W. Rosenheim*

Reading for the young child must of necessity be a shared activity. He cannot yet decode printed symbols for himself and so he depends upon a parent or an older brother or sister, or a nursery school teacher, to do it for him. If he is read to at home he can look at the book as it is being read to him, turning the pages if he wishes and responding to the pictures as well as to the spoken words. The presence of another person all to himself also enables him to talk about the story, to offer comments and ask questions while in the actual process of listening, or immediately afterwards.[1] It may be that such comments offered freely by the young child—often as much to himself as to his mother or his teacher—are an early form of the inner dialogue which often accompanies successful adult reading.

In *Books Before Five* (1956) Dorothy White notes that her impression is that young children ask different questions every time they read a

---

[1] It would be interesting to compare the comments made by a minus-five-year-old 'while listening to a short story' with those made by the fifteen-year-olds in James Squire's study, *The Responses of Adolescents While Reading Four Short Stories* (NCTE Research Report no. 2, 1964). See Volume 2 of *Reading for Meaning*.

story 'and find something new there much as I find something new every time I pick up *Emma* or *Middlemarch*'.

In a sense, then, for the child at this pre-reading stage, the adult is standing in for the author, enabling the child to enter into the kind of conversation outwardly which at a later stage he will engage in silently as he sits huddled over a book. In a paper for the Third International Reading Symposium, Ronald Morris (1968) has suggested that 'we fail to develop powers of reading effectively' because we pay insufficient attention to the personal response of the reader/listener to the writer/talker. He continues: 'In asking for response to be personal I am suggesting that in successful reading there is a constant to-ing and fro-ing between reader and author. The reader attends not merely to what he thinks the author is saying but also to the possible relevance to himself of what is being read. To read in this way is to read reflectively, to review what is being said in the light of one's own understanding and experience of life.'

The young child who only hears stories at his playgroup or nursery school is rather more limited in his scope for this kind of 'to-ing and fro-ing' between himself and the writer. He may be squatting on the floor with twelve or twenty other children, gazing up at the back of the book from which the teacher is reading and thus almost entirely dependent on the sounds of the story to convey meaning to him; and in a group the opportunity for questions and comments is not so great as in the one-to-one home situation.

How far the young child who never sees or listens to a book at home, and never goes to a play group or nursery school before the age of five, is for these reasons less well motivated towards reading once he arrives in his 'reception class', and by what means his first teacher can best dispel a lack of interest in books and their contents, will be questions to which we shall return later in this survey.

THE WORLD INSIDE

The function of phantasy in stories for young children

'If a book is to be read with any appreciation at all by children it has to contain those phantasies which are relative to their stage of development.' *Friedlander*

Our attitude to the function of phantasy in the emotional and mental development of the child generally will affect the degree to which we welcome or reject the presence of a strong phantasy element in stories and nursery rhymes for the very young. Do we, for instance, regard 'So he took him by the left leg and threw him down the stairs' as just a piece of nursery rhyme nonsense or do we regard it as a satisfying reflection for the young child of his own feelings of aggression—or do we take the view, as some experts in child-rearing have done, that a firm steering of the child's attention to the realities of the outside world is generally more advisable?

Directed and undirected thought

Perhaps it would be useful to remind readers of the distinction made by Jean Piaget in *The Language and Thought of the Child* (1926) between 'autistic' or 'undirected' and 'intelligent' or 'directed' thought. According to Piaget:

> Directed thought is conscious, that is, it pursues an aim which is present in the mind of the thinker; it is intelligent which means that it is adapted to reality and tries to influence it; it admits of being true or false (empirically or logically true) and it can be communicated by language. 'Autistic' thought is subconscious, which means that the aims it pursues and the problems it tries to solve are not present in consciousness: it is not adapted to reality, but creates for itself a dream world of imagination; it tends not to establish truths but to satisfy desires and it remains strictly individual and incommunicable by means of language.

Two points are raised by that final remark—that autistic thought 'remains strictly individual and incommunicable by means of language'. Experts in child psychology may agree that those thought patterns which are most closely related to the child's deepest needs and desires function largely at a subconscious level—but not, surely, *entirely* at that level. It is now generally acknowledged that disturbed children can externalise their anxieties through play—and one of the features of play is speech. For instance, the child who, while playing with a family of dolls, says that one doll is going to eat another doll up may be voicing a hidden anxiety about his own position in the family—and to this extent he has made explicit the autistic thoughts which are, at a subconscious level, preoccupying him.

Similarly young children who make a passionate—and direct—response to stories about wolves and foxes, giants and witches are probably responding at a deeper level to their own violent and destructive impulses. Certainly, children in the three to five age range often ask to hear stories of this kind, once they have been introduced to them, over and over again.

In *Literature and the Young Child*, Joan Cass (1967) says: 'Under five is not really the time for stories about fairies, ogres, witches, goblins and the like. One needs to be quite sure of solid things before meeting the magic of unreality and the young child's fanciful tales should not include the supernatural . . . It is creatures that are purely phantoms of the imagination which as yet the under five is not really ready for.' But if Piaget is right and the current of autistic thinking runs more strongly in these early years than at any other time, unchecked by the 'directed' or 'intelligent' cognitively based forms of thought which are only just beginning to develop, then it is *precisely* at this stage that the child will be responsive to and often even preoccupied by those symbolic creatures and occurrences which Joan Cass dismisses as 'purely phantoms of the imagination'.

Another educational psychologist, Ruth Griffiths, working in the 1930s, agreed with Piaget that it is possible even in young children to distinguish between 'concentrated attention' which 'brings the individual in touch with his environment', and 'autistic or unconscious thinking . . . often disguised as symbolism', but she held very firmly to the view that in the early years of the child's life before the ability to conceptualise has developed, it is often by means of this indirect thinking that behavioural problems are explored by the child: 'Of all the aspects of childish experience there is none that being universally recognised is yet so little understood in any scientific sense as that of phantasy and imagination. This largely neglected aspect of childish experience appears to be of outstanding importance, not only for the emotional development and mental health of the child, but as a significant factor also in intellectual development at this stage.' She maintains as a result of her records of such thinking, expressed by the children she observed through drawing and talking that: 'Often problems that will not yield their solution when attacked at the logical level, become clearer when the individual allows his thoughts to wander among adjacent topics. Thus valuable mental work is often achieved though at a slower rate and probably involving a smaller expenditure of mental energy.' Even in adult life Griffiths suggests that 'Frequently we drop back from "objective concentrated thinking" into a state in which we are less conscious of our surroundings' and in which 'the mind "plays" about its ideas in a less consciously directed way'.

In her book *I Could a Tale Unfold*, P. M. Pickard (1961) relates the child's need to project his repressed desires specifically to his response to literature. She agrees with Griffiths that: 'The phantasies rise spontaneously unbidden by the child' and similarly endorses her view that the outlet afforded to the child by such an opportunity to project what he has repressed to some extent releases him from the concentrated effort of repression to which much of his energy would otherwise be directed. She suggests that 'when we tell children a story we project characters and events upon which they can in turn project themselves'.

It is true of course that, as well as books, many television programmes nowadays offer the opportunity for children to project their inner phantasies; one only has to observe how three- and four-year-olds will improvise on television serials whose theme is the battle for power between a destructive force and an upholder of law and order (such as Captain Scarlet or Dr Who) for periods of up to an hour, sometimes even longer, to endorse the view that such material clearly fulfils a need in the child to explore situations which are fraught with danger and aggression.

In a paper, 'The psychological significance of children's literature', Jacquelyn Sanders (1967) makes a point about 'adult issues suitable for children such as conflict' which could apply equally well to books or to television:

> Since a story is not life, some very different issues can be dealt with through fiction without creating the anxiety that they do in real life. In this respect, phantasy is a method of presentation that has a great advantage, because events that are obviously unreal or very distant do not have as great an emotional impact as those that appear closer to home and therefore more possible.

This is not to imply that children can make a clear conceptual distinction between phantasy and reality at this age. It is rather, as Susan Isaacs (1932) remarked, 'that there is a progressive penetration of feeling and phantasy by experience, a progressive ordering by relational thought of the child's response to the world'.

Even at this early stage, then, stories can provide young children with an organisation of experience which because it is controlled in words and thus 'distanced' from direct first-hand experience is more likely to reassure them than to frighten—always provided that the story ends 'happily ever after'. It is necessary that Snow White should come back to life, that the grandmother should be disembowelled from the wolf—and that Little Black Sambo should regain all his smart new clothes!

THE WORLD OUTSIDE—FAMILIAR AND UNFAMILIAR
Recognising the familiar in stories

To provide material for his own projected phantasies is not of course the only function that stories can have for the young child. They can equally well confirm what he knows already by reflecting the familiar —'holding a mirror up to Nature' even at this early age. In her record of Carol's response to books between the age of two and two and a half her mother, Dorothy White, who was also a qualified children's librarian, notes: 'Much of our reading time at the moment is spent just listening passively while Carol points out "That's a boy. There's a girl. There's a mummy." '

Mrs White notes how even before the age of three her daughter related her own experiences to those which were depicted in books:

> The experience makes the book richer and the book enriches the personal experience. I am astonished at the early age this backward and forward flow between books and life takes place. With adults and older children one cannot observe it so easily, but here at this age when all a child's experiences are known and the books read are shared, when the voluble gabble which is her speech reveals all the associations, the interaction is seen very clearly.

When Carol was two and a half her mother records:

> This morning I read Beatrix Potter's *Tale of Tom Kitten*. After a series of failures and near failures in choosing stories lately I was happy to see something hit the target. Here were kittens tumbling about a doorstep in the dust, much as she likes to do herself where the gravel is wearing thin. Mrs Tabitha Twitchet expects friends to tea, Mittens, Tom Kitten and Moppet are to be washed, combed and given clean clothes. Here for Carol was a comprehensible universe . . .
>
> Now at the fourth reading she is starting to tell the story to me. 'He scratched', she says, pointing at Tom Kitten. She wants to hasten to the end of the story which by now has become a real climax. The pictures of kittens wrecking their bedroom did not

interest her until I explained that they were pulling all the clothes out of the drawers. This made naughtiness of a recognisable kind. Wickedness has to be in scale to be appreciated.

Today too she was enthusiastic about the pictures of the kittens being spanked and asked to have it again. As I realised today when her cold developed, she has been out of sorts and I have been short-tempered. I smacked her yesterday, hence the interest.

Exploring the unfamiliar

But listening to stories can extend the young child's experience of the known world as well as confirming it. *Peter Rabbit* provides Mrs White with an excellent example of how such an extension of experience takes place: 'the opening part where Mrs Rabbit takes her umbrella and her basket and goes to the baker to buy buns has stirred Carol to the depths. She is forever talking about buying buns (goods which in fact we never purchase) and every time an umbrella is dropped in the hall, Carol takes it, finds a basket and informs me that she is off to the baker's.'

On another occasion when Carol was four, her mother records: 'This afternoon we read Penelope Gibbon's *Riki the Eskimo*, a simple story of an Eskimo boy who takes a spear to his father at a distant fishing ground and returns home to a family feast in the igloo that evening. Carol had plenty of background for the story—the polar scenes of the magic cave last year seemed quite fresh in her mind; she has a bookish knowledge of bears, and she has been inside the canoe at the museum. Her questions were largely concerned with the gaps in her knowledge. Thus she was curious about the windows in the igloos and puzzled why the Eskimos should have no glass.'

Sometimes, however, stories fail for young children because they are too far removed from their personal experience. Perhaps an extension into the unfamiliar must be grounded in a confirmation of the familiar first; in other words a firm base is necessary before a projection outwards can take place successfully. For this reason *The Tale of Jemima Puddleduck* was not successful with Carol who lived in 'urban New Zealand' because 'too much had to be explained' so that 'the dead weight of information necessary before we could get on with the story killed the pleasure'. This remoteness from their own environment may well spoil such stories for urban English children too, although I must record that *Jemima Puddleduck* was one of the most successful Potter stories with my eldest child at the age of three or so because one of the main characters was a fox—and at the time he was strongly attracted to any fox or wolf story (*Pinocchio* which included *both* was his favourite).

In an article entitled 'A psychological basis for judging children's literature dealing with nature and science', Luitgard Wundheiler (1967) makes the point that 'children want books that give them the information they need in order to use objects in play. In regard to objects in nature this means that children want to know what acts will have what consequences.' Any adult who has been subjected to the spate of questions that young children begin to ask from the age of three or so may agree that even at this age books can be of interest to the child which explain simply, with clear and frequent illustrations, about rockets, or about where rain comes from—or about anything connected with his environment which it occurs to the child to investigate.

The provision of such books to stimulate the child's curiosity about what he sees and smells and hears and touches—along with stories and rhymes to satisfy his emotional experiences—is surely desirable, especially if we accept Jerome S. Bruner's hypothesis that 'any subject can be taught effectively in some intellectually honest form to any child at any stage of development'. The child's response to books can well be envisaged in the form of Bruner's spiral—the child returning steadily to reading at each stage of his development for both the confirmation and the extension of his experience, subjective and objective, as the world expands before him—'for the highest pleasures of literature . . . whether in adults' reading or children's combine the urgency and authenticity of life as we know it with the excitement and wonder of life as it may yet be known' (Rosenheim, 1967).

PATTERNS OF RESPONSE

I have suggested that three patterns which can be distinguished in the young child's response to nursery rhymes and stories are 'the tacit recognition of inner desires and fears', 'the conscious recognition of the familiar' and 'the exploration of the unfamiliar'. In an article entitled 'Response to literature' D. W. Harding (1968) suggests four rather different patterns which can also be detected from the reading preferences and the comments of young children: 'There appear to be four levels of response, emerging in sequence: briefly they are response to the quality and pattern of (1) sounds, (2) events, (3) roles and (4) worlds.' Harding then adds the following notes to explain in greater detail what each of these 'levels of response' can be said to involve:

Sound: When children bounce on mother's knee to a song or a nursery rhyme, when they join in the chorus, when they chant 'maximum capacity' round the room, and maybe when they chuckle at special words, names and puns, they are responding to the texture and rhythm of sounds. Such new actions seem to be both elements of their enjoyment and signs of it.

Event: Both rhythm and form involve a pattern of expectation, both for the satisfaction and the modification of the expected pattern. Stories for very young children embody a pattern of events within this rhythm or form. When a child corrects the storyteller and wants the story word-perfect, he is asking for confirmation of the pattern (in one respect or the other). At a later stage he may make up topsy-turvy stories with reversals of the pattern; finally he will improvise and impose his own.

Role: In free play or classroom drama, children take up the roles of characters in their stories, or perhaps continue the role-playing that the story involved them in: 'I'm Jack and this is the beanstalk and you be the Giant.' Sometimes children will replay the story, sometimes reshape and improvise on it, perhaps relating the roles and events more nearly to their own wishes.

World: While a story is being read aloud to a group a child may interpose: 'He's a funny boy' (about Ian in *The Silver Sword* perhaps) and the group may begin to talk about his background, his relations with the other characters etc. A new variety of talk develops to relate and organise elements of the world of that story or to relate the world of that story to the child's own world. It will tie in all the four kinds of response, giving some a new articulation.

Each of these features of response must be familiar to any parent who has ever made a habit of reading to small children. The strong rhythmic pattern of most nursery rhymes which invites the young listener to join in undoubtedly increases his pleasure in the performance:

> Hickery dickery ————
> The mouse ran up the ————
> The clock struck ————
> The mouse ran ————
> Hickery dickery ————

Here the sense of pattern is so strong that if the mother leaves the last word unsaid, the child is compelled, triumphantly, to chime in and add it for her.

Moreover, many nursery rhymes, like this one, reach an obvious and dramatic climax which leads the child into Harding's second dimension of response—an awareness of the pattern of form. Dorothy White notes on many occasions how Carol took a real and obvious pleasure in the climax of a story and James Britton has recorded how his three-year-old daughter already showed a grasp of the pattern of events (and much more) in *Cinderella* which she described as 'A big sad book about two ugly sisters and a girl they were ugly to'.

In Harding's third and fourth dimensions of response we can see how taking up a rôle can involve each of the three elements of response to which I have already referred—the projection of inner feelings, the recognition of the familiar and the exploration of the unknown: just as 'world' involves the child's organisation of experience at each of these personal levels.

What must be emphasised is that already, at the pre-reading stage, children are capable of responding to books in many different ways. They can respond to the *meaning* in a book in terms of their own conscious or subconscious experiences, and they can also respond to the *medium*, to the patterns of sound or to the patterns of the narrative. What they cannot yet do is to decode the print for themselves, but apart from this inability there appears to be *no fundamental difference* between their 'reading' responses and those of older children, or even adults.

THE NEED FOR MORE RESEARCH

As far as I know, apart from Dorothy White's book there is no research available which records:

the amount of time regularly spent by parents or nursery school teachers in reading to children under the age of five;

details of the books that were read and of children's preferences— for fact or fiction, for the familiar, or the absurd, or the horrifying or the funny;

the questions asked by young children or the comments which they freely volunteer;

any follow-up to see whether children with a rich pre-reading experience of books *do* learn to read more easily than children from bookless backgrounds—and whether having learnt to read they continue to read for pleasure outside the classroom.

So I shall end this section on the 'pre-reading period' with a list of questions by means of which parents and teachers, with very little expenditure of time and trouble, could begin to gather information. In this way a start could be made towards understanding more fully the value of books in the young child's environment from the day when he first clutches a book to himself as he toddles unsteadily round his living room.

POINTS FOR DISCUSSION

1 To what extent do pre-school children refer in play to characters or episodes from books which have been read to them?

2 Are their memories for details from books which they cannot read for themselves shortlived or retentive?

3 Are certain kinds of details remembered more consistently than others?

4 Are there marked differences or similarities in the length of story to which two-, three- and four-year-olds can listen before their absorption fades?

5 Is there any noticeable preference for certain *kinds* of stories at the age of two, three or four? Do young children, for instance, consistently show the same enthusiasm for stories about animals as for stories about people—or is this an adult misconception?

6 Are there any sex differences in the preferences expressed by boys and girls before the age of five? In other ways their play patterns often differ noticeably—would this be equally true of their favourite stories?

7 Are young children capable of enjoying not just story books, but also books which answer some of their 'why' questions simply and with clear illustrations?

8 Can the appeal of nursery rhymes for young children be defined at all clearly from the sort of comments children make about them and the favourites they establish?

9 Do all young children irrespective of intelligence or social background pass through a stage when they are preoccupied with

giants, or burglars, or wolves, or rockets—and does reading about them help the child, inhibit him, or leave him unaffected one way or the other?

10 Do small children ever refer to dreams or nightmares about characters in stories they have heard?

11 How old do children have to be before they can enjoy poetry?

12 Do 'children's' illustrations which make a strong appeal to adults make an equally strong appeal to the children for whom they were intended?

13 Can illustrations be classified in any way as having a noticeably strong appeal for intensity of colour, or clarity of line, or familiarity of detail—or the reverse of any of these features?

14 Does vocabulary have to be carefully graded for the listening comprehension of the under-five-year-old?

15 Must the syntax be simpler than their normal speech patterns for the same reason?

These and many other questions must frequently occur to parents, librarians and nursery school teachers, but so far researchers into reading seem to have neglected this vital time before compulsory education begins.

11 Reading readiness

Later in this book the various factors which affect the child at the start of his reading career will be summarised in some detail. However, the 'reading readiness' concept has had such an influence upon teaching practice at the infant stage that I have considered it to be sufficiently important to have a preliminary hearing.

The idea that children could not simply be taught to read as soon as they arrived in school, but had to be carefully prepared for direct instruction in reading skills and watched for signs of 'readiness' before they were confronted with the task of decoding written symbols first received official mention in various reports and articles in the 1920s. A. E. Sanderson (1963) notes the use of the term 'reading readiness' in this country in a Report of the National Committee on Reading published in 1925, and Nila Banton Smith (1963) notes its use in the United States in articles published in January 1927. It is perhaps significant that *The Language and Thought of the Child* was written in 1923 and published in this country in 1926, as it is in this book that Piaget suggests that there are clearly definable stages of maturational development through which all children (sooner or later) must pass. Sanderson also points out that much of the research in educational psychology about this period demonstrated that there were considerable variations between children, not only in intelligence, but also in rate of maturation and speed of learning. He suggests that the impact of these ideas resulted logically in the concept of reading readiness.

In *Children Learn to Read*, David H. Russell (1949) sees the concept of reading readiness as largely an outgrowth of the child study movement, from which the belief was widely popularised that there is an optimum time for any particular learning and that attempts at instruction before this stage is reached are usually laborious and unsuccessful. The application of this belief to infant education led educationists and teachers from the 1930s onwards to approach the teaching of reading more indirectly than formerly, placing it very much within the context of the child's general development. Infant teachers thus attempted to provide for the child in his first year at school a much wider range of experiences than the direct teaching of the '3 Rs' had previously

16

involved, designed to *stimulate* in the child a desire for more specific learning skills such as reading and writing as the need for these became apparent to the young learner.

ACTIVITIES DESIGNED TO FOSTER READING READINESS

Check lists

Russell, who was one of the chief exponents of the readiness concept in the USA, formulated a check list to help kindergarten teachers to discover whether or not their children were ready to learn how to read. This is given in Appendix A. It was designed to give the teacher a detailed profile of each child, and to assess the child's total development since this was felt to be relevant to his readiness to learn—and in particular to learn how to read.

More recently Elizabeth Standish (1959) has suggested that there is a minimum level which has to be reached by a child in all the following directions before the learning of literacy skills can successfully be accomplished:

1 his general level of learning ability or intelligence

2 the adequacy of his sensory equipment and stage of development of his perception

3 his language development

4 his background experiences

5 the strength of his interest in learning to read

An indication of the kind of classroom activities which are considered to prepare a child for the moment when he is taught directly how to read, can be gained from Ruth Reeves's book *The Teaching of Reading in our Schools*, sponsored by the National Council of Teachers of English in America and published in 1966. She states that the child should be able to remember things in sequence, and should also be able to follow directions responsibly. In the classroom:

1 Children should have practice in classifying.

2 Children should learn to observe closely in kindergarten and to use their imagination and powers of perception.

3   They should have plenty of apparatus to listen to, and should ask and answer questions about literature.

4   They should be encouraged to relate sounds to pictures.

Dixon (1967), in *Growth through English*, comes closer to relating the child's pre-reading activities to a positive enjoyment of books by suggesting that the first two stages of the learning-to-read process should be:

1   Much enjoyable listening to standard English—assimilating it with satisfaction through stories told by the teacher and later through her *reading* stories too.

2   Reading aloud by teacher and child of the child's *own* stories in his own language and preserved in that form by the teacher who wrote them down.

Dixon concludes: 'But in any case, learning to read and write leaves the child alone with language in a way which differs from his previous experience. This should not be made a sudden transition. The new activities should be preceded, accompanied and followed *by talk*.'

The keynotes of all these activities are clearly pleasure and the stimulation of interest in reading through closely related activities.

CHANGES IN ATTITUDE TO THE READING READINESS CONCEPT

Since the 1930s the importance of the concept of reading readiness has been widely accepted by teachers in this country as well as in America and many infant teachers (though not all) have been content to engage their children in pre-reading rather than reading activities for the first few months of their school life. Within the last decade, however, there have been signs that an increasing number of educationists have become uneasy about a policy which encourages teachers to wait until children qualify—on any kind of readiness check list—for direct teaching in reading skills.

It would now appear to be established that children well below either the mental or the chronological age of six *can* perceive the small differences of detail which are necessary if they are to learn how to decode written symbols successfully. Supporting evidence has been collected by Hunter Diack and John Downing amongst others in this country and by researchers such as Durkin, Denver and Holmes in the United States. In his article 'Is a mental age of six essential for reading readiness?' Downing (1963) refers to reading experiments with young children conducted by each of these American investigators and in a later paper[1] (1968) he cites the further researches of Shaw (1964) Sutton (1966) and Mason and Prater (1966) all of which lead strongly to the conclusion that 'the necessary mental age for beginning to learn to read is relative to the conditions under which the child must work at this task'. In an article entitled 'Formulae for beginning reading tuition' Southgate (1968) affirms that 'In those schools in which the staff consider reading of prime importance *and favour an early beginning* to reading tuition, a strong reading drive is permanently in force and most children *do* learn to read early and well . . .' whereas 'In those infant schools in which the staff are convinced of the value of delaying the beginning of reading tuition, little or no reading drive is in force and children's reading progress in their first year or two at school is noticeably slower.'

Morris's Kent survey (1959) would confirm this pattern of measurably greater reading progress amongst children who have received direct teaching earlier. Morris also suggests, however, that although word *recognition* skills are well advanced in such children their total *comprehension* of what they read may not be any greater than that of children who have had more opportunities to explore their environment through talk. How far a formal start is going to benefit the child educationally in the long run has still not been confirmed or repudiated by longitudinal research evidence.

Early help for the disadvantaged reader

However, though educationists in this country may now be willing to acknowledge that children *can* be taught to read before the age of six they are still inclined to be cautious about advocating the advisability or desirability of such a practice. Many would agree with Dr W. D. Wall that most children learn to read, without undue difficulty, by the time they are eight and that any pressures to speed the process up may well upset those children who, at a more leisurely pace, achieve the same ends as the fast movers. But although reservations have now been voiced about the readiness concept, it has certainly not been abandoned as irrelevant to the questions of *when* and *how* children should receive direct teaching in literacy skills.

What *is* certain is that children who leave school either semi-

[1] Both these papers are summarised in Appendix B.

literate or illiterate have *not* received the full benefit of any educational programme. Might they have done better if they had had individual and intensive teaching earlier? The point at issue is whether children, who are noticeably or measurably disadvantaged in any of the four major areas on Russell's check list when they first come to school, should receive intensive training in the skills which are necessary for literacy *from the very beginning*.

In an article entitled 'Early reading—some personal thoughts' Mr Keith Gardner (1966–7) has attacked with vigour the theory that 'late starters in reading make up their lost ground rapidly at a subsequent date'. He points out that pupils who have no real reading ability at the age of seven and a half years never become first rate readers throughout their primary school life, and notes further that since 1961 the population of non-readers entering the junior school (i.e. the group 'at risk') has increased by 12 per cent. He suggests firmly and cogently that 'a pupil who has difficulty in auditory discriminations is not so much a case for leaving alone and waiting for a magic moment, as a case for careful and intensive teaching'.

The most fundamental changes in attitude towards reading readiness have come chiefly from the United States where there has been an increasingly acute awareness in recent years of the problems which stand in the way of effective and successful development amongst disadvantaged children, i.e. those children with 'impoverished linguistic experiences' cited by Downing (see Appendix B) as part of that 'significant minority' who *cannot* begin to read at an early age. Researchers like Bernstein in this country and Loban and Strickland in the States have demonstrated that one of the chief problems educationally for children coming from culturally deprived backgrounds is not so much a lack of money—or music or painting or literature; it is the comparatively narrow range of speech functions which such children have learnt to operate which largely prevents them from communicating effectively at school and which increases, for children *already well behind their more fortunate compeers*, the difficulty of learning how to learn.

Members of the Task Force set up in the United States in 1965 by a special committee of the National Council for Teachers of English to investigate particularly the problems of disadvantaged children stressed the need to intervene *as early as possible* in what may have previously been falsely regarded as the child's 'natural' rate of development: 'In language and intellectual ability the greatest development probably occurs between conception and age three or four. . . .

At age six something can be done, but not so much as at four. Less and less can be accomplished as the children grow older as far as acceleration in intellectual development is concerned.' Because for this group of thinkers time wasted may be time lost, the use of diagnostic tests has become essential to pinpoint weaknesses so that immediate attention can be directed to them. The comfortable assumption made by the majority of the infant teachers in Morris's Kent survey, that they could tell 'by intuition' when children were ready to begin reading, would meet with little encouragement from members of this American Task Force. Samuel Kirk, for instance, has evolved an 'analysis of psycho-linguistic disabilities', whereby the child is subjected to nine tests which should isolate any weaknesses of communication.

Writers like Bereiter and Kirk emphasise strongly this need to use 'a lasar-like approach', bringing intensive attention to bear on those areas such as language which underpin the success or failure of a child in a learning situation at school because: 'By the time they are five years old, disadvantaged children of almost every kind are typically one or two years retarded in language development. This is supported by virtually any index of language development one cares to look at.'

It seems logical therefore to Bereiter to suggest that:

If a child who starts out behind is to catch up he has to progress at a faster than normal rate. It follows therefore that any educational progress that claims to be helping children to overcome their environmental handicaps must be able to show not just a normal rate of progress but a superior rate.

Because 'it is too much to expect that progress can be accelerated above the normal level in all areas of development at once', Carl Bereiter and Siegfried Engelmann (1966) have constructed a pre-school programme that tries through direct and intensive teaching to improve fundamental language skills 'because these are instrumental to the whole process of education'. 'Reading', according to Bereiter, 'provides the clearest example of this point. If reading were only of value once the child sets out into the world it would not matter if he did not learn to read until his last year of school. But because reading is instrumental to school learning, because progress in most other academic areas is held down to the rate at which children progress in reading, it is important that the child learn to read as early as possible in his school career. The child who falls behind in reading is held back in all other areas.'

Accordingly, Bereiter and Engelmann constructed their programme at a strictly functional level: 'We have not been very much concerned with many of those aspects of language which serve mainly social or expressive purposes . . . it has not bothered us so much that a child may not know the word "sheep" as that he does not know the word "not", for while in the former case a child might encounter occasional difficulty, in the latter case he is deprived of one of the most powerful logical tools our language provides—a tool moreover which it is *assumed* in school work that a child possesses from the very beginning. In our program we have been less concerned with the child's lack of empirical knowledge than with his lack of ability to derive knowledge from statements.'

With their experimental group, therefore, Bereiter and Engelmann set out to teach the children to recognise and *to produce for themselves* certain quite specifically defined logical statement patterns such as 'the ability to handle polar opposites' (if it is not . . . then it must be). After eight months of instruction all but one of the four-year-old children who were involved were able to meet all the linguistic criteria that had been set down—as a result of 'the continual use of pattern drills not unlike those used in the teaching of foreign languages to college students'. The difference, as Bereiter points out, is that in this instance 'the drills have been used to teach new language operations rather than to replace old patterns . . . the children are not merely learning a way of expressing themselves that is more acceptable to the teacher, but are acquiring tools that enable them to do things intellectually that they had not been able to do before.'

The conviction that a child's ability to make educational progress can be not just speeded up but actually changed by outside intervention was expressed clearly by A. R. Luria in *Speech and the Development of Mental Processes in the Child*, first published in the USSR in 1956 and in this country in 1959, when he warned that any theory which regards 'the maturation of mental abilities as *a spontaneously continuous process* not only shrugs off the problem of explaining the mechanisms of mental development, but also relegates educational influences to a very subsidiary place, understanding them at most as a means of speeding up or slowing down "natural maturation", *the direction of which is predetermined*'.

After reviewing those recent American studies which 'indicate that intellectual development may be importantly influenced by deliberate mental training', Downing (1968) suggests that 'at least we may conclude that more attention might be given to the effects of providing the experiences necessary for the development in children of those learning sets which would expand Hebb's "Intelligence B" attainment to the limits set by his "Intelligence A" capacity', and he reminds the reader in a footnote of the 'valuable distinction' which Hebb makes between 'Intelligence A—the intellectual capacity determined by the genes and Intelligence B—the individual's present mental efficiency including those cognitive abilities which have been established as a result of stimulation by the environment.'

POINTS FOR DISCUSSION

Clearly most children are likely to progress from the non-speaking, non-comprehending baby stage to a point when their physical, mental, psychological and social development will enable them to be taught the written language *but*

1   Are we clear as to what the *minimal* levels of development are in each of these areas?

2   Are diagnostic tests available in this country which can efficiently pinpoint areas of weakness in a child's general development when he first comes to school?[1]

3   If there are, do infant teachers use such tests at any point during the child's first term—or even first year—in school?[2]

4   How many of Sanderson's criticisms of 'R-r' tests are still valid?

5   Do some children 'naturally' have a slower growth rate in any/ some/all the four main areas of development, or are environmental as well as genetic factors occasionally/frequently/always involved?

6   Is an infant teacher justified in 'waiting' for a child to show signs of wanting to read before she attempts to teach him to do so?

[1] For a list of tests that are currently available see Appendix C.
[2] Both Dr Morris's surveys (1959 and 1966) indicated an apparent lack of concern about the diagnosis of individual weaknesses. None of the selected schools in her second survey and only *one* school in the total sample used diagnostic tests 'because it was generally believed that time given to testing could be spent more profitably in teaching'. Morris comments: 'Our intensive studies revealed that most teachers did not accurately ascertain the particular difficulties of their retarded pupils by other methods. Consequently because much of the instruction given was not directed to specific objectives it was not as effective as it might have been.'

Goodacre (1967) notes that 'Although the use of standardised tests in schools has increased during the last decade . . . such measures are confined to the assessment of older "infants" (i.e. $6\frac{1}{2}$ +), and the infant teacher (of five- and six-year-olds) depends largely on subjective estimates based on the reliability of her own power of observation to determine an individual pupil's reading ability *throughout his infant schooling*.'

7 Does it *really* matter whether a teacher gains a detailed assessment of a child's immediate capacities or incapacities for learning as soon as he comes to school, or is the time factor unimportant at the infant stage?

8 Is an intensive language-based approach which cuts out 'arts and crafts, group play, dramatic play, block play and so on' (Bereiter) ever desirable—and if so, for what reasons and for how long?

9 Do children who have attended a nursery school or a play group for at least a year before entering full-time schooling (a) show earlier signs of reading readiness than children who have remained in the home? (b) learn to read with less difficulty than previously home-based children?

10 Is it of any permanent educational value for a child to acquire literacy skills at an early age, even assuming that he is often perfectly capable of doing so?

III Factors in learning to read

'Reading is the first of the 3 Rs children must acquire as a basis for a lifetime of schooling and self-education.' *Ruth Strickland*

PROBLEMS EXPOSED BY RESEARCH

Failure rates

The Ministry of Education surveys conducted at a national level since 1948 have shown a steady improvement in the proportion of children who according to the test criteria used, were able to read 'satisfactorily' by the time they left school: 'only 20 per cent of the secondary modern school leavers studies in 1961 showed a reading standard as low as that shown by 30 per cent of the age group sample studied in 1952'. But in spite of this improvement, the proportion of children who never learn to read satisfactorily is disturbingly high.

The position appears to be very similar in the United States. Speaking at a conference on reading in 1962, James Squire, Secretary of the National Council for Teachers of English, said: 'I am not impressed with statistics which reveal that children taught in 1957 are accelerated six months in reading over similar children tested in 1937 . . . Considering the enormous effort that we have put into reading . . . the gains during the past twenty years should be far greater.'

In her follow-up study of 101 poor readers from the original Kent reading survey Joyce Morris (1966) emphasises two points. The first is that although on average the reading attainment of the children significantly improved few reached the normal standard for their age; and second that those who had the greatest problems to begin with continued to have the severest difficulties and in the opinion of the secondary school heads would never fully overcome their reading disability.

Morris concludes: 'At best the chances of second-year juniors with a reading problem eventually achieving average or normal competence is about 1 in 8, and at least *half* of them will remain very poor readers to the end of their school days (and beyond).'

If so many children are not taught to read adequately at the age when most of their contemporaries are acquiring the skill, it looks as though they will be incapable for the rest of their lives of reading very much at any level more complex than newspaper headlines and super-market advertising. Because any teacher must surely acknowledge that such reading failure imposes serious, even dangerous, limitations on such children (later adults), Morris's summarised conclusions are given in full in Appendix E.

Teachers' lack of theory

It is not perhaps surprising, in view of the tremendous educational importance that learning to read independently has for the child, to find more research into this aspect of English teaching than any other. Ronald Morris (1963) notes that 'The past thirty years has seen the production of more than three thousand experimental studies of the reading process', and since he made that comment at least a dozen major pieces of reading research have been published in this country alone.

But in spite of the vast amount of research which is now available in print—or perhaps because the sheer bulk of printed matter is so intimidating—there seems to be very little direct use made of research findings in either infant or junior schools. Goodacre (1967) noted, for instance, that many teachers rely heavily on the manual of instruction which accompanies the most popular reading schemes at present in use in this country. She noted further that: 'The reading scheme or series with its set of readers of increasing difficulty appears to be of immense help to teachers and to provide a source of security—especially to infant teachers straight from college.' Kenneth Jones (1968) found as an interesting corollary to this that student teachers at schools using his Colour Story Reading experiment were extremely reluctant to become involved with it and preferred to stick to the primer-based scheme which they 'knew about' from college.

It would also appear, however, that teachers learn how to teach reading principally from experience, rather than from study or in-struction. Goodacre notes: 'Some young teachers reported that they had had only limited instruction in the actual mechanics of teaching reading in their training colleges; this might help to explain the findings of Malmquist (1958) that teachers with twelve years of service attained distinctly better results in teaching reading to beginners than teachers with less experience, and that teachers with more than six years' experience attained better results than teachers with less service.'

Often the emphasis in Colleges of Education has been placed so firmly on *what* is to be taught that the actual process of 'teaching' and the dynamics of that process have been ignored. Books like *How Children Fail* (Holt 1964) and *The Exploring Word* (Holbrook 1967) are now in print to demonstrate to us the terrifying chasms which can yawn between the teacher and the class or between what we *think* we are teaching and what in fact the students are failing to learn.

Clearly experience is bound to increase a teacher's confidence and her insight into the problems which children encounter at this stage, but to rely so heavily on experience puts incredibly large numbers of children (taught by teachers of *less* than twelve years' experience) at a serious disadvantage, at what for them is possibly the most crucial educational period of their whole lives. When we remind ourselves, further, of the 'drop out' from the profession of college-trained teachers after only two or three years' teaching, the need to find other ways of improving their ability to teach reading successfully to infant and junior school children becomes paramount.

Confusion among teaching methods

The teacher has a wide variety of methods, devices and approaches from which she can choose. How she chooses should surely depend— partly at any rate—on research findings about the effects of different methods, different devices and different approaches upon children in the relevant age group. Unfortunately, if Dr Goodacre's London survey is at all typical of teachers elsewhere, children in their first two years at school are often subjected to a somewhat haphazard application of 'mixed' methods which fails to take into very clear account either social, psychological or linguistic factors:

> The most important finding of this survey amongst urban infant schools is that broadly speaking the *social* area of the school had little effect upon teaching methods, materials, standards or even school conditions ... Mixed methods were those most often reported irrespective of the social area of the school. Even the 'whole word' approach, often described as suitable for duller children, was found to be no more popular in the lower working class area than either of the other two areas ... Even when the controversial question of the use of phonics was studied, the social area of the school made no appreciable difference in regard to this practice ...

At the same conference at which James Squire expressed his concern about the apparent failure of research findings to produce more striking results, Mary C. Austin stated that: 'As a minimum, all kindergarten teachers must become better grounded in reading instruction if they are to appraise more effectively each child's readiness for beginning reading, and to provide a school program adjusted to individual strengths and weaknesses.' Even if, as Southgate's article (1968) suggests, there is no precise way of evaluating the variables involved in the learning-to-read process, a grasp at any rate of *all the* relevant factors could provide the teacher with the insight to map out her own reading programme, adjusted to individual strengths and weaknesses in the class.

THE CHILD

Physical, mental, psychological and social factors

The many studies that have been made into reading development which have focused on the learner and his problems fall into four main categories—those with physical, mental, psychological and social factors. There is only room to summarise them very briefly here, as the only possible alternative to an entire book devoted to factors involved in the child's own personal developments.

In the first category it is obvious that unless the child can hear, see and articulate efficiently, and can interpret the sounds and visual information he receives correctly, he is not going to learn to read easily. Every child should ideally be tested for these basic abilities early in his school life, in order that any defects can be dealt with as far as possible before they permanently affect his progress.

In the second field the consensus of opinion among researchers is that non-verbal tests do not in themselves provide a satisfactory measure of a child's reading potential. They may provide a useful diagnostic guide but should never be taken as an absolute. For example children may learn to read far better than their IQ test at five would suggest— and the reading from a later IQ test may not agree with the first.

It has not yet been established to what extent psychological problems are the cause or the effect of reading difficulties, but research all points to an undeniable connection between the psychological stability or instability of a child and his ability to learn. Morris (1966) found considerable evidence for a link between backwardness in reading and emotional maladjustment.

It has been well known for some time that there is a significant tie-up between the child's progress and certain parental factors. A positive relationship has been shown to exist, for instance, between the number of books in the home and the proportions of good readers in the school; the parents' educational and cultural background and their interest in and encouragement of their children must strongly influence the children's desire to read.

Material factors on the other hand, do not seem to have nearly such a direct effect—or at least not above a certain level of prosperity. Below that 'threshold of bad material conditions', however, they can have a serious effect on children.

The importance of language

But by far the greatest and most handicapping deficiency of the culturally disadvantaged child is found in the realm of language. 'Poor' English, lack of ideas and limited general knowledge among the adults of the family must affect the child's verbal ability and his drive to learn to read. Bernstein and Lawson in the UK and education-ists such as Loban, Strickland and Jensen in the USA have provided an extensive body of research which demonstrates very clearly the crucial importance of the *kind* of spoken language that the young child acquires in his pre-school years for his later ability to cope at all adequately or easily with the written language.[1]

It is perhaps surprising that it is only during the last decade that research has directed any detailed attention to the relation which the speech forms possessed by the young child when first he comes to school bear to the whole of his subsequent education and especially to his 'capacity for literacy'. As Andrew Wilkinson (1965) pointed out in *Spoken English*, the lack of attention which talk in the classroom has received until very recently is truly astonishing. The conviction with which the '3 Rs' were accepted as educational goals had the effect of dismissing talking as a respectable educational activity. If children were talking they must be wasting their time because they could not be concentrating so well on their reading or their writing or their numbers, and so talking was discouraged by many teachers. In some schools it is still assumed without question that learning is more likely to take place in a hushed classroom than in a 'noisy' one.

All that I have been able to do here is to give some indication of the areas in which researchers have touched upon factors which affect the 5-6-year-old's mastery of the written language when he is confronted

[1] Since this book was in manuscript a paper by Labor (1969) has been published in this country which challenges many of the linguistic theories referred to in the following pages.

with the twin tasks of learning how to read and write in his first years at school. I have grouped these findings separately, for the sake of clarity, under the headings: vocabulary, structure and language attitudes—although in many ways of course, this is an artificial distinction. All aspects of language are interdependent in practice and should always be considered in close relation to each other. This categorisation should not lead a reader to infer that in school any one aspect can be taught or tackled separately from the other two. There still tends to be too great an emphasis, for instance, on the importance of vocabulary as a measurement of reading ability considered in isolation from other aspects of the child's reading development. It is not the child's ability to recognise a word or even to produce a single definition of a word's meaning which will by itself reflect his capacity to understand or to enjoy a book, and we delude ourselves by talking about such tests as if they were accurate measurements of reading ability.

The extent to which a child's capacity, not only for speech but for the exploration through speech of himself and his environment, is limited or extended by the vocabulary and language structure inside which he operates and by his basic attitude to language and what it is used for, must now be acknowledged as a subject of the greatest educational importance. What follows may help to draw attention to the kind of observations a teacher can make in her own classroom.

VOCABULARY

Bernstein (1958, 1959, 1960, 1961, 1962, 1964 and 1965) has characterised in considerable detail differences which appear to exist from a very early age between two varieties of 'English as it is spoken'. Originally he called one kind a 'public' language and the other a 'formal' language; subsequently he referred to the use of 'restricted' and 'elaborated' codes of speech. Bernstein suggests that all social groups use a restricted code of language on some occasions but that the lower socio-economic groups make little use of the 'formal' language or 'elaborated code' of speech. Consequently some children will only be able to listen in to one kind of language use at home whereas other children will be able to listen into—and thus begin to assimilate—two widely different language uses. Vocabulary differences between the 'restricted' and 'elaborated' language codes that Bernstein has noted include: a rigid and limited use of adjectives and adverbs in RC[1] but a discriminative selection from a range of adjectives and adverbs in EC[1]; the infrequent

1 RC: Restricted Code; EC: Elaborated Code.

use of impersonal pronouns in RC compared to a frequent use of such pronouns (e.g. it, one) in EC; a simple and repetitive use of conjunctions (so, then, and, because) in RC compared to a frequent use of conjunctions and prepositions 'which indicate logical relationships' in EC.

Investigations with older children suggest that schooling appears to do little to minimise the language gap between children who come from culturally different backgrounds. Bernstein (1960) found striking differences between the vocabulary scores of teenage working class and middle class boys. Although the *non*-verbal mean raw score of the middle class (public school) sample was not more than 3 points higher than the equivalent score for the working class group, the difference between the verbal mean raw scores (as measured by the Mill Hill Vocabulary Scale) favoured the public school group by 18 points.

In another investigation (1962) in which Bernstein again used contrasting groups of working class and middle class boys, 'a relatively undirected discussion' on capital punishment was recorded and then analysed for language differences. No differences were found in the proportion of finite verbs, nouns, prepositions, conjunctions and adverbs, but the middle class group was found to use a higher proportion of passive verbs, total adjectives, uncommon adjectives, uncommon conjunctions and the personal pronoun 'I'. The working class group used a higher proportion of total personal pronouns and especially of the pronouns 'you' and 'they'.

Metfessel (1962) notes the following vocabulary defects in culturally disadvantaged children:

1 Culturally disadvantaged children understand more language than they use. Even so, by second grade the comprehension vocabulary of such children is only approximately a third of that of normal children, while by sixth grade it is about one half.

2 Culturally disadvantaged children can use a great many words with fair precision but not those words representative of the school culture. It has been estimated that something *less than half* the words known by middle class pre-schoolers are known to slum children. Even such common home words as 'sink', 'chimney', 'honey', 'beef' and 'sandwich' are learned by culturally disadvantaged children one or two years later than by other children.

3 Culturally disadvantaged children frequently are handicapped in language development because they do not have the concept that

objects have names and that the same objects may have different names.

4   He concludes: culturally disadvantaged children use fewer words
. . . than do kindergarten children of higher socio-economic status.

Loban (1963) noted that over the first seven years of schooling all children in his investigation, drawn from widely ranging social groups, increased the number of words which they used in speech according to yearly measurement tests, but that the culturally advantaged children 'became able to use more words' than the culturally disadvantaged children, and thus they maintained their initial linguistic superiority.

Loban also noted that all social groups in his sample used the same number of words from among the 12,000 most common words in the English language, that the 'low sub-group' showed a higher incidence of words selected from the next 20,000 most commonly used words, but that the 'high sub-group' 'continued to expand their vocabulary and thus gained ascendancy in the use of the least commonly used words in the English language.'

Jensen (1967) describes what he calls the 'associative network': 'Words in context acquire associations. These verbal associations have other associations and so on, to form an elaborate, ramifying verbal associative network. This network is thought to act more or less automatically and unconsciously as a broad source of transfer for conceptual learning and retention . . . Word association experiments on children indicate that low socio-economic-status children have a less rich associative network. Even the words they know and use have, in this sense, less associative meaning to them and the associations are not as structured in terms of hierarchical characteristics that facilitate categorisation, conceptual analysis and the like.'[1]

STRUCTURE

'It is not words that give meaning to the sentence; it is the sentence that assigns meaning to the words in it.' *Ronald Morris*

'Language imposes its structure upon raw experience and structures and organises it in ways that the subject is able to recall for use at a later time. This ability is limited for the person who either has not acquired

[1] The assumption that 'deprived' children have a less rich associative network than those in higher socio-economic groupings has now been challenged vigorously by Labor in *The Logic of Non-standard English* (1969).

or does not habitually use the logical and structural properties contained in formal language.' *Arthur Jensen*

In the important early paper (1959) in which Bernstein first set out in detail the differences between his postulated 'public' and 'formal' languages, he noted certain structural differences between the two kinds of linguistic usage that he was describing. A speaker using the 'public' language or 'restricted code' would make frequent use of short, grammatically simple, often unfinished sentences whereas a speaker using the 'elaborated code' would more often use grammatically complex sentence constructions 'especially through the use of a range of conjunctions and relative clauses'[1]. Other characteristics of the elaborated code as compared with the restricted were:

1   Accurate grammatical order and syntax regulate what is said.

2   Individual qualification is verbally mediated through the structure and relationships within and between sentences, i.e. it is explicit, where the restricted code-user tends to make greater use of implicit non-verbal methods such as gesture for conveying personal qualifications and attitudes.

Strickland (1962) in a study designed to analyse the structure of children's language from the 1st to the 6th grade (6–12 years) has made the following points about the language patterns actually used by the children studied by her research team.

1   Patterns of structure within children's oral language can be identified and described.

2   Some basic patterns appeared with great frequency and other patterns and combinations with less frequency in the free talk of children.[2]

3   The most used and apparently basic patterns appeared with high

---

[1] In his analysis of the capital punishment discussions (cf. p. 31) Bernstein found that the middle class group used a higher proportion of subordinate clauses and complex verbal stems than the working class group.
[2] Both Strickland and Loban agree that it is 'the structural elements *within* the basic patterns' that are used with greater dexterity by children from rich linguistic backgrounds. Loban found that the 'high' group used progressively more subordination than the 'low' group. Bernstein, in this country, found that middle class teenagers used a higher proportion of complex verbal stems.

frequency in all the age groups. (cf. the most used words in Loban's study).

4   The lengths of phonological units[1] used by children varied more within a grade than from grade to grade.

5   The number of language patterns used by children in the study ranged from 658 in grade 1 to 1041 in grade 6.

6   The use of language patterns when children were classified according to verbal intelligence, non-verbal intelligence and the total intelligence showed few outstanding differences when frequencies of use were compared.

7   Regrouping children according to the occupation of parents revealed no major differences in the frequency of use of the patterns studied, but some differences appeared in the use of patterns when children were grouped on the basis of the education of fathers and mothers.

8   The application of the 'Chi-square' technique revealed significant differences at the 1, 2 and 5 per cent levels between the use of subordination patterns and verbal intelligence, mental age, occupational status and parents' education at grades 1, 4 and 6. These ratings of significance differed from grade to grade.

Loban—The Language of Elementary School Children (1963)
Here are some of the structural differences which emerged in the patterns of language usage used by children from high and low socioeconomic backgrounds in Walter Loban's study.

Structural patterns
1   The low group used many more *partial* expressions (sentence patterns that are incomplete) than the high group.

2   Except for the linking verb pattern and the use of partials, the differences in structural patterns used by the two groups are negligible. This *similarity* in use of patterns is considered to be an important finding of this study, especially when considered in relation to the findings which immediately follow.

---

[1] A phonological unit is (a) a unit of speech ending with a distinct falling intonation which signals a terminal point; (b) it may contain one or several meaningful communication units; (c) in this study the term 'sentence' means 'phonological unit'.

Elements within the structural patterns:

1 Although both groups used the same basic structural patterns, the elements within those patterns were used with far greater dexterity by the high group.

2 The high group used progressively more subordination than the low group and in spite of (or as well as) this increasing ability to formulate complex sentences, they still ended up with a greater number of 'communication units' (a group of words which cannot be further divided without the loss of their essential meaning) than the low group.

3 For subject nominals the low group depends almost exclusively on nouns and pronouns. The high group can use noun clauses, infinitives and verbals.

4 For nominals used as complements, both groups use nouns and pronouns with the same frequency, but the high group invariably exceeds the low group in the use of infinitives and clauses.

5 Those subjects most proficient with language are the ones who most frequently use language to express tentativeness. Supposition, hypothesis and conditional statements occur much less frequently in the spoken language of those lacking skill in language.

Language mazes
Some of the most interesting observations in this study are about the phenomenon that Loban defined as the 'maze'. All the children in the sample became involved in such mazes and Loban describes the characteristics of this apparent breakdown in the speaker's ability to manipulate language structurally as follows: 'One cannot listen to these recordings or read the transcripts without noting how frequently the subjects, when they attempt to express themselves, become confused or tangled in words. This confusion occurs not only in interview situations but also in the daily talk of the children, in the classroom when they share experiences, and on the playground of the school. The language behaviour in question is not a matter of words tumbling over one another but rather a case of many hesitations, false starts, and meaningless repetitions . . . The linguistic troubles of the subjects resemble very much the physical behaviour of a person looking for a way out of an actual spatial maze. He thrashes about in one direction or another until finally he either abandons his goal or locates a path leading where he wishes to go. Sometimes he stumbles upon a way out: sometimes he has presence of mind enough to pause and reason a way out.'

Loban defines such mazes as 'a series of words or initial parts of words which do not add up, either to meaningful communication or to structural units of communication. They are unattached fragments or a series of unattached fragments which do not constitute a communication unit and are not necessary to the communication unit. Sometimes the mazes are very long, consisting of from ten to twenty or more words or fragments of words.'

Loban found from his survey that from the age of five to the age of nine groups that were both low and high in language proficiency continued to have difficulties with language tangles or mazes, but apparently all the 'high group' members were gaining control of mazes whereas the members of the low group varied more in their control. Loban notes further, however, that from the age of ten the low group did show 'considerable improvement in controlling words per maze'.

LANGUAGE ATTITUDES

'Language is considered one of the most important means of initiating, synthesising and reinforcing ways of thinking, feeling and behaviour which are functionally related to the social group. It does not of itself prevent the expression of specific ideas or confine the individual to a given level of conceptualisation, but certain ideas and generalisations are facilitated rather than others, that is, the language use facilitates development in a particular direction rather than inhibiting all other possible directions.' *Bernstein*

Throughout the 1960s, and as one of the pioneers in focusing interest on the part that language plays in any individual's life, Bernstein has steadily concentrated on the effect that social attitudes on the functions of language can have and do have upon the actual words and structural patterns of any given speaker. It is this difference in attitude to the possibilities that language holds out for communication that underpins the distinction between Bernstein's two 'codes'. Denis Lawton's detailed summary of the 'two codes hypothesis' can be found in Appendix D. In relation to this specific context—i.e. those language factors from his home background which can influence the child's capacity for learning—the following are brief notes on particularly relevant points:

1 In a 'middle class controlled environment' a 'dynamic interaction can be set up between the child and the parents' (the mother has

received special attention in Bernstein's studies) in which there is 'pressure to verbalise feelings in a personally qualified way'. This for the middle class child becomes part of his socialisation process and determines the level of conceptualisation possible.

2 This 'pressure to verbalise' now provides the link with education: for the middle class child, the school which links the present to a distant future does not clash with the values of the home. Moreover, the child's level of curiosity is high and his ability to switch from public to formal language gives him sensitivity to role and status and enables him to behave appropriately in a wide range of social circumstances.

3 In the working class family, the language between the mother and child is 'public'—containing few personal qualifications and employing concrete symbolism. This tends to limit the verbal expression of feeling, and the emotional and cognitive differentiation of the working class child is, therefore, less developed.

4 The working class environment is thus in conflict with formal education in the following ways:
   (a) There is a clash between the child's accustomed immediate responses and the 'mediate' responses required by the school.
   (b) There will be an inability to communicate with the teacher on the teacher's own level.
   (c) The working class child will resist extensions to his vocabulary and resist efforts to 'improve' his control over language.
   (d) He will experience difficulty in dealing with more abstract concepts (e.g. phoneme-grapheme relationships).
   (e) This low level of curiosity will be interpreted as poor application to work.
   (f) He will have little opportunity to enhance his self-respect.

Robert Hess, of the University of Chicago, has also found considerable evidence of these two modes of language behaviour (public/ restricted and formal/elaborated) in the parent-child interactions of lower class and middle class Americans, observed in situations in which the mother is required to instruct her child in learning a simple task (Hess and Shipman, 1965); and Arthur Jensen (1967–8) wrote: 'The language of the lower class mother does not provide the child with cues and aids to learning to the same extent as the language of the middle class mother.' Jensen notes the following processes 'which can be said to spring from the child's general orientation to language':

1 *Labelling*
The habit of labelling or naming objects and events in the environment which in middle class children leads to a very close relation between perception and verbalisation.

2 *Abstraction and categorisation*
The ability to abstract and to categorise things in terms of various abstracted qualities (e.g. sounds).

3 *Attentional ability*[1]
Like Bernstein, Holt and Kirk, Jensen notes the apparent inability that some children have—especially disadvantaged children—to concentrate on what is happening in the classroom. Jensen writes, 'This deficiency is not so conspicuous in kindergarten but becomes clearly manifest in the first grade as soon as reading is introduced and other structured cognitive demands are made upon the child.' Jensen continues, 'In addition I have observed a secondary phenomenon: there is an actual deterioration of the child's attentional ability usually beginning in the first grade. Some children begin actively to resist focusing attention on teacher-oriented tasks and activities. Normal attention behaviour gives way to a kind of seemingly aimless and disruptive hyperactivity.'

4 *Verbal mediation (inner speech)*
One of Jensen's most interesting hypotheses is that working class children are much less likely than middle class children *to talk to themselves* as an aid to thinking. Jensen is chiefly concerned to point out the importance of this 'thinking' process in solving so-called *non*-verbal problems, but its relevance to a task like the act of reading is immediately clear. Children who are not in the habit of 'talking to themselves as an aid to thinking' may well take much longer to master the skill of decoding printed symbols in a meaningful way, whereas children whose inner speech is already well developed may experience little difficulty in regarding reading as 'silent speech'. The age at which children develop the ability to think inwardly is not very clear—Piaget suggested that inner speech did not develop until the child was at least six or seven, although Vygotsky interprets the gradual disappearance of egocentric

---

[1] An excellent discussion of attention as the term is used here and of its importance to educability is to be found in *The Backward Child* (Burt, 1937), pp. 479–85.

speech at a somewhat earlier stage as an indication that the ability to talk inwardly is developing. From my own experience—unscientific but on a day-to-day observational basis—I would guess that if the child's overt speech is well developed then his ability to use inner speech is evidenced certainly by the age of four, and probably considerably earlier.

If we recall Diack's suggestion that the image on the retina is somehow converted by complex brain processes into 'silent sound', the question of when the child develops such an ability for inner thought is an important one for reading specialists to bear in mind and it would be interesting to have further research evidence which demonstrates the presence or absence of inner speech processes in the pre-school and 'infant' school child.

PAUSES AND HESITATIONS IN SPEECH

It used to be customary (and probably still is in some classrooms) for English teachers to draw attention to the pauses and hesitations which occur in a child's speech—when he is talking to the rest of the class about some topic or speaking in a debate—as if these were weaknesses which, with practice, could be overcome. Any kind of 'sound fillers' for these pauses, such as 'er' or 'sort of' or 'you know', was condemned because they lacked meaning or precision, and the suggestion was that a fully articulate speaker would never be reduced to such fumbling and stumbling. Tape recordings (such as that quoted by Wilkinson in *Spoken English*, p. 28) have now shown that hesitations and sound fillers occur in any kind of spontaneous conversation however articulate the speakers.

Indeed, those who have investigated this particular phenomenon suggest that speech pauses should be regarded as an important part of the thought process in which the speaker is involved rather than as *breaks* in that process. Goldman-Eisler (1954) demonstrated, for instance, that the more complex the process, the longer and more frequent the pauses in speech. Bernstein (1962a) corroborated this finding by showing from discussions recorded on tape that 'hesitation phenomena' occurred noticeably more often in the conversation of clever middle class boys than they did in the speech of the working class groups. He concluded that such hesitations (amongst other speech characteristics described in the same article) 'entailed qualitatively different verbal planning orientations which controlled different modes of self regulation and levels of cognitive behaviour'. Lawton regards this particular experiment as important because 'it showed that restricted code and elaborated code are not simply different "styles" of speaking on a par with dialect differences but are related to different kinds of dimension of verbal planning, the conclusion being that restricted code users were habituated to "short run" searches in their verbal planning operations'.

Loban (1963) connected speech pauses and hesitation with language 'mazes', (cf. p. 35). His observations tend to confirm those of Bernstein and Lawton that restricted code users are more likely to use 'short run searches in their verbal planning operations'. Loban observes that sometimes the speaker 'thrashes about . . . until finally he either abandons his goal or locates a path leading where he wishes to go. Sometimes he stumbles upon a way out: sometimes he has presence of mind enough to pause and reason a way out'. Clearly the speaker's expectations about the possibilities of language are going to affect the degree to which he perseveres in his attempt to formulate what he set out to say explicitly: 'Sometimes the subjects persevere with the ideas they are trying to formulate and at the end of the maze do achieve a unit of communication. Other times the subjects abandon the ideas they are trying to express, perhaps finding the problem too difficult or too tiring to express, or not worth the effort. It is entirely possible that in another situation where the motivation was much greater the same idea represented in the maze might find its way to a clear expression of meaning.'

If researchers like Bernstein, Loban and Jensen are correct, clearly one of the most crucial tasks that the infant school teacher—and subsequent teachers—will have to face must be to find ways and means of changing the attitudes to language held by many of the children who enter their classes. When the children are from homes where most if not all of the conversation operates on a 'restricted code' basis unless they are deliberately encouraged to try out a different 'wavelength', and to experiment with ways of making their feelings and ideas verbally explicit, they may reap depressingly little of the benefit which derives from the educational dialogue that all effective teaching and learning involves. And unless the teacher is aware of the *nature* of the linguistic difficulties (of differences in attitude as well as in vocabulary and structure) which confront many children, these will remain for much of their time in school 'on the outside'. Like so many of the children observed by John Holt, they may be bored because they cannot respond to the language forms demanded by the teacher, and afraid of failure because they sense dimly a difference of attitude which they cannot pin down but which estranges them to a large extent from much of the activity which we call 'learning'.

POINTS FOR DISCUSSION

To conclude this section on the factors centred in the *child* which may affect his ability to learn, and to become literate when once he goes to school, I have set down a number of questions which groups of teachers or students may find useful as a basis for discussion or for further investigation:

1 How thorough are the medical checks in a child's *first term at school* on his ability to see adequately, to hear adequately and to articulate adequately?

2 How quickly (if at all) do teachers ascertain the child's 'measured' IQ when first he comes into school and how far do they keep a check on its fluctuations (if any) over the first few terms of his school life, or at regular intervals after the initial testing?

3 How closely are (a) any *initial* and (b) any *later* differences between verbal and non-verbal intelligence scores observed and recorded?

4 What steps are taken in the infant school or department to remedy emotional maladjustment in children *directly*, in view of the acknowledged connection between maladjustment and unsatisfactory progress in literacy skills? How far are infant teachers trained at college to recognise the various and wide-ranging symptoms of maladjustment in young children and how much information have they received about the appropriate channels for dealing with it?

5 How far can the child's *attitudes* to language be diagnosed by the infant teacher?

6 In what ways can the infant teacher encourage children to extend their own use of the spoken language, especially if the children who are restricted in their language uses are likely (a) to find the teacher's way of using language unfamiliar and (b) to resist any pressure to change their own habits?

7 Is plenty of opportunity for spontaneous talk a sufficient impetus to all children to extend their own use of language or can situations be structured—at infant level—to challenge or to encourage the children into new forms of thought and expression?

8 How far *do* the language patterns and attitudes of the teacher (implicit as well as explicit) help or hinder the expressive development of the children in her class in either its oral or its written form?

9   If some children from linguistically rich homes already possess the capacity to handle the spoken language in a variety of ways how far does this help their initial progress with literacy skills regardless of the methods and materials that are used?

   (Loban's study (1963) showed a positive statistical correlation between reading, writing, listening and speaking.)

10   How far will the approach to reading and the choice of reading materials which the teacher does decide to adopt affect the children's attitudes to the functions of language in relation to themselves? Will the degree to which these first written forms resemble the speech forms already familiar to the child be an important factor in his response—or a relatively minor one?

11   How many infant schools or departments attempt any kind of serious co-operation with parents as far as the education of their children-is concerned? How many headmistresses encourage their infant teachers to explain to the parents the educational aims which they have for the children in their classes and the *means* by which these aims are implemented? How many schools ever consider enlisting directly the parents' help in giving the child active encouragement and positive help in the development of his faculties and interests?

THE TEACHERS

One of the few points about which all investigators of reading achievement seem to be agreed, is—not altogether surprisingly—that successful learning depends to a large extent on the teacher: if the teacher is 'good' the children will learn from her (or him) whatever approach or method or materials she decides to use. It would perhaps be useful at this point, however, to analyse rather more precisely what it appears to be that makes a teacher 'good' or 'bad', both in general terms and, more particularly, in relation to the teaching of reading.

General factors in teaching ability

Experience: It may seem to be a truism to state that an experienced teacher is better than an inexperienced one. But as is the case with most obvious remarks, on closer inspection complications appear. We still, for example, know very little about how much experience is required before it is possible to *use* it to teach as well as to learn from it. In addition, we do not know what other factors may be involved which enable some teachers to use their experience dynamically where others actually seem to be prevented by past experience from rethinking and re-experiencing present problems. It is probably not so emphatic-ally a question of 'how much' or 'how little' as of how responsive or unresponsive these adults are to the nature of the children and to the nature of their subject. How teachers see children will depend initially partly on their own experiences as children at school and partly on the kind of training they have received—what physical, psychological and sociological factors have been brought to their attention. How they develop their power of perception will depend upon the extent to which they feel genuine interest and concern for the children in their classroom, continually modifying and adding to their theoretical knowledge by a lively awareness of how children react—to each other, to the teacher and to the 'finding out' which it is the teacher's job to encourage.

Malmquist found that teachers with twelve years' experience produce better readers than teachers with six years' experience but we want to know *why* and *how*. As Mackay and Thompson (1968) emphasise in their paper on literacy: 'If the work of the gifted teacher is to be of some help to her colleagues she must attempt to understand (and to make explicit) why she is successful.'

Rapport: Recent detailed analyses, both of children talking and of children writing in school situations, have demonstrated that the child's subconscious feelings about the teacher undoubtedly influence the kind of work he produces, because it affects the degree to which he can allow himself to become involved in the learning situation. If the child knows that his teacher will listen to him attentively and will consider his words carefully and seriously, he is less likely to be afraid of being made to look silly or small and therefore *more* likely to seek to know and to find out:

Liking and trusting the adults who help is obviously important; we do things for people we like more readily than for those we fear and distrust. (Mackay and Thompson)

In a report on teacher/pupil relationships in *New Education* (July, 1968), the following comments of secondary school boys are reported:

Mark says of the usual classroom situation, which we term 'repres-sive': 'I've got to be very careful. I only answer on things that I really know, that I definitely know, that I've read out of a book like. And then I say this and this and Mr — says "Oh, that's very good, Hull". But I never answer unless I'm positive I'm right.'

To this Paul added: 'I've often sat in the classroom and someone's asked a question and I've had the answer in my mind and yet I haven't put my hand up. I don't know why. When he gives the answer I could kick myself for not putting my hand up. I think you're a bit frightened you're going to get it wrong or something and that the master's going to turn round and shout or something like that and say you're an idiot.'

If this sense of the teacher's responsiveness or lack of it affects *what* children learn (because it affects *how* they can learn) at secondary level, surely this must be equally if not more the case for five- six- and seven-year-olds whose sense of their own identity and confidence in their own powers when they first come to school is bound to be more precarious and easily upset. The extent to which the infant teacher conducts her lessons formally or informally, and the way in which she structures her class, have important implications here. The degree of formality or informality which she encourages in her relations with the children may be more important in this very personal respect than her choice of a reading scheme—or materials.

In a recent interview with the editor of *New Education*, Sir Alec Clegg describes one Junior School class with which he is familiar— 'where children are required to talk all day and every day'. He goes on to say: 'It is unlike anything I have ever seen. But it is a simple fact that this particular class—which draws on not too good a social back-ground—has sent to the grammar school each year for the last two or three years something like twenty-eight children out of thirty-eight, when I would have expected it to send about six. And last year (1967) every child but one scored an IQ mark above the hundred—above the national average.'

It is clear that the teacher here has such good relations with the class that she can allow them free rein and still maintain her control of the situation—with remarkable results.

Perhaps one of the secrets of rapport is summed up in the suggestion of Mackay and Thompson that the teacher 'should be able to employ in day-to-day classroom situations a flexible range of human relationships; engaging in fun, seriousness, permissiveness and firmness, praising, encouraging and understanding and becoming as aware of her own failures to teach as of the children's failures to learn. Her competence will be seen [felt?] by each child as her ability to help him succeed and here the teacher is not only an instructor but a learner'. They illustrate this point with the following quotation from Jerome Bruner: 'It is our task as learned men and scientists that discovering how to make something comprehensible to the young is only a continuation of making some things comprehensible to ourselves in the first place—understanding and aiding others to understand are both of a piece.'

The teacher's approach

How do teachers assess children's readiness to begin reading when first they come into the reception class?

How do they assess reading progress once the child has embarked on a reading programme?

What kind of standards (if any) do they expect the children to reach while in their class?

Does the social background from which the child comes influence the teacher's expectations about its progress?

Does the social background from which the teacher comes likewise influence her assessment?

These are all questions posed by Dr Goodacre in both her London surveys but particularly in the 1968 investigation.[1] Here in brief are her original findings from the initial survey:

How do teachers assess children's readiness to begin reading? Goodacre notes that 'teachers differ both in their desire for such data and in their confidence in the reliability of the information. Although the use of standardized tests[2] in schools has increased during the last decade, this report shows that such measures *are confined to the assessment of older "infants"* and that the infant teacher depends largely on subjective estimates based on the reliability of her own powers of observation to determine an individual pupil's reading ability *throughout his infant schooling.*

'Teachers certainly attached far more importance to *attitude* and *interest* in learning to read then to the development of the *perceptual abilities* as a sign of readiness; *48.5 per cent* of the items mentioned were connected with the child's attitude to reading activities: interest in all kinds of books: keenness to read: interest in the printed word

[1] For a detailed summary of Goodacre's first and second reports see Appendices F and G.
[2] A list of diagnostic tests that are available from the NFER is given in Appendix C.

generally: interest in pre-reading activities and materials: interest in stories from books. Only 7.7 per cent of the items mentioned discrimination of shapes generally, knowledge of letter sounds, awareness of left to right sequence or association of word patterns with pictures and ideas. 6.3 per cent of the items mentioned the importance of spoken language development and *under 5 per cent* referred to the child's emotional adjustment to the school situation.'

Readiness for what? A further interesting feature of the investigation at this point was that *whatever* the criteria of readiness stated by the various teachers ('interest' or 'perceptual abilities') *no* significant difference emerged regarding the type of introductory method used. *Whatever* the readiness criterion similar proportions of children were *introduced* to reading by either global methods excluding phonic instruction or 'mixed' methods inclusive of phonics.

How is reading progress assessed once the child has embarked on a reading programme? Forty-three per cent of the infant schools or departments in Goodacre's survey used standardised reading tests. Of the schools using them, however, 40 per cent did so *only in the last term* before promoting pupils to the junior school.

Schonell's tests were the most often mentioned—more than half the schools using tests, used the Schonell Word Recognition Test. Eleven used Burt's Graded Word Reading Test; only seven used a 'reading for meaning' test—six using the Holborn Reading Scale (Watts) and one the Neale Analysis of Reading Ability. Only three out of the 100 schools used *both* types of reading attainment test.

Six Heads, although they did not use standardised tests, made a point of mentioning that they recorded the pupils' progress by testing them for their knowledge of letter sounds or recognition of the words of the basic vocabulary of the primer.

Reception class teachers' comments on the use of tests: No reception class teacher used a standardised reading test, but fourteen teachers explained how they tested pupils at this age. Twelve tested word recognition by asking the children to name the words provided in the vocabulary lists at the back of the primer, or on flash cards, wall charts or other reading apparatus. Only one teacher tested for the knowledge of the letter sounds. Seven reception class teachers commented that they considered testing was of no value at this age. They may well have been correct not to place any emphasis on 'testing' the children at this early stage, but Goodacre points out that unless the teacher has a clear idea of what the child can do—and what the next step appropriate for its reading development is—she cannot be said to have a firm grip on the learning situation:

> The crucial aspect of all such learning situations is the necessity to maintain the interest to learn, while keeping the learning situation within the capabilities of the learner at that stage. The process needs to be one of constant reappraisal, the teacher providing opportunities for practice so that confidence is gained and the knowledge assimilated, all the while watching for signs of flagging interest or the opportunity to introduce the child to the next task in the sequence. The latter may prove particularly difficult as it necessitates a knowledge by the teacher of the progression and stages of learning involved in the teaching of the skill. Those familiar with teaching machines would recognise this as the knowledge of the necessary units of programming.

We may have reservations as to how far this skill-centred approach could maintain the child's interest by itself, but there is certainly a need for more precise knowledge about the nature of the learning situation— with particular reference here to the activity of reading and *how* the teacher is to recognise when genuine development and progress is taking place and when it is not. Perhaps Mackay and Thompson are on the right lines when they say: 'At present we know something of what the teacher does in her classroom, but we know all too little about how the pupil is reacting, interpreting and understanding her procedures. This complex process needs to be described objectively in carefully defined and consistently used terms.'

Teachers' standards and expectations: Two thirds of the reception class teachers in Goodacre's survey were found to set no specific standard; in most cases they believed each child should be allowed to progress at his own rate or that any uniform goal was unattainable since promotion to the next class was dependent upon age rather than ability.

Of the thirty-six reception class teachers who did aim at a specific standard, twenty-five referred to the 'introductory book' as their criterion or as one of their criteria: only three out of the thirty-six actually mentioned recognition of letter sounds and there were *no references* to signs of *understanding* the meaning of the material to be read or of *enjoyment* derived from the activity.

Does the child's social background influence the teacher's expectations? More pupils in the suburban, middle class schools were estimated by their teachers to be reading Book 4 or beyond than pupils in either of the working class groups, but also these schools had a larger proportion of pupils estimated to be reading Book 1 or below; i.e. 'poor readers' by their teachers' standards. If teachers' estimates of their pupils' reading attainments are compared with their actual *tested* attainment, they reveal an *under*estimation of working class pupils who appear to do better than the predictions suggested. In relation to teachers' estimates of pupils' attainment on the basis of 'which book they were on', the middle class pupils were superior to the working class although on the actual test the pupils in working class[1] area schools *showed superior attainment.*

Does the teacher's social background influence her assessment? To account for this discrepancy between the tested and estimated reading attainment of working class and middle class children, Goodacre advances the following (somewhat debatable) hypothesis:

> The teacher's values, attitude and expectations . . . are probably intimately related to her own social class origin . . . It may well be that the working class teacher's expectations of working class pupils are *lower* than those of a middle class teacher, as the former is overcritical and underestimates the potential ability of her pupils in order to emphasise her own social mobility and attained social status as evidenced by graining entry to the teaching profession.

Goodacre suggests further that 'the explanation for the similar reading achievement of the working class and middle class area schools in comparison with the significantly lower attainment of the lower working class children is that the working class teachers in the lower working class schools, by reason of their status anxiety, underestimate these pupils' ability as do the teachers of middle class origin in the same area, who do so because they are unfamiliar with such children and their level of achievement. Whereas the teachers in the middle class area, irrespective of their own social class origin, tend to over-estimate the ability of their pupils and depress the level of achieved attainment,

[1] Goodacre's 'second group' between lower working class and middle class.

possibly by reason of setting too high standards which produce too great a level of anxiety in the pupils or dissipate their interest.' However plausible or implausible such a hypothesis may at first seem, it is examined in Goodacre's second report in such detail that it deserves serious consideration; she is certainly correct in her assertion that this aspect of the learning situation has received very little attention from either educationists or sociologists.

The teacher's aims

In a paper presented at the Third International Reading Symposium and entitled 'Are today's teachers adequately trained for the teaching of reading?', William Latham (1968) suggests that 'the teacher be able to offer clear and relevant answers to the following questions:

1 What are my aims?

2 What actions are necessary to achieve these aims?

3 How can I assess (a) what has already been achieved, and (b) what my subsequent actions help the child to achieve?'

In the last analysis these are the factors which will decide the kind of reading programme that a teacher offers to her class and the kind of results that she reaps. She may be content to regard reading at this stage as primarily a decoding process, in which case form is likely to take precedence over content in the materials that she provides for her class. She may, on the other hand, place greater emphasis on the need to foster the child's capacity for *response* to the written language, in which case content should take precedence over form. She may come to the conclusion that decoding and responding are both important aspects of reading and thus create opportunities for the child to do both in her classroom (though not necessarily at the same time).

Undoubtedly many infant teachers in this country, perhaps the majority, take 'reading' to mean 'the ability to re-convert written or printed language into speech'; in other words, reading for their pupils is principally a decoding operation. Far fewer teachers at this stage would regard reading *principally* as 'the act of reconstructing from the printed page the writer's ideas, feelings, moods and sensory impressions'.

Now Latham warns that if reading is taken to be 'nothing more than the correlation of a sound image with its corresponding visual image', this will lead to a tendency to restrict infant teachers' training in the teaching of reading to those skills which are specifically connected with the successful analysis of phoneme-grapheme relationships. On the other hand, if 'reading' is taken to imply 'reconstructing from the printed page the writer's ideas, feelings, moods and sensory impressions', this will lead to 'a search for integrated programmes which will cover the *range* of skills required'. 'Such a search', Latham continues, 'may lead, when associated with the concept of reading as a developmental process, to a further logical integration of the process of communication.' Instruction in reading may, as Paul Witty suggests is already happening in the United States, come to be considered 'as part of a larger programme in communication that aims to lead children to speak clearly, write efficiently, listen intelligently and read critically. That is, reading comes to be seen and dealt with rightly as part of literacy.'

To adopt this second view of the nature of the reading process is not to suggest that alternative approaches to the teaching of reading would be eliminated. Latham appears to suggest for instance that his quarrel is chiefly with the *narrowness* of the infant teacher's skill-centred aims at present, and to argue in effect for *a wider range of skills* ('higher order skills such as aid comprehension and inference') to be taught. There would still be differences therefore between the teaching programme of a teacher who adopted such an approach and a teacher who taught on a *child*-centred rather than a *skill*-centred basis, even though both accepted Latham's wider definition of reading.

The alternative definitions of 'reading' given here drop away, for most children, as they move up the school, but the alternative *centres of interest*, the child and his needs or the subject and its skills, remain. In the second half of this book, it will become clear that 'child-centred' and 'skill-centred' teachers become involved in very different kinds of teaching. The English teacher's choice of reading materials at secondary level, and the way in which the novels, plays and poems chosen are presented to the class, will be very much affected by his or her implicit or explicit aims. What we must above all try to find out is whether the children's response is similarly affected—and in what ways.

Value-centred aims and skill-centred aims: In his UNESCO Survey of 'The teaching of reading and writing', Gray (1956) claims that: 'In planning any reading programme the specific aims to be attained are of major importance since they influence not only its nature and scope but also the content and methods of teaching.' He identifies two types of aims, the first group concerned with values, the second with skills. Gray states that value-centred aims are:

1 to extend the experiences of children concerning things within the range of their environment

2 to make their lives more meaningful through an understanding of the experience of others

3 to extend their knowledge of things, events and activities to other places, countries, people, times

4 to deepen interest in their expanding world

5 to develop improved attitudes, ideals and behaviour patterns

6 to enable pupils to find the solution of personal and group problems appropriate to their age level

7 to enrich their cultural background

8 to provide pleasure and enjoyment through reading

9 to develop improved ways of thinking and expressing ideas

10 to help them become more familiar with the interests, activities and problems of the community

According to Gray, skill-centred aims are:

1 to develop keen interest in learning to read

2 to stimulate the development of an inquiring attitude or a demand for meaning in reading

3 to develop accuracy in word recognition

4 to promote efficiency in solving simple personal or group problems as one reads

5 to develop habits of effective oral reading

6 to increase the speed of silent reading

Gray advises the teacher of reading to give greater emphasis to value-centred than to skill-centred aims, on the grounds that 'most if not all reading lessons should *help to enrich the experiences of children, clarify their thinking or further their development in one form or another*'. He adds that 'the nature and variety of the attitudes and skills that should be emphasised during any reading lesson are determined in large measure by the values sought'.

If Goodacre's diagnosis of the trend in London schools is applicable to the country as a whole, however, we appear to be placing increasing emphasis in our infant classrooms on skill-centred aims:

> When the type of approach used is described as being either child-centred or curriculum-centred there appears to be some evidence that during the past five years there may have been a change in infant teachers' opinions and practices. *The importance of the basic skills and the value of a controlled and planned classroom environment received more emphasis in these London schools than the individual freedom of the child . . .*

SCHOOL CONDITIONS

The child will of course react not only to the factors relating directly to the teaching staff: he will also be influenced by the school situation itself. Important factors are such 'concrete' details as the shape and spatial size of the building, the numerical size of the school as a whole and of classes in particular; and also include the educational resources of the school such as books, tape recorders and television.

Obviously all these factors are going to have an effect on the child's educational progress generally, but, thanks to the National Foundation for Educational Research, three research reports, by Morris (1959) and Goodacre (1967 and 1968), have now been published in this country which have specifically investigated the observable and measurable relation that school conditions can have to reading achievement. Because all three are now widely available I have confined my references here to the briefest of summaries and comparisons of the first two surveys, along with a fuller account of all three in Appendices F and G. I do, however, recommend first-hand reading of the very detailed records of their findings which both Dr Morris and Dr Goodacre have produced.

The only previous study which has attempted in any detail to take school conditions into account was that of Kemp (1955) who had found that 'the main factors determining level of attainment in the formal school subjects are, in *decreasing* order of importance: intelligence, socio-economic status and the numbers on the school roll. *Class* size, new buildings and informal methods were reported to have little relation to level of attainment'.

Dr Morris's survey of sixty Kent primary schools (1959)

Two of the chief aims of Morris's original Kent survey were, first, 'to study the association between nine school characteristics and the reading achievement of children aged between seven and eleven', and second, 'to observe and record those conditions of learning and teaching reading in Kent primary schools which would provide a reference for this investigation and future studies and also be of interest to educationists in general'.

Nine school characteristics were taken into consideration:

1 urban/rural location (criterion: whether the school was administered by urban or rural district councils)

2 socio-economic status of the *school catchment* area

3 type of school organisation (e.g. Junior 'Mixed' Boys and Girls, Junior and Infant school combined, etc.)

4 size of school

5 type of buildings

6 size of classes

7 whether there was a formal approach to the teaching of reading in the reception class

8 whether phonic instruction was given to five-year-olds

9 whether systematic phonic instruction was used as a *commencing* method for the teaching of reading

The relationship between school conditions and reading attainment: It became apparent from the Kent survey that good reading attainment was often associated with the following school characteristics: large schools; large classes (often with a comparatively unfavourable pupil–teacher ratio); a middle class neighbourhood; superior buildings; an organisation which separated 'Infants' from 'Juniors'; and an early *formal* approach to the teaching of reading. On this latter point, however, Morris comments that 'the high level of significance favouring "phonics" as a commencing method in schools of this kind' must be viewed with caution because it could be said to be 'due to a relatively large adjustment compensating for the lower non-verbal scores of schools using this method'.

It would probably be true to say that the only finding here which may cause any surprise is the apparently negligible effect of an unfavourable teacher–pupil ratio in large classes (given that the other factors mentioned are present). We should remind ourselves, however, that the factors which appear from this survey to be connected with successful reading attainment from the age of seven onwards will have to be shown to recur in further surveys if any firm reliance is to be placed on them. It may be that factors centred in the child rather than the school are always of prime importance—and that any kind of school which draws its pupils from a middle class catchment area will show better results than a school comprised largely of 'disadvantaged' children *regardless* of the school organisation or of the reading methods and materials that are used.

Also, school factors which were not considered in this survey may have as important an effect on children learning to read as any of the variables which do receive a mention. For example, the effect of phonic instruction was taken into account but not the effect of teaching devices such as i.t.a., for the simple reason that in the 1950s neither i.t.a. nor Words In Colour nor Colour Story Reading nor Breakthrough to Literacy Folders were in use in any infant schools. Further, the teacher was not considered separately as a 'school condition' in Morris's survey, nor was the structuring of the class within the classroom for teaching purposes.

Dr Goodacre's survey of 100 London infant schools or departments

Dr Goodacre (who was a colleague of Dr Morris at the National Foundation for Educational Research) was thoroughly conversant with the results of the Kent survey when she undertook her own investigation in 1959. Indeed, some of the questions that she put to Head teachers and infant teachers were specifically designed to elicit information which could be fairly closely compared with Morris's findings. What follows is a brief summary, first of additional information about some of the school characteristics investigated by Morris and, secondly, of additional points which provide information about the school conditions in which the London children found themselves.

Organisation—infant schools or departments? It became apparent from a review of the findings of the first Goodacre survey that school organisation had relatively little effect upon either the way reading was taught or the level of reading attainment. Apart from the basic difference of size (infant schools tended to be larger than infant departments) schools and departments differed from each other in only three major respects:

1 Whether there was an organised library for the sole use of the infant age range of children.

2 In certain physical conditions primarily involving space, evidenced by the difference in storage facilities and playing areas (in favour of the infant schools).

3 In the provision made for backward readers. More 'infant only' head teachers made special provision for these pupils (0.1 per cent level). Only one in four of the J.M. and I. schools made such provision in comparison with three out of four of the infant schools.

The socio-economic status of the school catchment area: On the basis of occupational distribution, Goodacre placed the schools in three different groups, summarised as lower working class, working class and middle class. The distinguishing characteristics of all three are described in detail in her 1967 report.

On the basis of this social grouping, Goodacre made the following observations:

1 There was no significant difference between the schools in the different social areas as regards their choice of reading method or approach.

2 There was no significant difference between the groups of schools regarding the choice of introductory method, or whether systematic phonic instruction was given to the reception-class pupils. In *each* social area there was a similar proportion of reception-class teachers who were in the habit of giving phonic instruction to all their five-year-olds, irrespective of the background, experience or mental ability of their pupils.

3 Social area appeared not to influence the choice of reading scheme. and *Janet and John*, with its middle class characters, was equally popular in schools in all areas.

4 The schools in the three social areas did not differ significantly in their use of reading apparatus or in the existence or use of organised libraries.

5 No significant differences were observable regarding the standards

of reading readiness or the proportion of children able to read at entry.

6   There was no significant difference between the 'groups' of schools in respect to the heads' estimates of book levels achieved by the end of the infant course.

7   There was no significant difference between the groups of schools in relation to the use of standardized tests or in the teachers' opinions regarding the application of the term 'backward' or their provision for such children. The higher the social area, the larger the proportion of schools in which special attention was paid to such children, but the differences were too small to be statistically significant.

8   When grouped according to social class, the schools did *not* differ significantly either in the mean age of school buildings or in the mean material environment score, neither did they differ significantly regarding amenities and facilities.

9   The pupil/teacher ratio tended to be more favourable the higher the social area (5 per cent level).

10 The *lower* working class areas had a larger proportion of young teachers (especially taking the reception classes), whilst the *working* class areas had the highest proportion of teachers aged over forty. The lowest proportion of married teachers occurred in the lower working class area but in neither case (marital status or age distribution) did the difference reach significance.

11 In their approach to the teaching of reading the schools did not differ significantly in their materials and methods, their estimates of readiness and their expectations regarding standards, nor in their material and staffing conditions. Nevertheless, in the pupils' reading *attainment* at the end of the infant course there were significant differences according to social groupings. These differences were shown both in the standardised reading test scores and in the 'book criterion' (also used by Morris). The lower working class schools were markedly inferior to the rest. There were *less* significant differences between the working and middle class schools: in fact when the three social area means were considered, the pupils in the working class area schools showed superior attainment.

In her conclusions Goodacre comments: 'The superiority of the working and middle class schools in comparison with the lower working class pupil is marked. The most interesting aspect of these results is the fact that the working class schools' attainment is *not*, as might have been expected, significantly different from that of the middle class schools *in relation to tested attainment*, but the *expected* superiority of the middle class schools is apparent when the measure is *the teachers' assessments*.'

The infant teacher's approach to reading: In the Kent inquiry 80 per cent of the schools (48 out of 60) had been classified as 'informal' in approach by the investigator on the grounds that they 'tended to recognise the importance of individual differences, encouraged self-discipline, delayed the use of primers until individual children were ready and encouraged children to learn by the provision of a rich classroom environment'. Of the London schools 73 per cent described *themselves* (i.e. were not necessarily so described by the investigator) as informal, so that there would appear to be no significant difference between the areas in the proportion of schools which were organised on an informal basis. Goodacre notes, however, that '*the picture alters when the London teachers' descriptions of these categories are considered*'.

On the basis of details of their approach sent in by the teachers, Goodacre has regrouped them as follows, not according to whether they are formal or informal, but according to whether they are primarily child-centred or curriculum-centred. *Child-centred* she defines as an approach in which interest is aroused by the teacher using the child's *own* interests, experiences etc.: stress is laid on learning through play; analytic methods are used for the teaching of reading in preference to synthetic. In the *curriculum-centred* approach, the child's interest is aroused *by the teacher*, who introduces material, likely interests and so on either orally or visually, for example by means of stories, verses or visual aids. Play is 'directed' and stress is laid on a primer from the beginning; a synthetic method of teaching the children to read is preferred to a global or analytic method and children are likely to be taught in groups rather than individually.

If the eight schools are omitted who were unable or chose not to describe their approach, this grouping in comparison with the previous self-labelling as 'formal' or 'informal' produces 38 per cent 'child-centred' and 62 per cent 'curriculum-centred' schools. However, thirty-six heads who followed a 'curriculum-centred' approach also described their approach as 'informal'.

The use of phonic instruction: In the Kent inquiry the majority of teachers seem to consider that 'too early an introduction to sounds may adversely affect fluency and comprehension at a later stage in the child's development and schooling'. In Goodacre's survey, the reception class teachers of thirty-eight schools state that they gave phonic instruction to *all* pupils, and in a further twenty-two phonic instruction was given to *some* pupils in their first year of schooling. In other words in nearly two-thirds of the schools in the survey phonic instruction was given to some or all the children before they were six years old.

Goodacre contrasts this practice with Schonell's dictum that 'it is not until about *mental age 7* that a child can intelligently make use of the breaking-down-building-up method of tackling new words'.

Comparison of the results of the Kent and London surveys

The pattern which emerges from Goodacre's analysis of the differences between schools when they are grouped, firstly on an *organisational* and secondly on a *social* basis, is more equivocal than that of Morris's survey. It indicates that we must be extremely cautious in the deductions that we draw about the effects which any given 'school' factors have upon the educational development and achievement of children. The London survey would not appear to confirm Morris's finding, for instance, that separate junior schools were more successful in terms of reading achievement than schools which combined infant and junior departments.

The relationship between reading achievement and social catchment area would, on the other hand, appear to be confirmed to some extent by Goodacre's findings (the tested achievement of the 'lower working class schools was markedly inferior to the rest'). But here too the complex interrelation of differences when working class and middle class schools were considered (p. 81 of the Survey) indicates that no clear overall conclusions can be drawn about the overriding influence of socio-economic to socio-cultural background.

Goodacre changed the original 'formal' and 'informal' labels with which teachers were asked to classify their approach, to 'child-centred' or 'curriculum-centred'. This raises some important questions about the relationship of formality and informality to both the child centred and the subject centred teaching situations. They will recur with some force in Volume 2, *The Reader's Response*, where the teaching of reading to the secondary age group is considered. The degree to which a child can be left to himself to discover through his own needs and interests a structure that will extend his knowledge or deepen his insights, and the degree to which such a structure must be planned for him, still requires a great deal of thought and patient experiment from any teacher who is genuinely interested in teaching, or in children, or in both!

Organisation within the classroom

Another school condition to which increasing attention is now being paid by curriculum planners and developers (although it receives no specific attention from either Morris or Goodacre) is the effect on the learning situation of various organisational possibilities. All teachers, at every stage of the child's life in school must group their class in one of the three following ways: they must:

1 teach the class as one large group

2 divide the class into small groups

3 divide the class into individuals

There are two questions that we can ask here. First, does the child learn more effectively with one kind of organisation rather than another regardless of the material that may be used? Second, which materials for use in a reading programme at the infant or early primary stage can be employed most effectively with which type of organisation?

The class group: There are certainly occasions when it is desirable for the teacher to bring her children together as a class—after all they share the same classroom and rapidly gain some sense of class identity ('I'm in class two now') which it is much better for the teacher to utilise than to ignore. Reading to the children offers one such opportunity: the infant teacher may gather them all round her at the end of the morning or of the afternoon to tell them a story which, if it is well told, they can share with jointly bated breath. The teacher may also ask her children as a class group for news items which can be shared and discussed by everybody before they are recorded in news sheets or 'experience charts'. Many teachers still present flash cards to the class as a whole or ask individuals in a class situation to decipher display labels or words written up on the blackboard. Whether the class group is the most suitable for this kind of work is arguable; such a 'black and white' confrontation, where being wrong is the inevitable alternative to being right and failure is the penalty for ignorance or uncertainty, is likely to force the child into forms of behaviour which he might otherwise avoid in order not to appear foolish in front of the rest of the class.

Some reading schemes give more scope for class teaching than others. In the Words in Colour scheme for instance, children are encouraged to come forward from the class to write on the blackboard the appropriate coloured signs for various sounds, and I have seen a Colour Story Reading lesson conducted from the blackboard in a similar sort of way. This is not to say that these schemes *necessitate* a class approach; they could equally well be used for a course of individual programmed instruction or for work in pairs (as some of Gattegno's word games in fact are). But at present blackboard work with the whole class is still more commonly employed than are individual sets of cards. It is cheaper, of course, and the materials involved are more readily expendable.

Individual work: A large proportion of the work which a child does in an infant class in this country is work which he chooses to do by and for himself. Drawing, painting, writing, sewing are all individual activities. However, what is chiefly of interest to us here is how far his decoding and reading activities can be accomplished successfully on an individual basis.

As we noted at the very beginning of this book, once the child has mastered the code, reading is most often a private activity. The more proficient the child becomes the more he will be able to retire to a corner to 'lose himself' in a book. Absorbed reading of this kind is one undoubted goal for the teacher of reading and time should always be available for children to look at or to read *any book* of their own choice at some point in the school day. There are still schools where teachers refuse to allow children to bring their own books or their library books into the class on the 'one-book-a-week-only' principle—if principle it can be called. I can think of nothing to support such an attitude if the teacher genuinely aims to interest the child in reading for pleasure.

The common practice of the teacher 'hearing' a child read a page from his reading primer every day is perhaps the most popular form that the individual teaching of reading takes in our classrooms in the infant school at present. Unfortunately, where the classes are overcrowded the teacher often does not manage to hear every child daily, so that if the child is keen to read he comes home disappointed because he cannot go on with his book until he has 'been heard'—and if the child is apathetic, he receives an insufficient incentive from this inadequate allotment of the teacher's time to make any further efforts to improve his own rate of progress.

Once the child has begun to grasp the written code for English he can work by himself on special workbook exercises for both encoding and decoding practice. Mackay and Thompson's scheme which encourages children to build up sentences of their own from the start is also largely an individual activity, although initially the child has to depend a great deal on the teacher (or an older literate child) until he has mastered the accurate recognition of the words in his folder. Similarly, once children using i.t.a. have learnt the code they often forge ahead with reading and writing on their own.

Of the materials which I shall describe in the next section the Talking Typewriter gives the clearest instance of the way in which the materials that are used for any scheme can impose a particular kind of organisation on the learner. The attention of the ERE or Talking Typewriter can only be directed to one child at a time or, in the terms used by Moore (1963), only one child at a time can be placed at the centre of this 'responsive environment'. Indeed, the privacy and seclusion which is provided by the enclosed cubicle in which the machine is housed is considered to be therapeutically valuable for maladjusted children. The pressures of responding to another *human* being are removed and the child is free to talk or to remain silent, to press the keys or to leave them, without any fear of arousing antagonism in his teacher.

Work in small groups: Perhaps the most effective kind of group work for the five- to six-year-old can be undertaken in pairs and there are many reading activities that can be shared by children working in twos from the very beginning. Stott (1962) and Gattegno (1962) have both devised decoding games for children to play together in twos, and the thoughtful teacher could work out extensions or modifications of these to fit in with whichever decoding approach she happened to be using. Games challenge children directly and thus often involve them more readily than workbook exercises or other forms of individual reading practice. The concept of reading as an act of communication is also made clearer if one child is reading aloud to another. Given that *what* he is reading is interesting and well written, as his decoding skills increase so should his ability to read with expression—which might be neglected if the words are decoded silently and never heard in their oral form. Schools organised on a family grouping basis have greater scope for working in pairs in this way but in any class some children move ahead more quickly than others and their talents could often be used more effectively if they were paired with a slower child and *encouraged* to help him or her along.

IV Teaching children to read— decoding methods

'Reading means getting meaning from certain combinations of letters. Teach the child what each letter stands for and he can read. Ah no, you say, it can't be that simple. But it is.' *R. Flesch*

'We . . . reached the conclusion that the best way of teaching a child to read is to devise a method that would bring him as quickly and easily as possible to insight and knowledge about letters—what various letters look like and how they are used.' *J. C. Daniels and H. Diack*

'Real reading occurs only when the child gets the meaning of whole sentences.' *Huey*

'Reading is much more than the mechanical recognition of words; it is a thought getting process and, as such, a logical development of language.' *Joyce Morris*

'A well planned reading programme cultivates an inquiring attitude and helps supply the necessary background. Beyond these considerations which relate to meaning and behaviour are the aesthetic abilities to judge and enjoy the quality of the matter read.' *W. S. Gray*

'Unfortunately, for reasons partly associated with divergent psychological theories . . . the verb "to read" has ceased to have an agreed meaning even among those concerned with education.' *William Latham*

We have already glimpsed briefly the division of opinion which these statements exemplify in our discussion of the aims which lie behind the infant teacher's interpretation of 'reading'. On the one hand the teacher's task can be viewed quite narrowly as a 'decoding' one: the child has to be taught the sound or sounds represented by letter symbols so that when these are placed in combination with each other he can recognise words. It is easy to assume that once he has mastered the code, to all intents and purposes the child can read. On the other hand, there are teachers and educators who object to the reading process—at any stage—being reduced to the mechanics of a decoding operation however complicated the skills involved in breaking the code may be. They would argue that if a child is to be motivated to read, *what* he reads (or attempts to read) at *any* stage in the development of the process must be meaningful to him and capable of exciting positive feelings of pleasure and satisfaction. It is what the words *convey*, once the bridge between the written and spoken language has been crossed, that is important for the child, and too much time spent in examining the construction of the bridge itself may mean that he never reaches the other side.

Moreover, reading experts with a knowledge of linguistics are increasingly concerned to stress the dangers of splitting off any kind of language activity into a category of its own. The written forms of a language are rooted in its spoken forms and to ignore what speech has come to mean to any particular child when the first attempt is made to introduce him to written language may prove to be the worst error a teacher of reading can make. As Geoffrey Greenwood, the originator of the Wolverhampton tape scheme, has said:

> If we take children who cannot think of the language of books as an extension of the spoken word because it is not their own normal mode of communication and if we drill them in word recognition skills we often do no more than boost their reading ages with short-term results and without bridging the gap between their world and the world of books. Where the child's normal mode of communication is limited to:
>
> > He's gor a ball
> > He's throwin' it
> > An thers a girl
> > Ers catch'n it
>
> it is difficult to transfer the idea of language to the written form of 'Tom is throwing the ball to Mary'. The vocal rhythms, phrasing and structure are entirely different.

However, although experts such as Latham (see pp. 49–50) and Greenwood have argued convincingly against categorisation, teachers in general have been little influenced by them. The emphasis still tends to be on teaching children to decode rather than to comprehend.

To some extent, the teacher's approach will be dictated by the total educational resources of the school. Her choice of a decoding *method* or of a reading scheme will depend upon the materials that she already has in her classroom—the number of tape recorders available, perhaps, or whether she has the materials for a particular teaching device such as Words in Colour. She may of course be able to persuade the headmaster to buy these—though I have talked to headmasters who have maintained that they could not afford to dispense with their current stocks of reading primers. But whatever the gaps in her equipment, the teacher is always free to decide for herself in most of the following respects: the kind of group structure that she will use most frequently with her class for reading activities; the amount of time that is made available to children for reading; the degree to which her children are encouraged to look at and to decode a single book from cover to cover or a range of picture books with a simple story line; the kind of written work that the children are encouraged to produce.

In an article Vera Southgate (1968) argues that an 'emphasis on the numerous factors reacting within the reading situation may help teachers to realise that reading results can frequently be improved without adopting new reading schemes, books or apparatus'. I would agree that no particular complex of factors can be pointed to as the 'ideal combination' for an infant reading scheme, but to suggest that the multiplicity of variables *absolves* the teacher from questioning and re-questioning the particular combination within which she works with her class, in my view, reveals an unjustifiable complacency about the whole question of decision-making on the teacher's part which contrasts strongly with the urgency of some recent American writing.

In my summary of the different ways that reading can be tackled at the infant stage, I have tried to cover as many as possible of the choices open to a teacher in this country in the hope that it will help her to make the most effective selection. Two other books have since been published, one by Donald Moyle (1968), the other by Southgate and Roberts (1970), both of which describe in considerable detail the range of materials and reading schemes that are now available for teachers if they care to use them. With this kind of detailed documentation now in print there should be little excuse for those fairly narrow and limited programmes which still characterise for many children their introduction to 'reading'.

However firmly any teacher believes that reading should primarily be for meaning there comes a point at which the child must learn how to decode and encode the written language. I have looked first therefore at the decoding *methods* that a teacher can choose to use and secondly at the *devices* which have been evolved in the 1960s to help the child surmount the literacy hurdle. In the next section I have briefly outlined some of the reading *schemes* which have been designed to introduce the child to the written language. Lastly I have returned to a consideration of the overall variations in the teacher's attitude to reading at this stage —and to whether there is ultimately any major division between a skill-centred and a child-centred approach.

Breaking the code—a table of techniques

DECODING METHODS	TEACHING DEVICES	READING SCHEMES
Synthetic	the initial teaching alphabet	reading primers
		alternative schemes:
alphabetic	the diacritical marking system	(i) i.t.a. +a wide range of 'real' books
phonic:		(ii) Words In Colour
(i) letter units	colour:	(iii) Colour Story Reading
(ii) syllabic units	(i) Words in Colour	(iv) Stott's Programmed
(iii) word units	(ii) Colour Story Reading	Reading Kit
		(v) SRA word games
Analytic	(iii) English Colour Code	(vi) 'Breakthrough to
the word method		Literacy'
the phrase method		
the sentence method	audio-visual aids:	
the story method	(i) Wolverhampton hardware tape scheme	
	(ii) the talking typewriter	
	(iii) the talking page	
	(iv) the language master	

SYNTHETIC METHODS

Synthetic methods start with the smallest indivisible unit—letter or sound—and then build units into words. On the whole it uses the *sound* unit rather than the letter, because this avoids the problem where a letter has more than one pronunciation.

Alphabetic Method

In the alphabetic method the names of the letters are taught but problems arise with irregularly spelt words and those which the child can *say* but which, as a beginner in the decoding/encoding skills, he cannot visualise. It is a *visual* concept, currently little used in schools but I suspect that parents still read ABC books to two-, three- and four-year-olds in an 'alphabetic way': 'ay' is for 'apple', 'bee' is for 'book', 'see' is for 'confusing' . . .

Phonic methods

Phonic methods, too, are basically synthetic in approach, but they differ from the alphabetic method by paying more attention to the actual sound or sounds which letters represent—and to *systematically* teaching the child the sounds which single letters and combinations of letters can make. With the 'letter unit' phonic method the children are taught the shapes and sounds of the letters separately—with the syllabic method the children are encouraged to associate sounds with small groups of letters (on the grounds that consonants can be accurately sounded only in combination with vowels).

> What we have proved and demonstrated is that we need a method of presenting the child's first formal reading experiences as a programme which will lead him as quickly as possible to realising that letters or groups of letters stand for particular sounds. In our programme which we have shown in several research studies to be highly successful, we do this by introducing him to reading *by means of regularly spelt words* which are so chosen that he is forced to examine their internal structure to differentiate between the visual pattern of words. It is very important to begin by establishing correct, fruitful methods of analysing word structure (Daniels).

Advantages:

1 Learning sound/letter combinations enables children to tackle the decoding of new words for themselves.

2 Learning sound/letter combinations also enables children to tackle encoding for themselves—in fact, writing must be highly confusing for the child until letter/sound patterns begin to emerge.

3 The use of a phonic method helps children to read in a systematic left to right direction.

4 The use of a phonic method defines more clearly for the children

a greater number of visual cues when they are faced with the written language than any analytic method.

Reservations:

1 Many English words do not have a consistent grapheme/phoneme (letter/sound) relationship and even though over 75 per cent of them are *very nearly* spelt according to a recognisable pattern, teachers may not be aware of the morphological rules which systematise the spelling of many of these words.

2 Splitting words up, however it is done, may encourage habits of slow, laboured reading.

3 A carefully graded reading vocabulary is necessary for any kind of systematic phonic instruction—this can impose severe limitations on the reading materials used by the children at this stage.

4 The mechanical nature of phonic methods places too little stress on the importance of comprehension and response in reading. For 'breaking the code' a knowledge of phonics is extremely useful—crucial perhaps—but it has no relation to any deepening or extending of the child's thoughts and feelings.

5 There is confusion not so much about *whether* to use phonics as *when* to use them. The diagnosis that teachers need to make before they can tell whether a child is 'ready for phonics' is still not clear, and some children certainly appear to have greater difficulty linking sounds together than others.

From research it is clear that the use of phonic methods does help progress in reading. It also appears that good readers use phonic methods instinctively, but poor readers need to be taught how to do so.

ANALYTIC METHODS

'Whole word', 'phrase' and 'sentence' methods are analytic in their approach to the teaching of reading in that they begin by encouraging the children to recognise whole words or even whole sentences, and it is only after a 'sight' vocabulary of some size has been built up that teachers encourage the children to analyse words into their component sounds and letters. Advocates of analytic methods emphasise that any approach to the teaching of reading should take into account that reading is a form of communication and that successful reading always involves a response to the meaning conveyed by the words. 'Reading is thinking under the stimulus of the printed page.' Unfortunately much of the material that has been used by teachers who employ such global or look-and-say methods is so devoid of meaning anyway that the printed page appears to offer precious little stimulus to any thinking child.

In *The Teaching of Reading and Writing*, Gray (1956) gives a useful summary of word, phrase and sentence methods of teaching decoding, the main points of which are as follows.

The word method

'In the word method words are usually presented in a meaningful setting (on a picture or as a label to some classroom object), and learned largely by the "look-and-say" procedure during the first few lessons. This procedure is based on the assumption that each word has a characteristic form by which it can be remembered. . . . As new words are learned they are used repeatedly in phrases and sentences . . . Various devices have been introduced to facilitate learning; for example, *word cards*, to develop a sight vocabulary and to build sentences. Cards with a word printed on one side and an appropriate picture on the other (cf. Stott) were used for self-corrective practice.' Gray does make the point, however, that: 'If a word method is not accompanied by the analysis of words into their elements it should not be classified as an analytic method.'

The phrase method

The phrase method is based on the assumption that phrases are more interesting, because more meaningful, than words. It has also been recommended in the belief that it fosters efficient reading since good readers recognise groups of words at each fixation of the eyes. This has, however, been questioned (cf. Anderson and Dearborn, 1952). Gray concludes: 'The phrase method has all the advantages and limitations of the word method. Whereas it places added emphasis on meaning, it is an uneconomical method of word mastery.'

The sentence method

The sentence method urges that 'the sentence and not the word or letter is the true unit in language, expressing whole thoughts which are units in thinking' (Huey). It is this method which lends itself most readily to the utilisation of the children's own experience—as they express their thoughts and feelings to the teacher in speech:

As the pupils engage in conversation they make many interesting statements about it. One of the statements is then written on the blackboard by the teacher and read 'naturally'—i.e. with expression, since it represents an idea that has meaning to the reader (Gray).

Morris (1958) notes that when the 'sentence method' is used, emphasis is laid on reading comprehension and contextual clues.

The story method

The story method 'is an expansion of the sentence method, using a sequence of sentences in the form of a story as the unit of instruction in early reading activities. As stories have a universal appeal for children it is claimed that the story method ensures keen interest in reading activities, thus overcoming some of the disadvantages of the word and sentence methods. It also provides a more complete unit of thought than the sentence because it carries the reader through the entire series of events, which have a beginning, middle and end. Hence it not only emphasises meaning but trains pupils to anticipate and follow a sequence of ideas. Because of its very nature the story provides much greater opportunity for discussion and the understanding of relationships than the sentence' (Gray).

In his more recent (1963) survey of reading methods, Ronald Morris suggests that although the 'story method' appears to have fallen into neglect, more attention should be given to its possibilities, on the grounds that more than any other method it allows the child to *respond*—to be caught up in the story *before* he is asked to transfer it from the spoken to the written mode.

Advantages of analytic methods:

1 Particularly through the sentence method, 'the child from the beginning practises reading as a process of obtaining *meaning* from printed symbols' (Whitehead, 1954).

2 The sentence method 'offers help to the pupil from the context and from the continuity of meaning that can be embodied in the material' (Schonell, 1945).

3 'Since whole words and not letters, sounds, or syllables are the natural units of linguistic expression, it seems logical that whole word methods should be used to introduce children to reading' (Morris, 1958).

4 According to Gestalt psychologists, the eye tends to see wholes before analysing into parts. Some words certainly appear to be 'one look' words for children (cf. Ashton-Warner, 1963, and see below p. 100).

5 The use of analytic methods does not imply, as Flesch for instance suggested, that the children's attention is never drawn to the elements of which words are made. Words *are* subsequently broken down into syllables and letters and the sounds which they represent.

6 Teachers who *deliberately* opt for analytic methods are more likely to aim to teach reading in a wider sense than just decoding. These 'reading for meaning' enthusiasts are suspicious of an approach which appears to reach its goal before meaning has necessarily been obtained. They distinguish between recognition and response, and are anxious to encourage the latter rather than the former.

Reservations about analytic methods:

1 Analytic 'look and say' methods encourage guesswork and only a superficial appraisal of the printed or written symbols.

2 Analytic methods do not provide the child with a tool for tackling new words for himself.

3 Teachers using analytic methods have not necessarily liberated their children from the limitations of a graded vocabulary. If they use reading primers, they will be introducing the child to new words in a limited, step-by-step way, added to which, the content of special 'readers' is often lacking in story material to which the child can respond.

4 Analytic methods give no help when it comes to learning how to write. The child would have to postpone any attempts at writing until the teacher judged that a large enough 'sight' vocabulary had been built up in the child's reading, for word analysis into letters and letter sounds to begin.

5 Analytic methods demand considerable opportunities and experiences in order to formulate the basic reading concepts underlying this type of (self discovery) pattern (Goodacre, 1967). Disadvantaged children are not likely to have opportunities and experiences that are in any way relevant to 'basic reading concepts' (cf. Greenwood, *Wolverhampton Tape Reading Scheme Report*).

6 The apparently clear outlines drawn by the Gestalt psychologists have become less definite. It now seems that their experimental

results and their theories may not, after all, provide a fundamental basis for the understanding of the nature of perception, but rather a one-sided and exaggerated view of certain of its less important features. If teachers are to feel confident about using whole word methods for beginning reading, a re-examination of the part played by Gestalt psychology in their development is very necessary (Morris, 1958).

7   Experts in theory and practice are still not clear about the point at which children using analytic methods are to be encouraged to start analysing. In Goodacre's survey, for instance, infant teachers made little use of diagnostic tests for this purpose.

POINTS FOR DISCUSSION

1   Analytic methods with their emphasis on the larger units which convey meaning—'phrase' and 'sentence' as well as 'word' units— lead more naturally to reading for pleasure than do synthetic methods. Are they, however, being allowed to do so in reading schemes which are based on the emasculated material which many reading primers provide?

2   It is difficult to see how teachers using analytic methods can introduce the children to *writing* words and sentences for themselves without drawing attention to individual letters. Should an introduction to writing be left until later? If not is it enough for the teacher to encourage the child to copy the shapes of written symbols *without* relating them to sounds? If the children *are* encouraged from the start to relate the shapes they write down to sounds surely it is logical to encourage them also to relate the shapes presented to them for decoding to sounds?

3   *When* to direct a child's attention to letter/sound and syllable/sound units has still not been established with any certainty. We do not know how far children are thwarted by their inability to 'make sense' of the wide range of symbol sound patterns when they are struggling with traditional orthography. i.t.a. has certainly demonstrated that a simplified and regularised system encourages much freer writing as well as more confident reading—it may be that early direct instruction into discernible t.o. patterns would have a similar effect. At present children are too often left to internalise for themselves what must be a confused and muddled model of the

orthography, and this has discernible effects on their spelling for many years—sometimes for life.

4　The child may even *enjoy* learning and exercising specific decoding skills (*vide* the children observed by Joan Dean using Dr Gattegno's decoding materials). How far, however, is his enjoyment of decoding activities related to the excitement and satisfaction of problem solving alone, without reference to the meaning of what he is reading?

It seems astonishing that there should be no longitudinal research by means of a matched experiment of these two methods—analytic and synthetic—in the same school or schools and over a number of years. As Schonell (1942, rev. 1961) and Southgate (1968) have pointed out, all attempts to compare different methods 'have revealed limitations', simply (or rather complexly!) because there are so many variables to be accounted for. This being the case, and with such a lack of clear research evidence, it is not surprising that teachers should use 'mixed' methods in an intuitive but scientifically haphazard kind of way.

At present very many teachers do mix these methods, and this is made easy by the fact that those series of primers which are most popular are designed to be used with either method. Unfortunately, these are very limited in vocabulary and as a result are written in a highly artificial English, lacking natural patterns of tone, pitch and intonation. The question of *why* teachers continue to use such inadequate material will be dealt with later.

v Teaching children to read—teaching devices

There are basically two kinds of teaching device, or 'contrivance', which can help children to break the code of the written language. First of all there are those which directly affect the look of the written language by introducing additional decoding cues of various kinds. Second, there is an increasingly wide range of mechanical devices which can be used to help the child initially to bridge the gap between speech sounds and letter shapes.

The idea that children (and adults) would find the task of encoding and decoding written English simpler and more satisfying if the sound/symbol relationships could be made more consistent is not new. The difficulty with the traditional orthography (the alphabet as it stands) is that we only have twenty-six letters (graphemes) to represent nearly fifty sounds (phonemes); thus in spite of the number of sound/symbol rules which written English does in fact follow, there are still sufficient inconsistencies to confuse and baffle the child when he first attempts to convert spoken sound to written symbols and vice versa.

THE INITIAL TEACHING ALPHABET (i.t.a.)

What I propose to do in this section is, first, to give a brief account of the various teaching devices which are now being used in this country to simplify the writing system in one way or another for the beginner. Then I shall note briefly the audio-visual aids that are now being used in a minority, but an increasingly large minority, of schools to help children to move smoothly from the sound patterns of speech to the visual patterns of the written language.

Through the 1930s, 1940s and 1950s very little attention seems to have been paid to the possibility of changing the actual writing system for young children in the initial stages of learning how to encode and decode for themselves. But as Edward Fry comments (1967): 'The current flurry of activity is probably directly traceable to the well publicized and well financed efforts of Sir James Pitman during the past few years.' Before 1962 very few teachers had heard of the Initial Teaching Alphabet (i.t.a. for short) yet by the school year 1965–66 it was estimated by the University of London Research Unit that approximately a thousand schools in the United Kingdom alone would be using i.t.a. in their reading programmes.

The initial teaching alphabet was devised by Sir James Pitman for the specific purpose of helping children to cope with the decoding and the encoding problem in the early stage of literacy. Originally it was called the Augmented Roman Alphabet because the twenty-six characters of the Roman alphabet which we use when writing in the 'traditional orthography' (t.o.) of the language were extended to forty-four so that every grapheme could represent one phoneme only.

i.t.a. was launched, amidst considerable publicity, in the early 1960s. A committee of eminent educationists was formed to advise on its use in schools, and in October 1960 Dr John Downing was appointed to conduct a research investigation into the effects of i.t.a. on the reading progress of school beginners. In September 1961 the 'First i.t.a. Experiment' was initiated in twenty schools in this country. In 1963 i.t.a. was introduced experimentally into the United States, and over the subsequent twelve months projects were mounted in many American schools. The i.t.a. schemes received considerable financial backing in both countries, and a Reading Research Unit was set up from 1960–67 and based at the University of London Institute of Education with the focus of interest placed firmly on this particular teaching device.

Comments

As a result of the carefully documented evidence that has been collected by Downing and his research team[1] it is now possible to make the following points about the use of i.t.a. as a decoding device for beginners:

1   Most children at the infant stage (about 90 per cent in the experimental groups) can learn an extended alphabet without much difficulty.

2   Having learnt such a code as i.t.a. which regularises the writing system, they have been able to read and write with greater confidence and flexibility than most children who learn traditional orthography.

3   It is clear that t.o. presents difficulties to all children in the initial stages of learning how to read; the average and high ability children in both experiments did better when they were using

[1] cf. also *i.t.a. An Independent Evaluation* (F. W. Warburton and Vera Southgate, 1969).

i.t.a. than when they were using t.o. The extended code did *not*, however, help the slowest children; even before the transfer hurdle, the bottom 10 per cent made little progress in i.t.a.

4   As i.t.a. does not appear to be a desirable teaching device for backward readers the importance of diagnostic tests at the beginning of the child's school career (and not just during his last term in the infant school or department) becomes increasingly important. No child should be presented with a new version of the orthography who is unlikely to profit from its use.[1]

5   For those children who *do* make good progress with i.t.a., acquiring an early confidence in their own ability to encode and to decode successfully, with a regularised writing system, the only qualification about its use would be with regard to the exact nature of the setback which they experience while they are transferring from the extended code to traditional orthography. We are given very little descriptive information in any of Downing's books about the effect of this transitional stage on the children's own attitude to reading and writing, and it would be interesting to know a little more about the extent to which they themselves are aware of any slowing down or loss of accuracy in their work over the transfer period. In the Second Experiment (though not in the First) when t.o. was used for the tests the i.t.a. children were slightly inferior on almost every occasion. How far this was (and if it was, how far it continued to be) reflected in their work generally, is not clear.

6   Even if 'i.t.a. children' do not maintain their lead (as measured by tests) over 't.o. children' after transfer, as long as they do not fall behind them in their reading and writing, the additional confidence and pleasure which the use of a simplified system can give in the early stages offers a strong argument for its adoption with average and above average children.

7   In reading as well as in writing the consistency which i.t.a. brings to the decoding of any word should make it possible to rely much less heavily on basal readers. This means that the child can be encouraged to read, for pleasure, stories which are genuinely interesting and well written. To use reading primers such as *Janet and John* specially printed in i.t.a. seems to be turning a blind eye to many of the advantages of a regularised coding device.

[1] But cf. Southgate's different view about backward readers in *i.t.a. An independent Evaluation* (see Appendix I).

8   The use of 'achievement categories' for the children involved in both the experiments, has indicated very clearly *the wide range of individual differences* in children at the beginning stages of literacy — whatever the writing system to which they are introduced. Downing (1967) stresses Dr Joyce Morris's earlier conclusion that probably about half the t.o. pupils and an important section of the i.t.a. pupils will need to be taught in the junior schools by teachers who are well qualified and experienced in methods of developing the basic skills of reading and writing.

9   There needs to be more research done to devise a simplified writing system which will facilitate transfer to t.o. The errors made by children at the transfer stage do not altogether bear out Sir James Pitman's theory that children read for minimal cues along the top coastline of print. A smaller unit of transfer than the upper half of the configurations of whole words should be considered for this purpose. A series of experiments in an experimental reading laboratory should now be conducted, either to improve i.t.a. in this respect, or to produce an entirely new system.

10   It is certainly not yet clear from the available research *when* is the optimum time for any attempt to persuade the i.t.a. child to read and to write completely in t.o. The whole question of whether the transfer should be early or late is confusing. Downing appears to waver between a preference for a relaxed unpressured approach which does not hurry the child into t.o. and the more recent hypothesis since the Second Experiment, that the more familiar the child becomes with reading and writing in i.t.a. the greater the degree of interference when he comes to switch to t.o.

11   In the First Experiment teachers of both the t.o. and the i.t.a. groups were allowed, and in fact encouraged, to use whatever methods of teaching reading they had previously found to be most successful. This could have been very useful but there seems to be little of recorded observation of the different effects which the use of phonic or look-and-say methods may have had on the children's progress. It was emphasised to the teachers that i.t.a. was a *teaching* alphabet and not a phonetic alphabet but no direction as to its handling in the classroom was given.

      In the Second Experiment, which deliberately sought more clearly defined controls than the First, all teachers were asked to use

Janet and John basal readers with their t.o. and i.t.a. groups, but again no attempt was made to define the teaching *method* that should be used. In answer to a questionnaire, five of the twelve teachers in the Second Experiment said that they did phonic work earlier with the i.t.a. class than with the t.o. class, but this was not considered to be a change of method but rather an acceleration in the time needed for the various stages, teaching reading in response to the children's interest and development. As such, phonic work was regarded by these teachers as an essential part of their method with both groups of children.

THE DIACRITICAL MARKING SYSTEM (DMS)

The Diacritical Marking System is exactly what its name implies—a system of indicating sound-symbol relationships by means of marks placed above, below or through certain letters. Phoneticians have used diacritical marks for years, just as they have also added to the number of symbols in the traditional orthography of any language, but Edward Fry (1967), the author of this particular system—DMS—states that it is specially designed as 'a method of temporarily regularizing the phoneme-grapheme relationship for beginning readers'. To this end the rules to which it is said to conform 'represent a compromise between a system accurate enough to satisfy a phonetician and what it is practical to teach a child in its first year at school'.

Edward Fry, who is Director of the Reading Centre at Rutgers—the State University—New Brunswick, New Jersey, has outlined the rules in a paper printed in the Second International Reading Symposium There are seventeen rules and in addition a plus sign to indicate gross exception; e.g. önce, äny. Fry claims that the seventeen rules 'take care of over 99 per cent of the phoneme-grapheme correspondence used in English writing', although for an *English* speaker his examples appear to be full of inconsistencies—or even downright mistakes: her, sir, fur—'note that the "r" in these words sounds the same as the beginning sound in red . . .'

Here are some examples of the rules for using—or not using—diacritical marks in Fry's system:

1 Regular consonants and short vowels are not marked. (This is in line with the fact that these are the most frequently used of these letters.)

2 Long vowels have a bar over: e.g. gō, mē.

3 Neutral 'a' (∂) has a comma over it: e.g. ȧgo, Canȧdȧ.

4 Silent letters are slashed out: e.g. mār̸d, māde̸.

5 Consonant digraphs have a bar under: e.g. s̲hut, t̲hat, c̲hat, w̲hen, si̲ng.

6 Diphthongs have a bar under: e.g. bo̲y, bo̲il, o̲ut, o̲wl.

7 The second sounds of consonants have a bar under: e.g. i̲s, g̲em, c̲ity.

Reservations

1 The most obvious objection to be made to Fry's description of DMS is the discrepancy between some of the examples which he gives and the rules which he cites for them. The 'r' in fur̲, her̲ and sir̲ is not the same when these words are said by an English speaker as the 'r' in red, neither does the letter 'y' represent a long 'e' in 'funny' nor the 'e' in 'enough' a 'schwa'. These discrepancies may be due to the difference in pronunciation between an American and an English speaker, but if this is the case, some of Fry's instructions about the use of DMS would have to be disregarded if the system were used in English schools and as Fry, Gattegno and Jones have all discovered, teachers are not always clear themselves about the sounds that the written symbols of their language represent. (Jones demonstrated, for instance, that many teachers believe that a short 'a' as in c̲at features in words like 'America' and 'about'.)

2 Some of Fry's diacritical marks require the child to make rather finer distinctions, e.g. 'd̲, l̲, and n̲ suffixes have no vowel, so the 'schwa' vowel is slashed out in such suffixes, e.g. able̸, happe̸n, live̸d, penci̸l; 'the "l" sound in "able" and "pencil" sounds just like the "l" in "love" and seems to follow immediately the preceding consonant'. To require a child who encodes 'pencil' to encode the grapheme/phoneme correspondence in this way may train him to become aware of the difference which often exists between the sound and the look of a word—but is it in fact making either the decoding or encoding process any simpler for him?

3 One sign in this system (e.g. the 'bar under') is used to represent *several* different correspondences; e.g. the *second* sound of various consonants—the *third* sound in the case of yes, diagraphs and diphthongs. It may be doubted whether in the initial stages such a

mark is an adequate cue for the child when it is used without distinction for dissimilar reasons.

4 The system is not comprehensive in the clues given for sound-symbol relationships. No indication is given, for instance, that the 'd' in 'stopped' sounds like a 't'.

5 The slashing out looks messy and the use of marks such as the comma over the 'schwa' may later confuse the child in his use of traditional punctuation.

A COMPARISON OF DMS, i.t.a. AND t.o.

In 1964–5 Fry conducted a research study with first grade children, some of whom were using the DMS system, some i.t.a. and some the traditional basal reader system. All used the same set of reading primers for the course. The data which he gives are concerned with 'the differences between means of the three method groups in a few of the most important tests'. Twenty-one classrooms in all were involved, seven for each system.

In fact there were no significant differences between the mean scores for any of the methods. The group with a slightly higher mean IQ (the t.o. group) also had a slightly higher reading achievement, as might normally be expected, but the chief finding was that 'the difference between classes is much greater than the differences between *method groups*'. Fry concludes: 'Possibly we should be looking for something besides the alphabet as being vital to the efficient acquisition of reading skills. We have a suspicion that that something is teacher ability.'

COLOUR

Where Pitman's device for regularising the written code uses additional orthographic symbols and Fry's device uses additional diacritical marks, other code initiators have used colour to make clear to the child the sound–sight patterns which do exist in the written language but which are not clearly signalled for the beginner, in the traditional ortho-graphy.

I have described briefly here three ways in which colour has been used in the code presented to the child.

Words in Colour

Words in Colour (WIC) was originally devised in the late fifties by

Dr Caleb Gattegno and it was introduced into English schools in 1962. It is in fact a scheme to introduce the child in a highly systematised way to all the possible sight/sound relationships that exist in our written language. Colour is used as 'the simplest means of distinguishing between the different pronunciations of identical letters or the identical pronunciation of different letters'. It serves as 'the initial visual clue to trigger the response in the mind of the learner' and Gattegno claims that colour reinforces both the auditory and the visual imageries of the child. Dean, who observed WIC in the classroom (see Appendix J) describes how children who could not recognise a word when they looked at it in black and white, could decode it correctly when they closed their eyes and were asked by the teacher to think of 'the mauve one' (t) 'the white one' (a) and 'the brown one' (p).

Forty-eight colour tones are used in the scheme—a different tone for each sound in the language—and all the possible grapheme combinations which produce these forty-eight sounds are written up in the appropriate colour on a series of wall charts. It is only the charts and the work on the black-board which is in colour, however. The children write in black though they are encouraged to play with words by recalling colour images of them. Gattegno states explicitly that the child's ability to recall the different colours which represent each specific sound provides him with 'inner criteria . . . to which he may refer for correctness of spelling, rightness of structure and for good writing'. He continues: 'Because colour has the labile quality of images and thought, its systematic use makes it possible to transform English into a phonetic language using 270 or so coloured signs (for all the possible sight/sound combinations) and to learn it as a phonetic language.'

Whatever the image associations may be, children seem to have no difficulty about operating with a range of forty-eight colours. This is almost certainly due to the carefully programmed and systematised way in which the children are introduced to the various colour/sight/sound combinations. According to Dean, the systematic introduction and exploration at each stage is as much a feature of the scheme as the colour. In the schools that have used WIC there have been no complaints at any rate, about confusion caused by colour blindness or by difficulties in distinguishing between one colour tone and another.

Colour Story Reading

Colour Story Reading (CSR) was devised by Kenneth Jones in the early 1960s and although when compared to i.t.a. the number of schools which have now used CSR is small, teachers of both normal

and retarded children have expressed enthusiasm about its possibilities (cf. Appendix K which summarises Jones's Research Report
on CSR).

Unlike Words in Colour, which uses a different colour for every
sound, CSR employs only three primary colours: red, blue and green,
plus black. Jones has been able to restrict his scheme to these colours
because he also uses background shapes to indicate certain sounds which
can be spelled in various ways. These background shapes are simply a
square, a circle and a triangle; although each of these can be red, blue
or green. Jones claims that: 'This simple concept of backgrounds
representing sounds has acted like a magic wand on the rag-bag of
sound/symbol disrelationships—the backgrounds have transformed the
colour symbol code into a precise instrument for coding and explaining
words in a simple and effective way.' For example, the words 'do',
'two', 'woo', 'drew', 'true', 'shoe' and 'through' would have the green
circle which represents any 'oo' sound drawn round the relevant letters
of each word—do, two, woo, etc. One background, the *blue* circle,
always indicates silent letters, the rest all symbolise a particular sound,
including the neutral vowel sound phonetically symbolised in CSR by
a red triangle. The letters inside any of these 'shape' backgrounds are
written in black.

When they are not printed or written inside a geometric shape, the
letters are allocated one of the three primary colours on the basis of
the following two rules: 'letters change colour when their sounds
change'; 'letters which have the same sound have the same colour'.

It is also true that because only three colours are used *some* letters are
identically coloured although there is no sight/sound connection
between them. This 'overlapping' might appear to the adult to be
confusing for the child, but a third factor as well as colour and background shapes is used by Jones as an integral and very important feature
of his system. This third factor or element is *story imagery* and it is
provided in nineteen specially written stories in which the author's
intention is to make available to the child a wide 'associative network'
in which colours, shapes and sounds are all linked by the story imagery.
Thus, to give one brief example here, a blue cat playing with a blue kite
(hard c and k are blue) turns red when a dog makes it angry and hisses
c c c c (in red). This use of the story imagery is in many ways the most
interesting feature of the scheme. It provides a striking difference to
Words in Colour, where the emphasis is continually upon the abstract
nature of sound/symbol patterns, and where picture imagery in verbal
or visual terms is deliberately avoided.

Jones used colour as a decoding device primarily because like Gattegno he was convinced that young children respond more readily to colour cues than they do to black and white. With the exception of television (where colour has now been introduced and is bound to be used more widely over the next decade) and any *printed* material which happens to come their way, children perceive and take their cues from a coloured environment. Consequently, Jones argued, why not introduce them to sound/symbol relationships in colour too, especially as such an extension of normal cues regularises these relationships and thus simplifies them. In an investigation with nursery school children into the visual matching of words to letters, the children scored about three times as high in the colour code as in black. An analysis of the coloured test showed that very few children appeared to be matching either by colour *alone* or by shape *alone* (this could be deducted from the errors). The great majority of children used both colour and shape.

Jones also suggests that the use of colour in the child's first approaches to reading involves his affective as well as his cognitive responses:

All the experimental work undertaken in this field shows that children are attracted by colour, especially primary colours. In the experiment referred to in the previous two paragraphs the majority of the children preferred the coloured 'words' and 'letters' and when asked why, gave such answers as 'because these are all different colours and those are all the same'; 'because green is my favourite colour'; 'that's pretty'.

English Colour Code

Unlike Words in Colour and Colour Story Reading, colour is restricted in the English Colour Code to vowel graphemes, on the grounds that whereas a large proportion of consonant graphemes have a completely regular link to the phonemes which they symbolise, vowel graphemes cover a wide range of possible letter/sound combinations.

D. V. Mosely, the author of ECC, originally used Perspex tiles as his basic materials, amongst which the fifteen most frequently used vowel sounds were represented by different colours. As in the other two colour-code schemes, whatever the letter combination, the same sound is always represented by the same colour. The one exception in ECC was the most common vowel sound of all, 'the neutral schwa', which was represented graphically by the use of italics. Wherever possible the name of each colour used included the vowel sound which the colour represented, e.g. red (short e), pink (short i), orange (short o).

Moseley makes it quite clear that he regards ECC primarily as a decoding rather than a reading aid, which can be used 'as supplementary material with other phonic schemes', as well as providing the basis for a complete remedial programme. In this respect ECC, like i.t.a., remains principally a device rather than a reading scheme.

In the first instance this particular colour code was designed and devised to give special help to backward readers who had difficulty both in differentiating between sounds and in blending sounds together. The author, who is an educational psychologist, has used ECC in programmes for the Talking Typewriter as well as in its present published form.

Materials. English Colour Code was published by the National Society for Mentally Handicapped Children (in 1970) in the form of a series of worksheets which incorporates the use of different colours for different vowel sounds, as the Perspex tiles did in the original research. The worksheets are laminated so that they can be written on again—if water-based felt-tip pens are used by the children.

Moseley stresses the importance of the spoken instructions which must be used with the cards, and tapes are provided with the work-sheets (reel to reel or cassette) as an alternative 'voice' to that of the teacher. He suggests that the use of headphones is desirable to cut out distracting background noise and states specifically that 'the course encourages selective listening'. Indeed the emphasis on phoneme-blending means that listening carefully to the tape (or teacher) is an essential preliminary activity to the visual decoding of words, with the help of colour, on the worksheets.

As it now stands, English Colour Code is similar in some ways to Stott's Programmed Reading Kit in so far as the worksheets are designed to take the child through an organised 'programme' of both encoding and decoding skills. Because the child is required to write on the worksheets from the start, Moseley suggests that 'a spelling test rather than a reading test' should be used to decide when a child requiring extra help should make a start on the cards. A table of 'spelling ages' and recommended starting-points is given in the teacher's manual.

Comments:
1 Because these workcards and instructional tapes are not closely integrated into a total scheme, ECC has a flexibility which enables

CHRIST'S COLLEGE
LIBRARY

it to be used with other materials as an extra aid for slow writers and readers, more successfully than either CSR or WIC.

2   The use of tape to free the teacher from the need to pay constant attention to the individual or the group is a good idea—given that the children are well motivated and freed as far as possible from other distractions. I would agree that headphones are desirable in a class situation and I would also guess that more concentration (even over a period of time as seemingly short as 15 minutes) would be gained by children working completely on their own with the materials rather than in a group.

3   Even though ECC is primarily concerned with code-breaking rather than responsive reading some of the sentences on the worksheets seem to be unnecessarily irrelevant to either the interests or the spoken language of school children: e.g. 'This wine is good'; 'Quench your thirst with orange squash'; or even (when we are soon to change to metric measures) 'Two pints make a quart'.

   Presumably the vocabulary used on the cards is taken from the book of word lists prepared by Moseley for the use of teachers and speech therapists. The five thousand or so words given in these lists is preferable to the mere hundreds that children are grudgingly allowed in reading-primers. Nevertheless, on one quick check of 'key' words quoted by Sylvia Ashton-Warner as words that children asked for as being of individual importance and interest, the following do not appear in Moseley's lists: 'skeleton', 'phantom', 'boxing', 'alligator'.

4   I find the attempt to link the colour used for a particular vowel grapheme with the appropriate sound in the name of the colour confusing rather than helpful. In several instances where the connection is not immediately obvious I am still not sure of the colour word that is meant to be used from simply looking at the worksheets.

5   There are intriguing differences in the use of colour in all three colour-coding devices now in print. For instance, neither WIC nor CSR attempts to link the name of the colour to the vowel sound thereby represented. More importantly, WIC deliberately discourages sub-vocalisation in favour of an 'algebraic' use of colour symbols, where CSR and ECC both stress the importance of making direct and frequent sound-sight connections—Moseley

through tapes and Jones through the *Nineteen Stories* record. It is interesting to speculate whether a child introduced to written language through Gattegno's method is likely to be a faster reader at a later stage—if he never picks up the habit of listening to 'what the symbols say' as he decodes them.

6   The devisers of all three colour reading schemes agree, however, from observations based on their own research, that the inclusion of colour (how ever differently it may be used) can provide sufficient additional information to produce better results as a code-breaking device than the uniform black of traditional orthography.

AUDIO-VISUAL AIDS

Now that the value of teaching children individually or in small groups is widely acknowledged, devices which combine the spoken and written mediums of communication would appear to have considerable potentialities for helping children to make sense of the audio-visual nature of language. Yet it has now become something of an easy generalisation to say that audio-visual aids are being increasingly used in education. It should be noted that there was no mention, in either Morris's or Goodacre's survey, of reading programmes in infant or junior schools which used tape recordings or films or gramophone records as teaching aids.

Although children are becoming increasingly accustomed to using mechanical aids at home—most five-year-olds are thoroughly used to watching television independently of adults—in most infant classrooms in this country there is not even a permanent record player. Overhead projectors and film loops may be used to good effect further up in the junior school and at secondary level, but at the moment the teaching of literacy is mostly achieved (if it *is* achieved) without their aid.

As with any teaching situation, there are difficulties of course—hardware costs money, and unless one's school has the dubious good fortune to be designated as 'experimental' for a period, it may not be possible to afford even one tape recorder per classroom, let alone film-projecting equipment or closed circuit television. If, however, the teacher *knows* how she wants to use a particular aid and has the enthusiasm to convince the Head that it will prove to be educationally valuable, the equipment may find its way into her classroom, especially if the school has an energetic parent-teacher association capable of fund raising when challenged. If on the other hand, a choice has to be made between books and machines it still has to be a very convinced teacher who opts for machines.

Certainly, schools programmes on radio and television are being listened to and watched by an increasingly large number of children year by year. In some areas, too, helpful LEAs have now made it possible for schools to group together in order to get the use of one kind of machine or another for their teaching programmes. One thinks for instance of the ILEA's closed-circuit television and 'fill in' courses, which are designed to familiarise teachers with the technical skills they need to manage complicated machinery, or of the ILEA's provision in some schools of a full-time skilled technician to service the hardware and keep it in running order—even more useful, perhaps, from the teacher's point of view.

The Wolverhampton Tape Scheme

Organised by the Wolverhampton Remedial Teaching Service, this scheme is one that has been notably successful and that relies upon hardware and the teacher's willingness to use it. Pre-recorded tapes are loaned from the Centre to which groups of about six children can listen at a time, through headphones, so that they do not interrupt or find themselves interrupted by the rest of the class. The tapes are primarily designed for non-readers or poor readers whose failure is considered to arise from a linguistically and culturally poverty-stricken background.

First used in 1955 and subsequently developed and modified over a period of six years, the Remedial Service developed the library to over 1,000 tapes in 1971. Its transfer to the Resources Centre entailed a certain amount of reorganisation, but it provides us with a good example of how a piece of generally useful hardware—the tape recorder—can be directly employed in a learning-to-read programme. Indirectly, of course, any television programmes, records, tapes, films or film loops that are used in school can influence the child's growing literacy by providing material likely to stimulate talk or simply by offering the child the enjoyment of listening to language being used to organise a wide variety of experiences.

The Talking Typewriter and the Talking Page

There are two machines both of which were being used with a very limited number of children in this country in the late 1960s which have been designed as specific aids to literacy for non-literate children.

The Edison Responsive Environment, the ERE or Talking Type-writer was invented first by Richard Kobler for work with Dr Omar

Khayyam Moore. The machine is an electronic typewriter with a multi-coloured keyboard and various attachments: a lit screen on which slides are projected during programmes; a window showing letters or words which are to be copied or have been typed; a microphone for reading back what has been written; and small amplifiers through which the supervisor can communicate from outside. The instrument is placed inside a soundproofed booth with several one-way mirrors through which the supervisor can observe proceedings. Outside is a large grey steel cabinet—the computer—which can be programmed for teacher adults or children from two and a half years of age. The lessons comprise listening, reading and typing either letters, words or sentences in English or in six foreign languages at varying levels of difficulty.

According to Dr John Henry Martin, Director of the Freeport Public Schools Experiment: 'The ERE is a computerised typewriter that reproduces several of the sensory responses of a human being. It talks, it listens; it accepts, it responds, it presents pictorial or graphic material, it comments or explains.' This particular computer's ability to offer a multi-sensory form of programming for individual learning is seen by Dr Martin as an important advance on the more usual forms of programmed teaching machines: 'Programming as the term is currently used is largely a linear concept of the presentation of printed material in planned sequences with or without pictorial material, with or without audio and with or without branching materials based upon a limited anticipation of the learner's responses.'

When exposed to the ERE, however, the child, initially at any rate, is given complete freedom with the machine. This is called 'freetyping' and all the child will usually do is bang the keys about, to see and hear the result.

'If the child is using the machine in order to learn to read, should the first key he happens to press be the letter "D", a "D" appears on the roll of paper in the machine and a voice says "D". The child may press "D" again—or he may hit any other letter—and each time he will be told what he has typed. Once he is familiar with the booth, the keys and the even voice which is there to guide but never to urge or correct him, he will be put on a programme.'

'Hello', the voice will say. 'As you know, this is the Talking Type-writer. We are going to play a game today. Type the letter C . . . C . . . C . . . green key . . . C . . . C . . . green key.' The child now finds 'C' by seeing it pictured in the window and looking for it among the green painted keys on the keyboard. A blocking device jams all the keys except the appropriate one and once the correct key has been pressed the voice again says the name of the letter. To quote Dr Martin again: 'Because incorrect responses cannot be completed on the "blocked" keyboard, this approach has aptly been called the "trial and success" method.'

'First, single letters are exposed. These are gradually coupled with other letters to form words. Later a whole printed line is exposed and finally several whole printed lines. When the space bar is depressed ERE will at that point pronounce and spell the word just typed. Similar rules hold true of the audio-recapitulation of a total sentence after a full stop, and even of total paragraphs and stories. At an "advanced" stage ERE (or the Talking Typewriter) must be able to ask the pupil to type certain words or letters based only upon the pupil's audio-reception. The only "help" given at this stage is that the appropriate keys are encoded in sequence. Finally there is the machine's ability to record the pupil's voice and to play it back to him in such a manner as to compare his own talk with the models pre-recorded in the ERE system.'

Dr Martin concludes his account of the machine's capabilities thus: 'Having built a word from its visual, tactile and audible components, having summarised it phonetically, having spoken it and compared one's own pronunciation with the pronunciation of the Talking Type-writer, a perceptual ring has been closed which not only results in the learning of the reading skill of the natural language, but also in the writing skill based upon the phonic analysis of the pupil's own speech.'

It is interesting that Dr Martin refers to the child as having sum-marised the word phonetically. In the articles which I have read describing some of the reading projects for which the ERE has been used, very little stress appears to be laid on the actual reading *method* which is programmed into the computer. The machine that I saw and heard spoke the names of the letters alphabetically but did not give their phonic sounds, although it would be perfectly possible to do this and clearly it has been done in Dr Martin's Freeport experiment. The approach tends to be synthetic, building up from single letters to simple then more complicated words and finally to sentences, but again no emphasis is placed upon this as an important feature of the machine's capabilities.

In her account of the Talking Typewriter in *Harper's Magazine* Maya Pines (1963) fills in the history of its evolution for us: 'The project is the brain child of a Yale sociologist, Dr Omar Khayyam Moore.' These 'learning experiments' with children have evolved from Moore's earlier work for the Office of Naval Research which was concerned with investigating the kind of 'human higher-order problem-solving' involved in mastering artificial symbolic languages. As his emphasis shifted from deductive to inductive processes his research with adults became more and more difficult. 'What he needed was a research laboratory in which an entirely new order of things had to be discovered, but rather than create a whole new environment that was strange enough he decided to reverse the situation and "go in for ignorant subjects instead" for whom our environment would be strange and unfamiliar—i.e. children from two and a half years onwards.'

Dr Moore set up his first 'Responsive Environment Laboratory' in 1958 at Hamden Hall Country Day School, a small private school near New Haven, Connecticut. Since then projects have been initiated in several of America's large cities (New York, Boston, Chicago)—at present in the United States more than seventy ERE machines are being used in over twenty such projects. Moore (1963) believes (along with other eminent American psychologists and educationists such as Deutsch, Bloom and Hunt) that the years from two to five are the most creative and intellectually active period of a human being's life. He maintains that children are capable of extraordinary feats of inductive reasoning if left to themselves *in a properly responsive environment*.

From the results which have so far been obtained from children coming from normal and from disadvantaged backgrounds with a wide range of problems, it would appear that the fully automated Talking Typewriter perfected in 1960 by Dr Richard Kobler is certainly a satisfactory environment for eliciting positive and constructive responses from the subjects. Those who have been involved in the experiments frequently emphasise the sense of release which maladjusted and severely retarded children appear to experience once they enter the soundproof booth and are left alone with the machine. Gitta Sereny writes of an eleven-year-old epileptic girl suffering from cerebral palsy and visual-perceptual disorders: 'I have watched Maureen many times—have seen her wide and delighted grin as soon as she steps into the room, have seen her *run* toward the booth and throw herself into the chair; have seen her lose all interest in everything "outside", have witnessed the curiously personal nature of her communication with this wonderfully passive "thing". She laughs with it and talks to it and she revels in being *alone* in this booth and in *charge* of the machine and her own actions.' Other writers have recorded similarly strong impressions that the impersonality of the machine, far from placing a distance between itself and the child, appears to be a positive advantage in encouraging them to lose their inhibitions and enjoy the sense of experimentation and subsequent achievement which this 'trial and success' approach provides.

Dr Moore has stated that he hopes that the less gifted children will benefit even more than the brighter ones from their sessions with a 'responsive environment' and again the special properties of the ERE— its infinite patience and absolutely consistent attitude towards the child—appear to penetrate their defences if they are emotionally maladjusted, or involve their wandering attention if they are mentally slow or retarded, more effectively than the most well-meaning human teachers. We must remember of course that only a very small section of the child's education is placed in the care of the computer, but nevertheless it is an extremely valuable and important section, and as Robert Weber (1966), Director of Program Development for the Responsive Environments Corporation, has pointed out: 'providing language arts proficiency for all students, at least until the present, has turned out to be the weakest link in the academic chain'.

There are now only two Talking Typewriters in use in this country, due to its expense (about £17,000), but the demand for its wider use continues to grow in the United States, chiefly on these three counts:

1 That it can give children from deprived environments the invaluable skills of functional literacy before they ever go to school—thus increasing immeasurably their chances of enjoying and understanding what education can give them from the start.

2 It has also been used successfully to teach illiterate and sub-literate adolescents and adults to read when all other methods appear to have failed.

3 If normal children can be taught to acquire the skills of literacy before the age of five, and Moore and his team have now convincingly demonstrated that they can, a rethinking of the educational needs of such children (along Brunerian lines) is urgently needed, above all for the years from two to five. The problem, Dr Moore believes, is to avoid missing this critical period: 'If I had a certain sum to spend on twenty Ph.D. candidates and twenty nursery-school children I'd use most of it on the youngest children—they're the ones who need it most.'

In this country the ERE machine has so far only been used in a very limited way—for recruits at the Army School of Preliminary Education in Wiltshire and for children with serious speech disorders at the Speech Therapy Training School in Portland Place, London. This unit has now been transferred to the Society for Mentally Handicapped Children in Newman Street, and placed under the direction of D. V. Moseley, the Educational Psychologist whose English Colour Code has already been mentioned in this section of the book.

The Talking Page is a further invention of Richard Kobler and it is now available along with appropriate reading programmes from Rank/REC Ltd. The Company are willing to rent sets of their Talking Page machines to British schools at the cost of £72 p.a. each.

Basically the Talking Page is a record player—the disc slots into a desk-size box on top of which there is a 'page' divided into fifty lines on which a written text (or diagrams) can be printed. The great advantage of this machine is that any one 'line' of the text can be selected for immediate playing back and listening to by the child, simply by moving a lever on the side of the box to the appropriate line number. Thus any line can be returned to at will without waiting for the record to play through to the end, and a five-year-old child can mechanically select the required groove with a precision which even the teacher could not match manually.

It is possible to programme the Talking Page with any kind of material that is amenable to this kind of treatment but the relation of written symbol to spoken sound is of course particularly valuable for the child who is learning how to move from one kind of language to the other.

The Language Master

The Language Master machine (Bell & Howell A-V Ltd) was introduced into this country in 1964. It consists of a special magnetic recorder accompanied not by spools of tape but by sets of cards. A typical card carries three sorts of information: a picture of some common object or action, its name or a suitable caption in print, and a recording of this caption in the teacher's voice. Thus, as with the Talking Page, visual symbols and speech sounds are immediately linked together for the child as soon as he feeds the chosen card into the appropriate slot. While looking at the picture and the text, he hears the spoken word or words from a built-in loud-speaker.

Children can work with this machine either singly or in groups and it has been used recently to explore the possibilities of individual and group learning by Mrs Bay Tidy, O.B.E., in a scheme financed by the Nuffield Resources for Learning Project and in co-operation with

Coventry College of Education.[1] Blank cards can be obtained for use with the Language Master as well as cards that have already been printed, which clearly gives the children and the teacher scope to follow their own interests as well as a previously devised programme. One group compiled a 'speaking dictionary' for instance and other possibilities must occur to pupils and staff if they have the machine as an incentive in their classroom.

[1] Details of this study, entitled *An Examination of some Self-Instructional Reading Programmes and Media* are available from Resources for Learning Project, Nuffield Lodge, Regents Park, London NW1.

VI Teaching children to read— reading schemes

'To guarantee that the child psychologically experiences literature as a useful tool, the first books that he reads are of crucial importance. In many series of readers this aspect has been overlooked: the learning of the mechanics of reading has been emphasised, leaving the content often shallow, occasionally inane.' *Jacqueline Sanders*

'If reading is to be accompanied by a sustained flow of thought in the mind of the reader, it will not be sufficient to remove strange words and unfamiliar grammatical constructions, since it is possible to use simple language to write nonsense, to tell a boring tale or to express complicated ideas.' *Ronald Morris*

A teaching *scheme* as opposed to a teaching *method* or a teaching *device* is a *programme* which is mapped out for the teacher (or which she can map out for herself), in order to enable her to take the children in her class day by day, week by week and month by month through a certain pattern of learning how to read. A teaching scheme may utilise a particular decoding method or a particular decoding device, it may place an emphasis variously upon talk, or upon writing, or upon breaking the code thoroughly and completely by means of special games and exercises.

READING SCHEMES BASED ON PRIMERS

By far the most popular learning-to-read programmes in this country are still based upon special 'readers' or reading primers of one kind and another. I have therefore chosen to look at primer-based schemes first before proceeding to describe some alternative kinds of reading courses for those who are no longer completely satisfied with graded sets and series of readers.

As Goodacre has noted, one of the attractions of the primer-based scheme, particularly for the inexperienced infant teacher, is that it gives a sense of security and appears to provide concrete evidence of the child's progress.

Mackay and Thompson (1968) describe clearly in *The Initial Teaching of Reading and Writing* how the teacher often appears to believe that 'reading progress may be "measured" by reference to the serial and page number or by the ability of the child to recognise the words listed on the final pages'. (My five-year old son was at first extremely proud of the grubby bit of card on which lines of page numbers had been crossed through to mark his progress through the Introductory Book of *The Happy Venture Readers*.) Mackay and Thompson continue: 'For the teacher of a class of forty children (in a crowded room), it is understandable that knowing that most of her class are at least up to "page three of Book Two" is comforting and reassuring.' It is a fallacy, however, to assume that this knowledge can tell the teacher very much about the child's reading progress. It may tell her how large his sight vocabulary is but whether he is reading the words as a result of familiarity, rote memorisation or phonic insight can not be ascertained simply by knowing that the child is 'on page three of Book Two'.

But have primers any other, more genuine advantages which justify their being used rather than the alternative devices, schemes and teaching aids which are now available? We need to ask three basic questions here: Do these books provide the child with the most efficient means of learning how to 'break the code'. Do they give him insight into the basic structure of written English? And do they offer him enjoyable and interesting reading material?

Are primers efficient code-breakers?

The answer to the first question must, to a large extent, be no.[1] No primer series, for instance, uses colour extensively or systematically to give the child an extra means of grasping basic word patterns when he is first confronted with the task of deciphering written English for himself.[1] Neither do the most widely used primers make any attempt to group words in the text according to their phoneme-grapheme structure although the *same* words are frequently repeated in the text and in Schonell's *Happy Venture Readers* 'phonetic lists' of words are given at the back of Book Two. But the opening remarks of *Out and About*, one of the early *Janet and John* readers, illustrate what I mean about the words in the text offering no clues to the phoneme-grapheme regularities which the written English code does in fact contain: 'Look, Janet, look. Come to the shop. I see a horse.'

[1] This criticism which is specifically related to the value of primers as successful decoding aids for the child, would not apply to the *Royal Road Readers* or any similar series which is based on phonic principles.

If one turns to the back of many of these readers the *word lists* can be even more confusing than the arrangement of the words in the text:

e.g.	box	weed	chick	sweet	this
	duck	such	nest	must	king
	long	wish	shop	free	chin
	plum	doll	sleep	dress	song

In some schools children are required to read these word lists faultlessly before being allowed to 'progress' to the next book in the series. But accurate word recognition is not the only—or even the best—way of noting a child's increasing literacy. Mackay and Thompson observe, for example, that 'an insistence on word recognition entirely ignores the knowledge children need but may not have of the structures of which these words form a part'—and in the case of the word list just quoted above one might add that 'the knowledge which children need but may not have of the structures which form part of the words' is equally overlooked. This insistence that every word must be correctly recognised before a primer is discarded means that a child may be forced to stick to the same book for a long (sometimes devastatingly long) time. He is not allowed even to turn to page 4 unless he is word perfect on pages 1, 2 and 3. Under such a rigidly controlled system even children who opened their first primer with enthusiasm to do some 'real reading' soon tire and—not surprisingly—lose interest.

Do primers give insight into the basic structure of written English?

The highly repetitive nature of the prose in these readers, combined with an almost total lack of conjunctions to link any of the brief (often curt) statements together, renders it absolutely impossible for the child to reconvert the written symbols which confront him into natural sounding speech. Primer English is unlike any other kind of English that the child ever meets: 'This is a shop. You see it is a toy shop. We will go to the shop with Mother. "Mother will get us a toy" said May.' The language here has the clockwork quality of a mechanical toy and would be more suitable perhaps if Daleks were introduced to 'emit' the words in jerked-out staccato bursts of Dalek speech.

Although the sentences are unnaturally uniform in their brevity even in the later books of these primer series, a research investigation conducted recently by Professor Strickland (1962) in the United States indicates that no distinct pattern is followed when it comes to the introduction of extended language structures, and that no account appears to be taken of the structural speech patterns most commonly used by the children for whom each book is intended. Here is the summary of her findings, which are drawn from an analysis of how far the language used in four of the most popular basal reader series in the USA reflected the speech patterns of their readers and how far they appeared to be introducing new structures systematically:

1 The basic subject, verb, object pattern was the *only* language pattern to appear in the samples taken from practically all of the books.

2 Other basic patterns (e.g. subject, passive verb, complement) appeared from level to level within a series of books *in what seemed a random manner.*

3 There was some evidence of expansion from level to level in each series in the use of elaborate patterns within a total sentence unit.

4 Some movables[1] appeared in the patterns used in each series of books, beginning at about 2nd grade (age 7) level.

5 There was *no clear arrangement* for introducing elements of subordination in any of the series.

6 Patterns which appeared in the primer samples taken differed from series to series *and from book to book within a single series.*

7 Patterns of sentence structure appeared to be introduced somewhat at random.

8 A structure pattern once introduced seemed not to be followed up with further elements of the same or similar sort. Thus there seemed to have been no provision for mastering patterns of structure through repetition.

9 There appeared to be no scheme for developing control over sentence structure which paralleled the generally accepted scheme for developing control over vocabulary.

Strickland also discovered that:

1 The length of phonological units (speech sentences measured by intonation) used by children varied more *within* a grade than from

---

[1] The patterns of stationary elements (Subject, Verb, Object/Complement) were designated as SLOTS and elements which could appear in different locations (e.g. adverbs, adverbial phrases or clauses) were designated as MOVABLES.

grade to grade and therefore appeared to be unsatisfactory as a measure of maturity of language.

2 The number of language patterns used by children in the study ranged from 658 in grade 1 (age 6–7) to 1041 in grade 6.

3 Children at *all* grade levels made *some* use of movables; the movables of *place* and *time* appeared with greatest frequency and children combined immovable language elements with movables *in a wide variety of ways.*

How simple should the language structure be in a child's first reading material?

'It is not the words that give meaning to the sentence: it is the sentence that assigns meaning to the words in it' *Ronald Morris.*

The assumption that all children on their arrival at school must be presented with identical forms of the written language of the simplest kind requires serious reconsideration. Some reading experts advance the view that it is in fact desirable for the child to 'begin again at the beginning', so that he can learn how to comprehend written English much as he learnt how to comprehend spoken English—being introduced first to nouns, then to nouns plus verbs and thus, gradually to the more complex structures which he is already manipulating with considerable ease in their spoken form. Beatrix Tudor Hart suggests, for instance, in a paper given to the First International Reading Symposium (1964) that although by the age of five or six the child is capable of quite complicated speech utterances, in fact, the only words of which he is aware as separate entities are 'concrete nouns and active verbs together with a few concrete adjectives and adverbs', and that *for this reason* 'the child's approach to reading should be graduated following the natural course of the development of speech. Beginning with single nouns, through short "noun-verb" sentences to more complicated but single sentences, each describing one meaningful and understandable incident. . . .'.

This is, of course, exactly what reading primers provide:

> Nip will run to get the ball.
> He will bring it to Jack.
> Jack said: 'I will throw the ball.
> You can hit it.'
> Dick did not hit the ball with his bat.
> The ball hit the tree.

One can say that each of these sentences 'describes one meaningful and understandable incident' but taken together with no linking words to fuse them into a related whole the total effect is something like that of a very old film—disconnected and therefore jerky. Although consecutive in meaning they are not finally *about* anything.

It is certainly true, as Mackay and Thompson have clearly demonstrated, that when young children take their *own* initial steps in constructing written sentences, they first select the lexical items which carry most information and often omit the grammatical items altogether or add them in an apparently unrelated string at the end of their 'sentence'. Thus Tudor Hart is correct when she suggests that 'come along into the garden' carries the same meaning for the small child as 'come garden'. To remove the grammatical words completely—or almost completely—however, when the child first comes to look at language written down, is to deprive him of the means by which he can arrive at the relationship between the lexical and the grammatical for himself. If, on the other hand, children are given *from the start* a set of words which have a full range of language functions they can discover for themselves how they fit together:

> The children begin to realise that sentences of the 'mum home' kind are incomplete and the missing words are added at the end to produce *mum home my is at*. At first sight this appears to be almost nonsensical but when asked the child will read aloud *my mum is at home*, inserting the missing words in their correct places and sometimes indicating them at the end of the stand. Or the child may make the sentence on his stand by selecting first the lexical items (the words with a low transition probability) and then, taking up the grammatical items later, insert them in their correct places by moving the words selected first to make room for them (Mackay and Thompson).

Sylvia Ashton-Warner called the single words which her children asked to be written down on a card *for themselves* 'captions' because they were '*one-word accounts of the pictures within*'. If a child selects on cards the two words 'mum' 'home' and puts them together, they are a symbolic representation of a much wider range of personal pictures which the child will describe *with many more words* if he is asked to *talk* about them. Thus the child using one of Mackay and Thompson's Word Folders who composed *my dad said to me you can go upstairs* added *in speech*: 'My dad said to me "You can go upstairs" yesterday because he didn't want me downstairs at the time. I was sitting in my nanny's sitting room watching the telly and my dad didn't want my television on. I was watching Secret Squirrel and my dad wanted to watch a film.'

Perhaps it is important to make a clear distinction between words-written-down *which the child asks for* and which he subsequently composes into 'captions' and then 'sentences' for himself, and which arise out of and are set in a context of his own personal store of picture images and spoken vocabulary; and words or sentences which are fabricated by a primer writer to produce an artificial simplicity which in no way represents a more complicated thought/speech process.

'Dick has a ball' or 'Janet held a doll' are comments which can hold little meaning for the child because they have no context; they are comments in a void; they have no connection with his own experience. 'Here is Dick' is not a caption for the child in the way that 'My mum is at home' could be; moreover, when the primer 'characters' speak they do so in carefully correct English which no child ever uses and thus lose whatever slim chance they might have had of being assimilated into the child's personal imaginative experience:

'I am to play bat and ball with Dick', said Jack.
One day John said, 'Let us play shops, Janet.'

Are reading primers worth reading?

Since the child's own written captions and simple sentences hold more meaning for him than those presented to him in a primer, does the primer offer him anything else once he has broken the code? What is there in them to please, amuse or interest him, or to encourage him to appreciate the value of written communication? Can we feel confident that a process of communication is actually going on as the child points his finger or his card at these words and says out loud:

Mother came into the shop.
Janet came too.
Mother saw something green.
She saw something red.
This is what she saw.
'I shall have this', said Mother.

Janet and John

or these:

I had a little dog;
His name was Buff;

> I sent him to the shop
> For a bag of snuff.
>
> *Beacon Readers*

or these:

> (Mother)   'The sun is out and there is no school' she says.
> 'You will want to go out in the sun.'
> Peter jumps out of bed. 'Good' he says.
> 'No school and the sun is out.'
>
> *Ladybird Key Words*
> *Reading Scheme*

Key words

In her description of how she taught Maori children to read, Sylvia Ashton-Warner distinguishes very firmly between *organic* words which come from the child and represent his inner feelings, thoughts and desires, and *inorganic* words which are imposed on the child from outside: 'Pleasant words won't do. Respectable words won't do. They must be words organically tied up, organically born from the dynamic life itself. They must be words that are already part of the child's being.' She goes on to quote 'a recent publication' on the approach of the *Janet and John* series which claimed that 'A child can be led to feel that Janet and John are friends' and she comments: 'Can be led to feel. Why lead him to feel or try to lead him to feel that these strangers are friends? What about the passionate feeling he has already for his own friends? To me it is inorganic to overlook this step.'

It is interesting to notice the difference between Ashton-Warner's use of the expression 'key words' for those words which spring from the child's inner vision; words which 'centre round the two main instincts, fear and sex'—words like *ghost* and *kiss* and *bomb* and *knife* and *Mummy* and *Daddy*—and the reading primer writer's use of the expression 'key words' to refer to those words which *occur most frequently* in the written language. The introduction to the *Ladybird Key Words Reading Scheme*, for instance, assures the teacher or the parent that by the time the child has read the whole series he will have *been presented* with a total number of nearly two thousand key words. It is important that the teacher of English at *any* stage should ask the question: does it *matter* whether key words to literacy are organic or inorganic, the most meaningful to the individual child or the most commonly used by all children? Word recognition tests are mostly based on the latter, but the 'one look words' for Ashton-Warner's children were not 'come, look, can, go, run, little, dog, horses . . .' but 'skeleton, spider, butcher, together, walnut, peanut, porridge, beer' —a mixture impossible to arrive at by presenting children with the words which they are most likely to come across: such words reflect rather the tremendously varied range of possibilities that individual choice allows.

After the 'uncontrolled' vocabulary of nursery rhymes and young children's stories the language of reading primers must strike parents and children alike as strangely attenuated and lifeless. Children run and hop and jump but they never scream and kick and yell. In many series there is a dearth of adjectives and adverbs for the first two or three books at least—colourful words which often help considerably to suggest feelings and movements and visual images. Even their 'mummies and daddies' or 'mums and dads' are constantly referred to as Mother and Father which, with the absolute correctness of their speech ('John do come here'), all adds up to the creation of a world which is far removed from the rough and tumble, the excitement and the harassment of everyday life.

The families of the primers are all too often prim. They usually come from a middle class background (often of a pre-war 1930s era). Janet and John, Dick and Dora, John and Ruth, Peter and Jane and their friends all climb trees in large gardens, play ball with their dogs, accompany Mother to the shops and make polite requests for sweets or toys, go sailing with Father or paddling in country streams—and hardly ever have a hair out of place, although occasionally they fall and cut their knees. But they never squabble or fight or argue with 'Mother' about whether it's time to go to bed or to play out or to watch television. In fact they are so preternaturally well behaved that one is tempted to say that they bear no resemblance to *any* normal children of any social class. It is extremely difficult for a talented adult writer either to create or to draw the reader's sympathies towards a wholly virtuous character but primer writers seem to be happily oblivious to such difficulties as their children play decorously beneath the apple tree alongside the well-tended herbaceous border.

In the course of writing this book, the Macmillan *Nippers* series edited by Leila Berg, has been produced to the accompaniment of a mixed chorus of praise and derision from the press. But at least the children quarrel and have 'mums' and 'dads' and play in what must for many young readers be a more recognisable environment than the world of Janet, Dora, Jane, Peter, Dick and John. In March 1970 Longman published twenty-four small booklets to be used in conjunction with Mackay and Thompson's *Breakthrough to Literacy Scheme* which are based on actual conversations with young school children about 'the new tooth', 'our baby', 'falling over' and similar experiences which are likely to spring from natural topics of conversation and interest.

The illustrations

In view of the generally high standard of children's book illustrations nowadays, the plates which are still used for several primer series are incredibly old fashioned and outdated. Mother's skirts are well below her knees, little boys have baggy pants and sun hats, and the toys are all of the sensible wooden variety. Perhaps the children don't notice the absence of familiar objects or the change in fashion—perhaps these characters are so unreal anyway that their funny clothes and hair styles are accepted unquestioningly. There is certainly nothing in the use of colour, brushwork or line to stimulate the child's imagination—although if one breaks away from the primer world into the wider world of *books* one example after another comes to mind of beautifully presented pictures which spread across the page in all sorts of interesting ways, full of dynamism and excitement and genuine artistry. There are of course (and thank goodness) a growing number of exceptions. The *Nippers* series are pleasantly illustrated in a range of subtle colours which strike a modern note, and the *Through the Rainbow* series published by Schofield and Sims make attractive use of colour photographs in their earlier books—their children grow visibly older too in the books catering for older age groups. The Longman *Breakthrough* series of reading booklets referred to in the previous section are most imaginatively illustrated by a series of expert and experienced children's book illustrators. The result is that each booklet has a character of its own, which is an added attraction rarely found in the normal run of reading primers.

Is the distinction between 'real' books and 'readers' necessary?

The effect of 'putting children on to primers' is to push 'real' books into a peripheral position—often literally! They are displayed neatly on shelves or in the book corner, but the book which each child keeps in his drawer and which he reads to his teacher is not one that he has chosen from either of these sources—it is Book One or Book Two or Three or Four—a book without a character of its own in fact.

For the child who has been used to having a wide selection of his own books at home that he can look at or listen to, this sudden narrowing of his field of choice to *one book* which he is expected to read word-perfectly page by page before he can tackle another must bore him if he is intelligent and depress him if he fails to make much headway. In a class of forty the pace at which he moves through his primer may be further impeded by the fact that the teacher cannot hear every child read to her every day. For the child who has not been used to a wide variety of books at home, his restriction to one book for 'reading' will not suffer from the contrast but it can hardly be an incentive to him to add reading to his voluntary spare time activities.

Story telling and 'real' books in the classroom

In *The Initial Teaching of Reading and Writing*, Mackay and Thompson suggest that one of the most important functions of picture story books in the classroom is that the strong story line, reflected closely in the illustrations, may encourage the child who has enjoyed listening to the story *to retell it himself*. They remind the reader that some children find it extremely difficult to maintain a subject through continuous discourse and they point out that 'the frequent use of picture story books for this purpose may well be one of the keys to the development of a new range of speech skills. Such is the child's interest and involvement in the stories that new ideas, new language skills, new aspects of grammar and new items of vocabulary are learned without conscious effort . . . The way in which parts of a text hang together (aspects of thematic organisation, cohesive elements, the use of reference, substitution, conjunction, anaphora and other discourse elements which organise sentences into a cohesive text) become available to the child through the reading and telling and discussion of stories'.

Children learn to talk by listening in to whatever the people around them happen to be saying. No doubt children whose parents make special efforts to talk slowly and distinctly to them at first—even the most disadvantaged—pick up speech sounds by the time they come to school unless they have some special physical or mental defect. No parent, however, attempts to introduce a child systematically to the eight different 'parts of speech'; nor do parents make a conscious effort to introduce phrases, clauses, simple and complex sentences in any kind of graded order for the child—and yet between the ages of one and four children learn, as Chomsky and others have shown, to operate these structures for themselves more effectively than the most expensive computer that man has yet devised. We do not know *how* all normal children achieve such an impressive feat of learning at such an early age but *why* they learn would seem to be fairly clear. The incentive to express themselves in this way—symbolically—through patterns of sound must be very strong, and so must the opportunity for talk and for listening to other people.

Similarly, children must be given a strong incentive to express themselves symbolically through written symbols. If children are to realise fully the possibilities for extended expression and communication that are open to them once they have mastered the written as well as the spoken language, they must be presented with a constant supply of fascinating books and not with a single dog-eared reader. It is ironical at a time when the books for this age group are being produced by such imaginative and creative artists as Charles Keeping, Brian Wildsmith, John Burningham, Helen Oxenbury, Renate Meyer and Maurice Sendak that in schools the child's attention should be largely focused upon materials that are both visually and verbally inferior. One suspects that fewer children would learn to *talk* successfully if they were put in a room with a Dalek for a teacher . . . What I am really suggesting is that we may still be placing far too great an emphasis on vocabulary grading and nowhere near enough emphasis on the child's own interests. Reading and writing only matter to a child if they are closely related to his own needs; at present the most popularly used reading schemes may be more closely related to the apparent needs of the teacher—for a system which enables her to follow the child's 'progress' from Book One to Book Five or Book Ten . . .

It would appear that most primer series in fact fail to meet adequately the requirements of either the keen 'decoder' who is best suited with a closely structured but comprehensive sight-sound introduction to the orthography, or the teacher who believes that no child should be forced to read a book which he does not personally enjoy.

Are 'real' books available for five- to six-year-olds?

The short answer to this question is yes, certainly. An increasing number of first-rate children's picture story books are being published every year by an increasing number of publishing companies. Further there are now a number of publications in both book and magazine form which help the interested librarian, teacher or parent to inform herself of the best that is available.

Outstanding reference books include *Four to Fourteen* by Kathleen Lines, *Intent Upon Reading* and *Open the Door* by Margery Fisher and *A Guide to Reading for the Under-Fives* by Eileen Colwell. Similarly, since the early 1960s Hamish Hamilton have published annual volumes of book reviews by Naomi Lewis entitled *Best Children's Books* of the year, which cover a wide age range including five and six.

From the magazines that are now available, teachers could persuade their schools usefully to subscribe to any of the following:

1 *Growing Point*—nine issues a year from Margery Fisher, address: Ashton Manor, Northampton (subscription £1.50, single copies 20p.)

2 *Books for Your Children* by Anne Wood—four issues a year, address: The Editor, 14 Stoke Road, Guildford, Surrey (subscription 60p annually for 4 issues, £1.20 for 2 years).

3 *Children's Book Newsletter*—a bi-monthly review of new books chosen by the review panel of the Children's Book Centre, address: Children's Book Centre Ltd, 140 Kensington Church Street, W8 (subscription 17½p. a copy or £1.05 for a year).

The National Book League also produces annual pamphlets entitled '100 Books for Children' arranged in age groups 3–6, 6–9, 9–11, 11–14, which give titles, publishers, prices and a very brief description of the books which are listed.

In Appendix O I have listed under the names of more than fifty publishers those books which are in my opinion suitable for use (not just wall decoration) in Infant classrooms.[1] I have divided this Appendix into List A and List B. In the former I have included genuine story books which with very few exceptions print no more than three sentences at the most on each page. What text there is is speakable and would sound like a story if it were read on to a tape for children to listen to as they turned the pages of the book and enjoyed the accompanying illustrations.

The books in List B mostly have four or five sentences to a page but they are still predominantly picture story books, attractively and imaginatively illustrated, and all encouraging the child to explore his own feelings about himself and his surroundings through fantasy and through fact. There are funny stories, sad stories, fantasy stories,

---

[1] I am convinced that far greater use could and should be made of tape recordings in all infant classrooms to help children at the initial stages of literacy to relate sounds to visual symbols in a way that is both meaningful and enjoyable. Any normal five- or six-year-old could handle a cassette tape recorder without difficulty and it is quite possible for a small group of children to listen to a recording of a story on earphones without disturbing or being disturbed by other activities taking place inside the same classroom. I have indicated in some instances on my list of books, where a tape would be especially useful (for example, with the 'Nebuchadnezzar' skipping rhyme, or with the Ezra Jack Keats picture story version of *The Little Drummer Boy*); ideally there could be a class 'library' of tapes to pair off with books that were popular favourites in the classroom.

familiar stories and reassuring stories as well as factually scientific books written simply and clearly to satisfy the child's increasing curiosity about how things work.

I have grouped the books in both sections under an alphabetical list of publishers. I have in the majority of cases only included titles that I have myself read and enjoyed. It is therefore a personal selection and I am very aware that there are many other interesting and attractive books that are available for the five to seven age range. My list is only the tip of the iceberg—an indication of the riches that are available and that *should be used* in schools. The cost should not be exorbitant as any permanent classroom collection can always be supplemented by further books on an extended loan system from the Schools Department of the County Library.

ALTERNATIVE SCHEMES

If, as appears to be the case, special readers fail by and large to provide the child with the most effective means of learning how to 'break the code', fail to give him an insight into the basic structures of written English and on top of that, often fail to offer him enjoyable and interesting reading, it would seem reasonable to suggest that infant teachers consider alternative schemes that are available in this country for incorporation into their learning-to-read programmes.

It should no longer in effect be so much a matter of which *method* (phonic or look-and-say) as of which *devices* a teacher decides to employ—and when. On the basis of the thinking that has gone into the preparation of this section of the survey I would be very much inclined to suggest that from the start the teacher adopt a two-pronged approach to reading. On the one hand the infant classroom should provide a wide range of the kind of simple, attractively illustrated *story* books that I have just been describing—along with tapes of the stories to which the children could listen if they chose—and on the other hand the same infant classroom should tackle the decoding aspect of reading *directly* by introducing one or more teaching device. It is not unrealistic to envisage a school in which two or three such decoding devices would be available, and the children grouped on entry on the strength of diagnostic tests to use the device most appropriate to them.

In this way, there would be no break for the child who has learnt to enjoy listening to stories at home, when first he comes to school. There would still be plenty of opportunity to enjoy books *from choice*, and listening for meaning would change smoothly into reading for meaning as the child became familiar with the written code. A direct, device-assisted approach to decoding would introduce him more quickly and more clearly to the visual patterns of our language than most primers do, and would also enable him to tackle the *encoding* problem more decisively and confidently from the start.

i.t.a. plus 'real' books

i.t.a. is a more adaptable device than either WIC or CSR and for this reason perhaps no particular scheme (so far as I am aware) has been especially evolved for it. Indeed to use primers specially printed in i.t.a. is to ignore the advantages of a regularised coding device. Certainly more schools are now using i.t.a. than any other of the devices which I have described, and an increasingly long list of specially printed story books are now available from the i.t.a. publishing company and also from a number of other publishers.

Words in Colour

The WIC reading scheme is intended to teach the child principally to decode. It gives the child a thorough knowledge of all the phoneme-grapheme combinations that he will find in the English language.

The author describes his concept of the reading process as 'algebraic': 'In our approach we use the word "algebra" to mean the way in which words and sounds can be made up from combinations of signs and transformed by combining the signs differently.' The children are started off working at forming combinations of sounds with the restricted language of five vowels. Children learn to read and write this fully phonetic restricted language *in which there is not yet a word* that is part of English before going on to add the four consonants 'p', 't', 's' (is) and 's' (us). With the following thirteen signs plus the mute apostrophe many combinations are formed—some of them words in the English language, many not. Gattegno (1962) supports and approves of this 'algebraic' approach for the following reasons:

1 It maintains the game-like activity.

2 It gives exercises which are intellectual in character.

3 It establishes from the beginning the analytic–synthetic method of forming words.

4 It increases awareness of what is being done and the sounds which are being uttered.

5 It helps children to recognise that words have to be *formed* and to see how they are formed.

Gattegno firmly repudiates the use of 'drill and repetition' and advocates instead the use of 'game-like activities': 'Children will be asked to *play seriously* a number of games, each game having a particular function, complementary to that of the others.' One example cited by Joan Dean[1] is 'the game of changing one word to another by changing a sign at a time. It is played with special rules which make it possible to add or insert a sign and to reverse a word as well. Thus one might get from "must" to "stop" for example, in this way: must, most, post, past, pass, pats, pots, stop'. From her observations of WIC in the classroom Dean comments: 'These games are undoubtedly valuable elements in this approach.'

I have already described (p. 80) the reasons given by Gattegno for introducing 48 colour tones into his scheme in the section on teaching devices and I shall not therefore refer to it in detail again here. According to Dean: 'The systematic introduction and exploration at each stage is as much a feature of the scheme as the colour.' She also comments that 'each step is simple and brings a measure of success, so that we have the effect met in linear programming of reinforcement of learning by success'.

The vocabulary is necessarily graded very stringently. Teachers are limited, if they make books for the children other than the basic primer, to words which are within the phonetic range which has already been learnt. Dean quotes an example:

> it is a teddy
> it is Pat's teddy
> sit up teddy
> teddy sits up

The *Book of Stories* which is published as part of the WIC material is not brought into use until the key consonants and a number of vowels have been introduced to form words and sentences—so that initially, if Gattegno's own advice is followed closely, the children are introduced to reading without reference to 'real' books of any kind. If, however, his scheme is regarded as a *decoding* scheme rather than a *reading* scheme, and over the period in which it is used extra *listening*

---

[1] International Reading Symposium 2, Oxford, 1966. Dean's observations in this paper are summarised in Appendix J.

story time (via tapes or the teacher) is provided, this need not be a serious drawback.

Gattegno has stated his belief that children are capable of much more intellectually at five than we normally assume. The WIC approach as he plans it makes no concessions, for instance, to word-picture associations. The 'reading' books which go with the scheme, as Dean remarks, are 'baldly phonetic with no illustrations at all until the *Book of Stories* is reached, and this only has nine black and white drawings'.

Gattegno claims for WIC (as Jones (1968) claims for Colour Story Reading) that because of 'the game-like character of the method the teacher can stand back and allow the children to find out for themselves', but it is difficult in view of the tightly controlled nature of the material to see how they can discover very much for themselves, unless a highly individualised classroom structure is being operated by the teacher. In the initial stages, at any rate, the child has an extremely narrow field within which he can operate so that his scope for 'finding out' in this area must be considerably diminished.

WIC materials: For the classroom there are twenty-one coloured wall charts, which will be put up at the appropriate stage in the course. Once on the wall, the charts remain in position so that children can refer back to a word on a previous chart when they are in difficulty. Another coloured chart displays the whole set of coloured signs that represent every possible sight/sound combination in the English language.

For the teacher there is a book on the theory of the approach, (the Background Book) and one on its practice (the Teacher's Guide). For the children the materials are as follows: three Primer books which give practice in sound combinations, a Word Building Book for each child formed of sixteen progressive charts. On these are shown the signs which have been progressively introduced on the Wall Charts and in the Primer Books. A set of Worksheets for each child based upon material described so far, but including 'additional challenges and techniques for self-education'. A *Book of Stories* for each child 'contains forty progressive ... stories for continuous reading'. It can be introduced only when the children are *about halfway through Primer 2*.

The children will also have a pack of Word Cards on which words are printed in black on coloured cardboard. Each grammatical category of words is symbolised by one colour and several words are printed on more than one colour if they have more than one grammatical function.

The advantages and disadvantages of the scheme: I shall conclude this section on WIC by quoting the list of advantages and disadvantages cited by Joan Dean (1966) in her paper to the Second International Reading Symposium. Here first are the advantages:

1   Colour really helps.

2   Children can really do something from the beginning. They seem to enjoy the exercises of solving a problem which is within their capacity and teachers using this scheme have remarked that their children do not like to be told a word but prefer to puzzle it out for themselves.

3   It develops to a high degree the ability to discriminate between different sounds and letter shapes. WIC makes both children and teachers very conscious of sound and the need for careful listening and careful looking.

4   It develops the ability to play with words and to see relationships between them. (What kind of relationships: structural or semantic—or both?)

5   Children who have learnt to read by this method are in a position to review the possibilities of spelling for any word. Only experience will help them to choose the right spelling from these possibilities however.

6   There are no blending difficulties because the consonants are *always* given with the vowels and never by themselves.

7   The scheme is systematic.

Here are the disadvantages of the scheme:

1   The scheme starts in a formal way and deals at the outset with sound combinations which are meaningless. This again seems to throw onus on the teacher to *see that children are learning in a reading environment* where many other aspects of learning to read are evident. I should perhaps add that Dr Gattegno would not agree with me here. He would prefer to concentrate on teaching children *with the scheme only* until they could read.

2 It may be a matter of weeks before children grasp the possibilities of decoding sufficiently to be able to enjoy using the scheme.

3 The ability of some children to grasp abstract concepts may be underestimated by many of us, but there are certainly some children for whom the lack of any visual or story aids could be a hindrance as much as a help.

Colour Story Reading

Although colour is the most noticeable feature of Kenneth Jones's reading scheme—as it is of Gattegno's—like Gattegno, Jones regards the use of colour as a decoding device which he has incorporated into a more complex reading programme. The CSR scheme is based on three stages of presentation:

1 enjoyment of listening to the *spoken* word in the form of *The Nineteen Stories*

2 development of visual awareness and learning

and

3 development of phonetic awareness and learning

Eventually all three stages co-exist, and if the scheme has been successful 'mutually reinforce each other in a triangular pattern of learning:

imagery

symbol   sound'

The symbols in Colour Story Reading consist of the twenty-six letters used in the traditional orthography along with the three background shapes, the circle, the triangle and the square with which Jones encloses a letter or a group of letters which represent a particular sound. Both letters and background shapes are printed in red, blue or green—and the letters inside a shape are always printed in black.

Where Gattegno has indicated by the use of colour forty-eight different *sounds* which occur in spoken English, Jones, by the use of colour and shape, has differentiated forty-two. Where a letter represents more than one sound it is printed in more than one colour or provided with an additional background shape and where various letter combinations produce the same sound, the same background shape is always used; for example, the green circle that represents an 'oo' sound would be used in too, two, through, blue.

The sound/symbol relationships are closely associated with each other in the story imagery. The green circle is first introduced in a story about a magic green balloon which murmurs 'oo' 'oo' as it floats along, and the red circle is featured in a story called *Ernest and the Fireworks*; Ernest frequently says '-er -er' when he speaks and in the story he is pictured lighting fireworks which are surrounded by a round, red glow.

The story *imagery* is therefore used in the CSR scheme 'to reinforce the link between the letters, sounds, shapes and colours' and in many ways it is the most interesting feature of the scheme. This is a striking difference from WIC, where the emphasis is continually upon the abstract of sound/symbol patterns and where picture imagery in verbal/visual terms is deliberately avoided.

In the first stage of CSR the children are simply encouraged to enjoy *listening* to *The Nineteen Stories* because initially, Jones suggests, 'the child is concerned with enjoyment and the acquisition of a rich imagery on which to base future learning'. The author claims that the wider the 'associative network' the easier it is for the child to retrieve the information that he requires:

As Osgood (1955), Bugelski (1942), Gibson (1942), Underwood (1945) and others have demonstrated, *paired* associate learning can be psychologically unsound when there is no logical or natural connection between the pairs of items to be associated. This situation occurs in traditional 'look and say' learning (associating a word-shape with a word-sound) and traditional phonic learning (involving linking a letter-shape with a letter-sound). The 'story' element provides a mediating structure of concepts and colours linking sight and sound which reduces or eliminates harmful interference caused by paired associate learning.

Mr Nen and His Friends—The Nineteen Stories. The six main characters in these stories, Apple, Egg, Ink, Orange, Umbrella and Lemon, enjoy a series of adventures and excursions together, which in the world of children's reading primers are a refreshing blend of phantasy and realism. The characters do not belong to any class or social group, and as they are animated objects and not human beings they suffer no parental restraint, although Mr Nen stands in as a father or perhaps uncle figure and they live in his house and go for rides in his car. Above all, after the first three stories, the friends speak in natural, recognisable and lively English. All the stories are within the experience of most children of five to six. The friends have a party, they go to the shops in Mr Nen's car, visit a railway station, have a picnic and so on. But during these outings interesting and strange things happen. They are not just dull flat accounts of boringly familiar events: signposts speak and balloons float home by themselves; the friends see the cat turn from blue to red; and on another occasion they keep meeting a green square that materialises from nowhere every time they say a word containing an 'ar' sound. Judging from teachers' comments this mixture of phantasy and realism is highly successful. The children not only enjoy listening to the stories, they also enjoy using them as a basis for drawing, painting and acting.

Materials to be used with the scheme comprise *The Nineteen Stories* (in black print to be read by the teacher to the children), records of all the stories, a wall chart of the different colour symbols (letters and backgrounds) systematically arranged, and three short reading books for the children, printed in colour and referring to the characters and events from *The Nineteen Stories*. Jones suggests that a picture of the green net which figures in Story 2 with the caption 'This is *the* net' is more meaningful to a child who has heard the story than the caption 'This is a net' or simply 'net', because he can link the net immediately with a story that he knows in which Mr Nen caught fish with the green net at the seaside. A 'treasure game' for young children using the coloured shapes and letters has been published by Nelson for use with CSR.

Both Jones and Gattegno claim that the schemes which they have planned enable children to discover the relationships between phonemes and graphemes for themselves. Both make use of games which the children can play in pairs or small groups and both point out the advantages of colour as a cue for individual learning. Instead of saying 'that letter says . . .', the teacher can ask the child in WIC to imagine the 'mauve one, the white one and the brown one': in CSR she can utilise colour and imagery by asking 'what sound did the cat make when it was angry and changed colour?'—thus the child is helped to arrive at the relation between sounds and symbols for himself.

Jones conducted a two-year investigation (1965-67) into the use of this scheme of 'phonetic colour' as an aid to learning to read and spell. The work was financed by the DES and carried out in association with the Reading Research Unit at the University of London Institute of Education. The main experiment covered nineteen schools—each school acting as its own control by using the same tests and as far as possible the same teacher with the reception class in the year *prior* to the experimental group's course using CSR. I have summarised the Research Report for this experiment in Appendix K.

Comments on Colour Story Reading:

1   From personal observation and from teachers' comments (Research Report 1967) it is clear that children enjoy the stories and remember the details. Jones' hypothesis that a wider associative network facilitates retrieval of information appeals to common sense as well as to psychological theories.

2   To adults, the scheme at first sight appears to be far more complicated than it does to non-reading children. To the child the initial similarity of symbols which are all printed or written in black may be far more confusing than the colour patterns of either CSR or WIC.

3   The use of colour and background symbols does initially reduce the speed with which the child can write—if he chooses to use colour himself. On the credit side, however, the distinct pattern made by words in colour visually may help him to retain the image of the whole word in his 'mind's eye' more readily than if the word is printed or written in a uniform colour.

4   The paucity of material is at present a drawback. Currently there are only three children's books in colour with a limited vocabulary and sentence structure. The child cannot even read the *Nineteen Stories* in colour, although listening to the records on which the stories are well and unaffectedly told by Peter King they may well be motivated to do so. Any infant teacher who prefers to use the experiences described by the children themselves is not of course so hampered as those who rely heavily on reading primers.

5   The drawback for a great deal of teacher-presented material in colour (writing down for each child in the class just one or two sentences perhaps . . .) is also primarily one of speed. It takes longer to use four pens than one pen, especially when background symbols have to be drawn as well.

6   *But*—this is the only decoding device that I know of which has incorporated into its accompanying reading scheme material which has some connection with the pleasure and enjoyment of

'reading' in the wider sense of the word. The Mr Nen stories should appeal to young children *as stories* (they certainly did to mine) and not just as useful decoding material, but at the same time the sound–symbol relationships which have been built into the stories provide the child with the decoding information which he requires in order to read independently.

7 It would be interesting to run an experiment using concurrently two reception classes in the same school, or as Jones did in his pilot study, two classes in succeeding years (harder on the teacher in this instance!), one of which would use Colour Story Reading and one Words in Colour. Though both schemes make use of colour they have many dissimilarities and it would be fascinating to keep a close record of children's reactions to both—as well as a record of their ability to decode in black by the end of the course.

Brimer's experimental evaluation of coded scripts in initial reading

In 1967 M. A. Brimer, a Senior Research Officer in Education at Bristol University, published a paper in which i.t.a., WIC, DMS and a device called 'Coloured Words' were compared with t.o. under rigidly experimental conditions. Five groups of children—one for each code—were presented in an exactly similar way with one hundred single words to be 'learnt' at word recognition level. The tests took place over fourteen days. Brimer found that, first, there was no significant difference between scripts for *oral* reading—except in the case of colour scripts which were inferior to t.o. Second, the Diacritical Marking System gave better recognition results than t.o., 'Coloured Words' showed no significant difference and i.t.a. and WIC were significantly inferior. However, it must be remembered that the coding device was used in the case of WIC with a total disregard for the scheme of which it is part. Also, the length of time to assimilate the words was short. Therefore the fact that children learnt the words coded in t.o. on the whole more successfully than words coded in other ways cannot be extended into any kind of valid generalisation.

A longitudinal comparison of children using different coding devices as a part of their reading programme would certainly be more difficult to control experimentally, as John Downing's first and second i.t.a. experiments have both clearly indicated. The less control there is, the more diverse the variables; and the more control there is, the less satisfactory the teaching situation. In spite of its drawbacks, however, such a longitudinal comparison would provide teachers with a fund of knowledge about the ways in which children are helped or hindered by these various devices and schemes which at present we very much lack.

Stott's Programmed Reading Kit

This reading scheme was formulated initially by D. H. Stott for use with backward readers. It is carefully structured to lead children step by step to a clear understanding of the various patterns that sound/symbol relationships form in the English language, and thus to break the code. It involves thirty 'card games' which children can 'play' in pairs or small groups.

To quote Dr Stott's account of his scheme in the *Times Educational Supplement* (22 February 1963) the 'three broad principles' on which the material are based can be described as follows:

1 Ready-made grammatical generalisations are of small value to slow children. To be effective, any rule has to be gained from the experience of language data—which has to be prepared in concentrated (or 'programmed') sequences.

2 A classroom method and classroom materials had to be evolved which demanded frequent responses and which checked each response as it was made. To utter more than twenty words without asking the class to respond or set down a word was a waste of time.

3 Since learning a (written) language is a long and often discouraging job, the pupil must be constantly egged on by success. At each step he must be proficient enough to provide correct answers.

Briefly, the card games (which I have described in greater detail in Appendix L) move from those which aim to make children aware of letter/sound associations, to those which give the child practice in 'blending' or fusing sounds together into simple words and syllables, to a third group of games which introduces the child to 'the fluent reading without tension of sentences mainly composed of simple phonic words, and the perfecting of sight habits of a number of common words'. From this point words in which the sound units are dependent upon the combination of two or more letters are introduced on charts, accompanied by a series of games to practise recognising these words. The sentences on these cards are 'designed to include as many as possible of the most frequent words used in children's reading'. A group of card games designed for learning and practising the

'Lazy E' come next, and finally there are syllable cards called 'Long Word Jigsaws' to give the child confidence to tackle long words and to show how the phonic sight habits already acquired can be used in reading them.

The Programmed Reading Kit sets out unpretentiously to unlock the code of the written language sufficiently for slow children to decode a basic vocabulary with confidence for themselves. The pace is deliberately unhurried to prevent bewilderment, anxiety and finally the withdrawal from the whole reading situation which reluctant readers often seem forced to make.

The Kit could certainly also be used to advantage with children of average ability at an early stage in their reading programme, to introduce them through the games to the ways in which sounds can be encoded into letters and words and subsequently decoded into sounds again.

But however backward children may be in deciphering the written language, care should be taken to see that this is not their *only* form of 'reading' activity. Stories which have a strong emotional appeal should be available for these (as for all) children, to listen to on records or tapes and to look at in plenty of attractively illustrated books, so that their decoding activities with the Kit are placed in a context of 'real' reading.

A disadvantage of the Kit is that it gives little opportunity for much personal response (apart from the satisfaction of winning the games), and even less scope for self-expression. It is true that with non-literate children this comes chiefly through talk, but perhaps when they reached the stage of decoding simple words successfully Mackay and Thompson's Word Folder could be introduced to encourage them to use the written language *for themselves*.

Stern and Gould, in their formulation of 'Structural Reading' (see Appendix M) have much in common with Stott in their approach to the initial stages of learning how to read.

SRA word games

A Canadian organisation called Science Research Associates Limited has also produced a set of word games as part of its 'Reading Laboratory Programme'. There are ten 'laboratories' in all and nine of them are chiefly concerned with 'developing the child's powers of comprehension' once he has gained some mastery of the written code. The first box of cards, however, is designed 'to provide extensive practice' in decoding skills along much the same lines as Stott's Programmed Reading Kit. Playing the games enables pupils to teach themselves and one another the correspondence between the sounds and the letters that make up their language. The cards are attractively and colourfully presented on thick cardboard with plenty of illustrations.

Breakthrough to Literacy

'A literacy programme must see its end in the ability of the learner to handle written materials of all kinds for a multitude of uses, both literary and non-literary.' *Mackay, Thompson and Schaub*

This 'literacy' programme differs from the four reading schemes just described in that it is not solely concerned with reading. David Mackay, Brian Thompson and Pamela Schaub have attempted to take into account the child's potential ability to use *every aspect* of the written language. They suggest that in order to foster literacy skills in non-literate children, teachers need to know more about how children *learn to be literate,* and more—in a precise sense—about the nature of the written language itself (see Appendix N).

It is true that if the infant teacher cares to look at it, a vast quantity of 'reading' theory and research is available, but research into how young children learn to write down their own thoughts is almost non-existent. Does it for instance help them to copy down sentences that have been constructed for them by the teacher, or do they gain more insight into the nature of the written language if they are encouraged to discover how the system works for themselves? And do we as teachers in any case know enough about the structures of the written language to be able to provide the child with a model of the ortho-graphy that he can grasp as a whole instead of piecemeal through his reading primers? Mackay, Thompson and Schaub not only raise these questions, they begin to answer some of them, and I have summarised their very useful account of the distinctive features of our own writing system in Appendix N.

In the following section I describe first the differences between the spoken and the written language which the speaking but non-writing child has to assimilate before he can become literate and which this group of linguists set out with admirable clarity in their book. Subse-quently, details of the literacy scheme which has now been evolved by the team for use at the infant stage are set out as the final alternative to the widespread use of reading primers.

A definition of literacy: Mackay, Thompson and Schaub define literacy as 'the ability to operate effectively with the writing system of a language'. They then define some of the abilities of a literate adult:

As a reader:

Fluent reading (both silent and oral) for a wide range of purposes with a wide range of appropriate responses.

Wide range of reading techniques appropriate to the purpose, among which are strategies for dealing with failure (e.g. ability to use a dictionary, to use reference books and to consult and discuss with other readers).

Ability to make critical evaluation of texts (to verify information, to recognise expressions of opinion and prejudice in the text, to assess the writer's attitudes, strategies and purposes).

Ability to add to his stock of knowledge by relating present reading to past experience.

As a writer:

Ability to communicate within the range 'self'-centred to 'subject'-centred (poetry, letter writing, technical writing etc.).

Ability to predict a reader's reactions and to write with a specific audience in mind; to write to produce a specified effect—effectively; to anticipate reactions to the text (e.g. defining or not defining terms for lay or professional readership).

Ability to correct and amend original drafts and to examine self-produced material critically.

Ability to use appropriate forms of written language.

Language myths are some of the mistaken assumptions that non-linguists are apt to make about language:

1   written language is 'superior' to spoken language;

2   English spelling is 'a mess';

3   words *per se* have meaning;

4   when we learn a language we learn primarily a vocabulary;

5   similarly, when we learn to read and write we learn discrete words;

6   some dialects and some accents of a dialect are 'better', 'rougher' or 'more slovenly' than others;

7   language *change* represents a debasement—especially when reproduced by certain newspapers, advertisers, novelists and radio announcers.

Differences between the spoken and the written language: For the child to learn to relate the familiar spoken language with the unfamiliar written language, it is clearly important for the teacher to know exactly what the two language modes have in common and how they differ. I quote in full the summary of these differences from *Breakthrough to Literacy*:

1   Speech consists of sound made by the speaker's vocal organs and received by his listeners' ears. Written language consists of marks on a writing surface made by a writing tool and received by the eyes. The child does not hear the sounds of spoken language as separate units nor the words of spoken language as separate items. The written language shows the letters as distinct shapes on the page and words are isolated by the use of word spaces.

2   Spoken language occurs in time, while written symbols occupy linear space. Further, written symbols are ordered lines from left to right and the lines are read from the top of any given page to the bottom.

3   The production of spoken sounds may be seen and felt as complex movements of the speech organs. The writing of symbols is not part of a child's experience in the same way. When the child begins to learn to read and write his motor control is likely to be at a stage near to scribbling and it is tempting to compare this with the early stages in learning to speak: that of babbling. But scribbling results not only in a later ability to form the limited set of letter shapes used in writing but also in the ability to represent an unlimited range of objects and pictorial patterns in drawing and painting.

4   Speech is almost always a social act. Most speech acts are dialogues and the situations which give rise to them are shaped unconsciously by the speakers. Writing, while it is being produced, is almost always a solitary act in which the writer is isolated from both people and situations. He is alone with his ideas and his ability to express these in written language.

5   There are many features of spoken language which are ignored in written language. Intonation, for example, is of considerable importance in English grammar and many shades of meaning are carried by intonation patterns. The written language has only very limited resources with which to indicate these patterns and relatively infrequent use is made of them. Similarly, rhythm, stress, the weak

forms of words and other features of spoken language appear, if at all, only in the most restricted way in written language.

6 Both spoken language and written language are complex in organisation and patterning. However, they differ in *substance* (spoken sounds as against written marks); in the *organs* used to produce and receive them; in *form* (the lexis—vocabulary—and grammar of spoken language are different in many respects from those of written language); and in the *situations* and *purposes* for which each is used.

7 Both spoken language and written language are symbolic; but written language is, as Vygotsky (1962) puts it, 'a second degree of symbolisation'. That is to say, in writing, as opposed to speech, we are entirely removed from the objects and situations to which the language refers. Vygotsky goes on to state: 'Our studies show that it is the *abstract* quality of written language that is the main stumbling block, not the underdevelopment of small muscles or any other mechanical obstacles.'

Children and the orthography of their language: Mackay and Thompson suggest that some children, somehow, are capable of internalising for themselves 'a model of the orthography that works. That is to say: they can spell correctly when they write and recognise spelling patterns correctly when they read'. But 'many other children make sense of it (the orthography) slowly and indifferently, and some retain throughout their lives so rudimentary a model that they are never able to do much about reading and writing. For them English teaching is remembered only in terms of dreaded spelling tests and composition and reading books that bored and confused them. They make up a large part of the population that believes it was "never any good at English".'

The writers also warn the non-linguist who may be hoping for too much too soon that '[it] will be likely to take *several years* to master [English orthography] [one is tempted to say that it *should* take several years], for there are many words that are out of reach of the young child and some of these will certainly involve patterns and conventions not needed until he has had considerable experience of written language'. They add—and this is most important—'There is another reason for the time taken to become "a good speller". Spelling patterns and all the other conventions of the writing system are *only one part* of the overall patterning with which the learner is dealing. They do not exist separately from the patterns of grammar and lexis and meaning, and if the child does not also have *some understanding of the larger issues from the beginning*, the more difficult it will be for him to become literate.'

The importance of production by the child: When they came to apply their theory of literacy, this team record how 'the emphasis we came to place on *production* in the first stages of learning to read and write is one of the places where we depart from the basic assumptions of traditional teaching methods in this field'. Here are some of the most cogent reasons which they put forward to support this emphasis:

1   It is only when the child attempts *to express himself* in written language that we (the teachers) can observe how he learns to manipulate written forms.

2   If the child dictates and the teacher writes down his dictation for him to copy it is the teacher who is coping with the transfer from spoken to written mode, not the child. 'The gap between success in writing sentences unaided and copying what someone else has written is great and it is not always easy to discover the sources of difficulty a child may encounter on the way. Neither can the teacher know accurately what to praise since she does not know what the child has done for himself.'

3   By enabling the *child* to show us what he is doing in the process of producing an acceptable written sentence, we are more able to help him to gain control of written language.

4   By giving him words on cards that he can pick up to build up into sentences, the child is enabled to discover for himself the correct structure of a sentence—he can see it taking shape and move it around when it 'sounds wrong' on being read aloud. The two writers of this paper affirm: 'We believe that all children try to get things right and that they arrange for themselves self-imposed practice precisely to master a skill until they are able to use it with ease and understanding.'

The stages of learning to write: Mackay, Thompson and Schaub analyse them as follows:

Since the initial vocabulary has to be learned from its visual pro-perties, it is hardly surprising that during the first stage many of the children *simply list words they recognise*. Words such as *with, dad, boy, girl, children, go Denis,* may be put into the stand and read back to the teacher *and talked about* . . . The child has learned to associate the black patterns on the cards with the sound patterns he makes with his mouth. In the particular example cited here, the child also 'read the word list from left to right, showing awareness of one of the conventions of written English'.

The child then begins to produce meaningful sentences, *but omits items with low information content*, thus producing a kind of telegraphese. For example, many children produced 'baby little' or 'children school' and read them as 'the baby is little' or 'the children go to school', either not noticing that some words had been left out or considering the omitted words so unimportant that they could be added when reading the sentence aloud. The team found many partial sentences of this kind using only the words that carry the message (lexical items), but the children produced *no examples* of sentences made wholly from words with a high transition probability (the grammatical items). That is to say that, while children will make sentences of the kind 'mum home' for 'my mum is at home', the same sentence is never produced as 'my is at' and read back as 'my mum is at home'.

The children now begin to realise that sentences of the 'mum home' kind are incomplete and the missing words are added at the end to produce 'mum home my is at'. At first sight this appears to be almost nonsensical but when asked the child will read aloud 'my mum is at home', inserting the missing words *in their correct places* and sometimes indicating them at the end of the stand. Or he may make the sentence on his stand by selecting first the lexical items (nouns, adjectives, main verbs) and then taking up the grammatical items later, *insert* them in their correct places by moving the words selected first to make room for them.

The team add: 'It should be clear by this stage that we are at least as interested in the mistakes the child makes as in his ability to produce acceptable sentences. It would be wrong to dismiss what *appears* to be a random selection of items when in fact it is organised in a way that is peculiar to a child at that stage in his development.'

Often the children will produce partial sentences and we have noticed that in these cases there seems to be an emphasis on the noun phrase. They frequently make strings like: 'boy and girl', 'my mum and my dad and the children', 'my big teacher', 'my baby'. These are simple labels, sometimes modified by adjectives and often preceded with the satisfying egocentric *my*. Mackay and Thompson continue:

'This is worth noting because later on some children may produce sentences where the ordering of the nominal and verbal groups is deviant. Sometimes we have found that this is due to the children setting up the nominal group first (e.g. *my little teacher*) *and then saying something about it*, even though in the *normal* grammatical ordering the nominal group may come at the end of the sentence (e.g. *my little teacher I love* instead of *I love my little teacher*). Traditional grammar would suggest that this is a confusion of subject and object; however, the child may feel that the "object" of the sentence, in this case my little teacher, is the real theme of the statement and knows that this can be shown by placing it first in the sentence sequence.'

The three investigators make it clear that this is not a dogmatic outline of stages through which all children must pass. Those stages that have been noted result from their own observation of the learning patterns of the children in the first experimental group to use their scheme. They agree 'it is quite possible that we omitted stages in this process or that we have described a "stage in learning that is common only to a few children". ' Clearly as the number of children using this approach increases it will be possible to state with greater confidence those stages which seem to occur more or less commonly.

Mackay, Thompson and Schaub suggest that 'it is more valuable to look positively at the orthography than to bemoan its shortcomings'. They set out the following list of sight/sound features that must be mastered by the child if he is to internalise effectively an accurate model of the orthography of his own language:

1   Listening to speech sounds—especially where there are differences in the speech sounds of the accents of teacher and children.

2   Learning to understand differences in the sets of speech sounds used by speakers with differing accents.

3   Learning how to think about the rules of the orthography and their exemplification. Learning how to discuss these and ask questions about them.

4   Learning the rules by proposing spelling patterns and noting how these may differ from conventional spelling. Learning to formulate rules as a result.

5   Learning spelling patterns as a reader. Recognising spelling patterns and knowing how to pronounce the spoken words these reflect. Learning how to add appropriate strong or weak stress to each word.

6 Learning spelling patterns as a writer. Learning how to represent one's own pronunciation of words in spelling patterns. Learning the *one visual form* for words or syllables which may have a number of weakly stressed spoken forms. Remembering the list of words which belong to each spelling pattern—which means that, for *lexical* words, word meanings have to be associated with the spelling of homonyms.

7 Learning that letter shapes are not just geometric.[1] They also have the special property derived from their position in space. For example, letter 'n' is not letter 'n' when it is upside down; letter 'f' is not letter 'f' when turned horizontally through 180°—unlike a teapot which undergoes no change of *identity* with change in its position in space. (The team suggest that ideally the shapes in the Word Maker should have been in three dimensional form to give children the opportunity of arriving at the one and only spatial placement for each.)

Materials

Materials which the child could use to compose his own sentences had to fulfil the following conditions:

1 They should be easy to use, easy to store and easy to maintain.

2 They should exclude from the skills involved in producing written language those concerned with handwriting and spelling.

3 Therefore the apparatus should be a word store and the items in it should be selected from those widely used by children of this age. It should make it possible for children to produce a very large number of sentences. There should also be provision for children to add words of their own choosing so that each child would draw on private experience in addition to that shared with other children.

4 In place of the line of typewritten *letters* the apparatus should provide a line of *words* held so that the child could carry it about the classroom. For this purpose it should include a stand which would make it possible for words from the store to be set up as a text.

The Sentence Maker: To fulfil these conditions, Mackay Thompson and Schaub designed and produced a *Sentence Maker*.

This consists of a triptych of card with the selection of words and

---

[1] cf. Lynn's similar point about 'b' and 'd': a chair is still a chair whether the seat points to left or right. The child's early experience tells him to ignore the direction. It is necessary, however, to learn that the direction in which the loop on 'b' and 'd' points does matter in reading.

affixes (e.g. -ing) printed on two folds; the third fold is a blank store for the personal word collection of each child. Each fold has lines of pockets to hold cards on which the words are printed. Each word is also printed on the pocket so that when the child withdraws these words he will be able to match them back into their appropriate positions. In this way he is helped to master the processes of word recognition and spelling. The current word lists for the Literacy Programme as they are arranged in the Sentence Maker are:

Side 1   home mum dad television bed baby
         brother sister boy girl children friend
         teacher school picture storybook house
         morning night day time birthday party
         cat dog shop car a a the the and very
         pretty big little good bad naughty some
         happy new all lot this I I my my they
         you me it we our he him his she her

Side 2   am is are was were will be been can
         do did work make made read write paint
         have has had come go came went said
         play walk run jump skip watch see saw
         want got get sleep kiss love like cry
         yes no es s s ed ing ? . - not n't for
         down up by on to in out at of there
         why because when what with after but

Side 3   Made up of blank pockets which can be used to store the per-
         sonal words required by individual children.

I have seen children in one of the Pilot Study schools using their Sentence Makers with much confidence and enjoyment. If a child is especially pleased with a sentence that he has constructed, he will pick up the wooden stand in which the word-cards are placed and walk round the classroom with it so that he can show or read off 'his sentence' to his teacher and anyone else who is willing to stop and listen.

The Word Maker is of similar design to the Sentence Maker except that it is smaller and has only two leaves. The pockets are printed with a range of written symbols and these are printed on cards which are stored like the words—consonant symbols on manilla card and vowel symbols on white, laminated card. All symbols are printed in the same colour and they are arranged as follows:

Left Hand	*Right Hand*
b b c c ch d d f f g	a a a e e e
gh h j k l l m m n n	i i y o o u
p p qu r r s s s	two blank pockets in which
sh t t th v w x y z z	to make and compare words.

The Word Maker also allows the child to try out spelling patterns without being 'committed' to the attempt in the way he would be if the word were written down. Thus an attempted spelling can be changed with no trace of the 'wrong' spelling remaining. It also enables the teacher to see the state of the child's knowledge of the orthography —the state of his model—and to see the outcome of his thinking. Because of this she is the more able to help where help is most needed.

Stages in the use of the Word Maker:

1 Refining techniques of word recognition: replacing the child's random 'looking' by systematic awareness of all the units of which a word consists.

2 Learning the meaning of letter and symbol.

3 Learning invariate consonant representations.

4 Learning alternative short and long vowel representatives for simple vowel symbols a e i y o u.

5 Learning that symbols may have more than one value. (Symbol 'o' is one that needs to be dealt with early in any teaching programme because it involves some of the first words which children need to use. In order that they do not become confused without knowing why they *are* confused it is wise to give them the information that some symbols are like this, leaving the details until later.)

6 Learning the meaning of *marker symbols*. It is likely to be of more use to children, in helping them to formulate the principles of the orthography, to give them a term like *marker* than to give them one like *magic*. Referring to the final 'e' marker in 'take', as the 'fairy e' or the 'magic e' is to take a condescending view of the nature and quality of the children's thinking.

7 Learning complex vowel symbols and beginning to collect the words that belong to each.

8   Learning the range of values of these complex vowel symbols. In words containing the vowel symbol 'ea', most words have one regular pronunciation as, for example, in *bead*. However, this symbol has other pronunciations and the words involved may be needed early in children's writing.

9   Learning about syllable structure and consonant clusters.

10   Learning spellings of words each of which may be the only example of that spelling pattern. For example: *women, people, pretty*.

Mackay, Thompson and Schaub suggest that 'teachers may find that children are helped in the task of remembering all the information they have to collect and systematise in their heads if this is also collected and systematised in a series of spelling charts. These charts may be built up as children's knowledge grows. If each large page exemplifies one piece of information and is read with a key word and its illustration to remind slower children (for example, a page to exemplify the symbol "sh" might start off with the word fi*sh* and a picture), this may become a reference point to which such children may return until they have achieved successful memorisation.

'As such knowledge accumulates in the child's mind, he builds up expectations of what written words look like. As he becomes more and more fluent as a reader and writer he will make increasing use of these expectations (and similarly formed expectations of *groups* of words and clauses) in order to predict what is going to happen.'

Project readers: These are the conditions that Mackay and Thompson set down for themselves before preparing a set of twenty-four books for Stage One of their programme:

1   That the books should be related to the *life and interests* of the five-year-old, his arrival at school and the impact of this important event on him. Home and school become two interacting circles from which the child views the world . . .

2   That the *language* of the texts should be related to the linguistic resources of the five-year-old. This meant that at this earliest stage, the written word should represent certain features of children's spoken language; it should use similar sentence structures and

cohesive elements while maintaining a sentence length that made appropriate demands on the child's reading skill.

3   That sentences should be *normal* written English sentences: that is, they should *look* natural, and sound natural when read aloud. They should be good models on which the child can build his own resources. *This does not preclude the use of an extensive range of sentence types.* It meant, for example, that our texts had to exclude the repetition of words when this was not demanded by the nature of the story or its style.

I quote here from Mackay and Thompson's paper (1968): 'Many of the small books which form part of the materials we have prepared are based on conversations with children from the reception classes of a North London school. The resulting "stories" were written down verbatim and subsequently re-written to retain the essential quality of the originals while conforming broadly to the usages of Standard English. In this way we hoped that the resulting texts would be closely related to the linguistic resources of the children, to their interests and to their notions of a "story". They are sociologically indeterminate in the sense that in them we have attempted to avoid situations or events restricted to one social class. But in another sense they are not so: to the extent that each story attempts to reveal the child's view of his world. In this sense they are, sociologically, children's books. In them we have attempted to make use of things common to all children; e.g. falling over, dressing up, losing a tooth, etc. The books, intended to be read first, overlap with the texts that we have found children produce when using the word folder. The child's reading is therefore preceded by work which has made him familiar with all the vocabulary items and sentence structures. In this way we have attempted to exclude aspects of practice (i.e. the repetition of words and sentences in a way that is not demanded by the literary form of the story) that distort the text and give it an unnatural quality. Similarly, we have not attempted to concentrate on any particular spelling pattern nor on "high frequency" items. We make no claim to have discovered the ideal vocabulary for use in early reading books; we believe it does not exist. It is not difficult to visualise another set of books with different lexical items which would be equally satisfactory. In the later books which are read by the time children are beginning to master our writing system, the subject of each story dictates its set of lexical items and the fact that these are set *in a context to which the child can refer* makes it easy to identify new words. The teacher helps this process by reading the story to the children first. She then discusses new words with them and may prepare special cards on which these are written, so that children can match cards and words in the text.'

The authors suggest that: 'We know far too little about the sort of illustration that appeals to small children. However, it is likely that primer illustrations should support the text with no extraneous detail, depicting the action clearly . . . When the child is reading on his own, clear simple pictures can offer help in providing clues to the situation and reducing the struggle with a difficult word in the text.' I have already referred (p. 102) to the high quality and attractive character of the illustrations in the 'Breakthrough' books. They are not in fact as simple as the original line drawings that were used in the pilot study booklets and some of them are full of fascinating extraneous details . . . We might in fact learn more about the kind of illustrations that appeal to children and are directly helpful to them at this learning-to-read stage if a careful record could be kept, in some of the schools using these materials, of the children's responses to and comments about the picture as well as about the text.

As well as the forty-eight initial reading booklets, the Sentence Maker and the Word Maker, there is also a set of twenty-four *Nursery Rhyme Cards* (two nursery rhymes to a card), illustrated with the same panache as the readers; the cards are accompanied by a long-playing record ('Sally go round the sun') so that it is possible for a child to listen and look at the same time. Finally there is a *Magnet Board* along with a collection of stick-on pictures 'designed to provide a source of interest and discussion and to help the children start to use simple written language . . . Various scenes both indoors and out can be set up on the board and the children can move the figurines about and describe what is happening'. The pictures include everyday objects and people, like a cooker, a bus, a baby, a 'mum', and some fascinating monsters and fairy tale characters, too.

Creativity and language: Finally, Mackay, Thompson and Schaub have this to say about their literacy programme for young children:

> Our concern has been to make it possible for children *to read and to produce meaningful language*. We have tried to avoid the charge laid at the door of earlier linguistic approaches to the teaching of reading and writing, that the written language presented to the children was far removed from their interests (and from their own linguistic

resources), and different in kind from that found *beyond* the school-room. It was not difficult to avoid using the language of the 'put the pin in the tin bin, Min' construction which was designed to direct the child's attention to the *substance* of written words. It was much more difficult to write sentences that were 'right' in all respects. We have found that children wrote sentences which seemed to us at first sight to have little to do with conventional notions of 'what children want to write about'. Thirty years ago many infant teachers were convinced that small children wanted to hear about elves, gnomes and fairies. The current emphasis on 'creativity' in the infant school is a reflection of the ascendancy of 'private' writing in some junior schools. Writing of this kind is important and, since it is highly motivated, is very useful in any literacy programme, but it must not be considered the *only* valid use for the child's newly acquired skills. The children in our experimental classes made many sentences like *my dad said to me you can go upstairs*, where there *seemed* to be little motivation for writing in terms of 'the interests of the child'. To the modern infants' school teacher, accustomed to the 'reading through experience' approach, there may seem to be an artificiality about the sentence and a confirmation of her suspicions about the lack of 'child-centredness' in this particular linguistic approach to the teaching of literacy. This fear is seen to be unfounded when the child fills in the context for us (in *talk*, notice—a medium which she can manipulate with much greater ease and speed). With this particular example the little girl told us, 'My dad said to me, "You can go upstairs", yesterday, because he didn't want me downstairs all the time. I was sitting in my nanny's sitting room watching the telly and my dad didn't want my television on. I was watching Secret Squirrel and my dad wanted to watch a film.' This would support the investigators' thesis that 'at the stage when children are not able to produce more than one sentence this one sentence is often only a part of a "story" the child has in his head and the sentence he produces is often a dramatic highlight from it'. I am sure they would agree, however, that there is a fundamental difference between the single sentence or 'caption', to use Sylvia Ashton-Warner's expression—which children produce themselves out of a much fuller context to which they can refer through talk if they wish, and which they certainly have in mind when they write the word, phrase, or sentence—and the kind of simple sentence much favoured by reading primers which has no genuine anecdotal context and therefore no 'flavour' or 'feeling' about it: 'Can you see the dog?' 'It is fun to see the dog with the ball.'

Comments on the Breakthrough to Literacy programme

1   Where most approaches to the teaching of reading concentrate on the 'substance' of the language (i.e. the medium in which it is written down) at the expense of the meaning, focusing the attention of the young child almost exclusively on decoding and encoding skills, this approach pays serious attention from the very beginning to the ways in which the child's own experience can be extended and organised by means of the written language.

2   The authors of the scheme never lose sight of the fact that their aim is to enable children to become literate—through expressing themselves in the written language as well as through reading about the thoughts, feelings and knowledge of others.

3   The child's first excursions into the written mode are closely connected with his own talk. Talk is encouraged as the context from which exploration of the written language springs. The children make up their own sentences; the reading books are about things that really happen to them seen from their point of view. They are not commanded to 'Look at Fluff!' or to 'Throw the ball!', nor are they told that 'Sam has a hat or a cat'. Much of the material is based on conversations with the children—on *their* anecdotes: 'I was running to school with my friend' . . .

4   The reading books are written in the kind of sentences that Mackay and Thompson have observed children make up initially for themselves *when they are using the written mode*. They lack the fluency of speech, although an occasional conjunction 'then' or 'when' or 'but' or 'because' across the middle of the open page perhaps, linking one sentence to the next, could easily increase the flow without flummoxing the child.

5   The suggestion that children are better equipped to learn how to read after they have experienced the pleasures and difficulties of producing something in the written language themselves is an interesting one and should be looked at further, especially where it is possible to compare the progress of such a group with one in which reading comes first and production second.

6   The observations of the mistakes that children make when first they start to compose sentences for themselves in the written

language bear out the hypothesis that difficulties of transfer from spoken to written language do not lie solely in the decoding/encoding problems which are involved. With this approach, the child's attention is focused initially on *sentence* building not *word* building and many of the difficulties are seen to be structural within this broader context—learning how to use grammatical items as well as lexical and how to find the appropriate places in each sentence for these words with a high transition probability which don't seem to convey much meaning at first but which turn out to be useful links between one lexical item and the next.

7   After introducing the child to the written language positively by encouraging him to express himself in the written mode by means of the Sentence Maker, the authors of this scheme do advocate systematic phonic instruction along with the use of the Word Maker on the grounds that the child is more likely to be able to surmount his initial difficulties with the orthography if he is given some means of expressing them. They encourage letter building play and include in an appendix to their book some extremely useful notes on English spelling so that the teacher, who may herself have a somewhat erratic notion of the systematic patterns which *do* exist in our orthography, has a reliable source to which she can refer both herself and the child.

8   The distinctions which are made by the team between the *substance* and *form* of a language—and between *letters and symbols*—should also help the teacher by giving her a firmer grasp of what she is about.

9   Similarly, the analysis of the real differences which exist, especially for an uninitiated child, between the 'meaning markers' of speech (stress, pitch, intonation, flow) and the 'meaning markers' of writing (punctuation and little else) increases our awareness of the gap between spoken and written modes of expression which must be bridged. Here again Mackay and Thompson have shown that it is not simply a matter of breaking the *code*, but of breaking the *silence*—learning how to give the marks on the page the strong or weak stress, the lift or dropping of the voice, which brings the text to life and prevents it from remaining as it does for so many children for so long, a sort of debased plainsong, intoned monotonously and drearily as though it were in truth the utterly foreign language that it is made to sound.

10 It is consistent with their stress upon the importance of using meaningful language with the child in the written as well as the spoken mode from the start that Mackay, Thompson and Schaub encourage the use of 'real' books in infant classrooms along with their own attractive booklets.

11 It is particularly interesting that these three linguists do not advocate the use of a rigidly or systematically graded vocabulary. They make it clear that teachers should be aware of the systematic patterns which exist in our everyday conventional use of the orthography but they do not suggest an overly protective simplistic approach. Like Gattegno they affirm that young children are capable of grasping quite difficult concepts if they are encouraged and provided with the means to do so.

VII Planning a reading programme

When she comes to plan out her reading programme the infant teacher should ideally be free to incorporate into her scheme as many different reading materials as she likes. Goodacre discovered in her London survey that only eighteen out of 100 schools offered the children a choice of two or more schemes—and both of them were tied to a standard series of reading primers. There appears to be an assumption among many teachers that all children are just as likely to learn by one scheme as they are by another, but on the whole research evidence does not bear this out. It is true that Brimer (1967) found no statistical differences between the various devices that he used experimentally with different groups of children, but then he was not using it over a long period in the context of the children's general level of literacy. More extensive observation of classes which have used i.t.a., WIC, CSR and Stott's Programmed Reading Kit all bear testimony to the fact that the children are more involved and consequently make better progress as the result of the change from the most traditional approach which makes no use at all of a reading *device*. It may be that no one scheme is better on every count than any other. However, it may well be true that some children find the use of colour illuminating when first they start to puzzle out the written language where other children derive confidence and pleasure from discovering their ability to manipulate an extended alphabet. It would be encouraging at any rate to see in all infant classes a wider range of reading aids than is commonly found at present—at the very least a selection of decoding games and a large stock of interesting, imaginatively illustrated books.

I should like to conclude the 'Learning to Read' part of this survey by summarising in some detail two American studies in which courses based on a standard and graded reading series were compared with other kinds of reading programmes. A range of standardised texts were used to assess the performances of the children undergoing the various kinds of programmes so that some idea could be gained as to whether the kind of teaching that the child learning to read received really did make any difference to his later achievements.

'AN INDIVIDUALISED v. A BASAL READER PROGRAM IN RURAL COMMUNITIES'

Conducted by Doris U. Spencer, Professor of Education and Director of the Reading Center, Johnson State College, Vermont, 1967.

In this study an Individual Reader programme was compared with a Basal Reader programme to answer the following questions:

1 Does the Individual Reading programme result in higher achievement than a Basal Series system when the pupils follow the individual programme through into the second year?

2 In which areas of reading do the major differences occur at the end of the first year and of the second year?

3 Does one method serve the high ability or low ability pupils better than the other?

4 Does either method favour one sex more than the other?

The Basal Reader Program followed closely the graded reading scheme and suggestions for further reading of the Scott Foresman Basal Program. Pupils were instructed in ability groups according to the Teachers' Manual.

The Individual Reader Program was designed to determine specific needs and interests and to concentrate instruction on points of weakness. The programme used reading materials gathered from all possible sources *but* it also used an intensive *phonics* programme which began with concentrated instruction on letter names and sounds.

The second year used reading materials as much as they wished, and also had a phonics programme consisting of frequent diagnostic checks of phonetic and structural analysis skills and concentrated practice at points of weakness. Teachers kept records of books read, reading levels and skills that had to be mastered.

Classes using either method spent a comparable amount of time on reading and related activities.

Results

Children in both groups were tested for reading ability at the beginning as well as at the end of the year. The results showed highly significant differences on all sub-tests (word knowledge, word discrimination and spelling, Reading Comprehension, Arithmetical Concepts) at the first grade level, favouring the Individual Reading Method. These findings were in direct agreement with the results of the 1964–65 first-year classes who had been taught by the same approach. The individual method served all ability levels equally well although girls were shown to be superior to boys. At the end of their second year, Individual Reader pupils were significantly superior to Basal Reader pupils on all 'post' measures except the Arithmetic ones. When only the pupils who had been with each scheme for the full two years were compared, the disparity was greater.

Conclusions

Among the conclusions drawn from the study by Professor Spencer, the following are relevant to our present concern with the effects of different approaches to the teaching of reading:

1 An individualised, intensive, phonics programme aids reading more effectively than the less formal, more widely spaced basal reader phonics.

2 Individual reading is more effective than the basal method since pupils may progress at their own rate.

3 Individual story reading gives children the chance to try their skill for themselves and so promotes interest in reading.

'THE EFFECTS OF PLANNED RECREATIONAL READING PROGRAMMES'

In this study, Donald W. Pfau (1967), Assistant Professor of Education, University of Maryland, found, as did Professor Spencer, that an approach to the teaching of reading which gives direct phonic instruction along with a much wider option of books for reading than any basal reading scheme provides, appeared to have very promising results. He suggests that 'although there is obviously a syndrome of agents operative in causing many capable readers to appear disinterested in reading, much of the problem can be traced to the fact that young children *encounter too many reading programs which are devoid of intrinsically rewarding reading experiences*'. He believes that 'there should be a clear cut distinction between reading done . . . to develop skills and abilities, and reading done to expand interests and improve "tastes"' and to this end he would like 'each child in the classroom to have daily informal opportunities to select and read independently from a variety of materials so that he may form the habit of reading by actively using the skills he has learned'.

Because very little research data is available to substantiate 'a consensus of opinion that recreational reading programs are especially desirable in their impact on the total reading and language development of children', Pfau designed a two-year investigation 'to measure and report the effect of a planned supplementary program of recreational reading on the amount of interest displayed in reading'.

The experiment

A group of 170 six-year-old children in their first year of compulsory schooling were randomly selected and assigned to experimental and control groups in five different socio-economic school communities. Subjects in all groups remained together through the two-year span. In the experimental group approximately thirty minutes a day was set aside for recreational reading activities in addition to the regular basal programme. Provision was made for the child to follow up his reading by engaging in various kinds of interpretative activities if he so desired. These individual and group activities were designed to provide each child with a means of extending his book through various forms of communication in order that he might gain the pleasure often needed to develop a desire for further reading.

The control group was instructed by the basal approach to teaching reading along with the usual opportunities for further reading provided by the basal programme.

Results

At the close of the second year the findings indicated that by every standard the interest in reading of the total experimental group differed significantly from that of the total control group—at the 0.001 level. The experimental group children made significantly more trips to the library and withdrew a significantly greater number of books. They tended to mention reading or a reading-involved activity a significantly greater number of times when questioned in a free response interview about what they liked doing both at home and at school, and selected a significantly greater number of reading-oriented items when subjected to the Reading Interest Inventory (developed for use in the experiment).

Teachers' opinion

Pfau notes that 'teachers expressed the opinion that the experimental programs rendered the children more fluent in all aspects of the language arts program (speaking, reading and writing) by broadening concepts and ideas which facilitated verbal 'written and creative interchange'. The study did not reveal significant differences between experimental and control groups in spelling and oral language fluency, but teachers reported that these areas of the programme appeared to proceed with greater ease and interest in the experimental group.

VIII Teachers' discussion

If it is true in this country as it appears to be in the United States that reading is not a habit which the majority of the population acquires to any great extent at school (and is not even acquired *at all* by more than 10 per cent of them), and if, as teachers of English or the 'Language Arts', we are still convinced that reading is a valuable as well as an enjoyable activity, we must be prepared to keep under constant review the possible factors *in our classrooms* which may prevent a child's acquaintance with books from ever developing into a friendship.

I have tried, in this section of the survey, to describe those methods, devices and schemes which can be used by Infant teachers in this country at the 'Learning to Read' stage, and to comment as far as I was able, on their apparent advantages and limitations. I am certain that many teachers will disagree with some of the things I have said (a characteristic of the profession is their inability to agree unanimously), but that does not matter. What does matter is that teachers should have some means made available to them for discussing as a direct result of their own practical experience what I have only been able to survey in theory. Talking continues to be important as an accompaniment to reading and this book or any section of it will only be of *real* help if it is used as a basis for discussion amongst the genuine experts, the teachers themselves. A Teachers' Centre with a warm room, easy chairs and a kettle is the necessary catalyst for any decisive changes in the way our children are to be introduced to books and to reading at school. There is certainly much to discuss and every encouragement should be given to the teachers to use their 'language arts' upon each other.

QUESTIONS FOR DISCUSSION

1   How far should diagnostic testing of specific abilities or disabilities (sight, hearing, speech, general co-ordination, etc.) be conducted, recorded and taken into account in the *reception* class of an infant school or department?

2   How far should teachers take into account or make any attempt to

change the demonstrable sex differences which at present exist between boys and girls when it comes to learning how to read? Should boys be given special encouragement or does the discrepancy in performance not matter in the long run?

3　Should infant teachers regard or disregard the measured IQ which could be and sometimes is obtained by an educational psychologist for the children in their classes? Is an intelligence quotient a help or a hindrance? How far are teachers' attitudes at present affected by such a measurement?

4　What other factors affect the teacher's attitudes to her class? Her own social background and schooling? The social background of the children? Their talk (accent; fluency, ability to communicate in her terms)? Their appearance? The teacher's temperament? The size of the class? The resources that are (or are not) available? The general atmosphere and values of the school?

5　How important is it for the teacher to be aware of a possible 'communication gap' between herself and some (or all) of her children? How can she recognise such a gap and if she does, what can she do to close it?

6　Is it going to make much difference to the learning situation if the teacher's aims are skill-centred rather than child-centred? Are the children likely to learn more, or less or just about the same?

7　Which combination of reading methods, devices and schemes would work most effectively? We still do not know, as so little experimentation has been done with a combination or choice of approaches operating inside the same classroom or school.

8　'Real' books or 'readers'—does it really matter? Will the answer depend upon whether the teacher's aims are child-centred, value-centred or skill-centred?

9　Do children need some kind of system or structure from the start, or should they be encouraged (or left) to discover any inherent system or structure for themselves?

10　Would any increase in the amount of hardware (tape recorders, record players, Language Masters, etc.) make very much difference to which children learnt to read effectively, or not?

11　Would a richer supply of software (more books, a choice of reading schemes and devices) be confusing or helpful for the teacher and her class?

12   Which schemes or devices are most likely to encourage the child to write as well as to read? Do teachers agree that early self-expression in the written language is as important as the development of an ability to read?

13   Should we have a greater sense of urgency about developing literacy skills in children who drop progressively further behind in the infant school? How often should the reading scheme or device be changed if it is apparently having little effect on a child? How detailed should the case history be on a child who appears to be having learning difficulties after one, or two, or three terms in school? Who should compile such a profile—and what kind of actions might it lead to?

14   Are we ever in danger still of working on the assumption in our classes that some children are 'bound' to do better—and some to do worse . . .?

Appendices

Appendix A

PROFESSOR DAVID RUSSELL'S READING READINESS CHECK LIST

Factors regarded as relevant to a child's state of Reading Readiness

Physical readiness

Vision: Does the child rub his eyes frequently, squint, hold materials in an unusual position or complain of frequent headaches?

Hearing: Does the child follow directions without repetition of them, respond easily to hearing games and use accurate speech sounds especially when corrected?

Health: Does the child show undue fatigue, susceptibility to illness, irritability and inability to concentrate?

Motor co-ordination: Does the child handle his clothes easily? In the use of tools in construction, in bouncing a ball and in other games do his eyes and hands work well together?

Mental readiness

Mental maturity: Does the child's mental test results show him to be sufficiently mature to be included in the group that have succeeded with a particular teacher before? Can the child give reasons for his opinions about his own work and the work of others? Is his memory span sufficient to allow memorisation of a short poem or song? Can he tell a story without confusing the order of events? Can he express a grasp of a story through dramatic play and rhythms?

Mental habits: Has the child established the habit of looking at a succession of items from left to right? Can he interpret pictures? Does he grasp the fact that symbols may be associated with pictures or objects? Does he recognise likenesses and differences in words? Can he anticipate what may happen in a story or a poem? Can he remember the central thought as well as important details?

Socio-emotional readiness

Does the child work well with the group, taking his share of responsibility?

Co-operation: Does he co-operate in playing games involving several children?

Independence: Can the child take care of his own clothes? Can he work by himself without asking for help? Can he find something else to do when he has finished one task?

Sharing: Does the child share materials without monopolising their use? Does he bring toys and books from home that other children may use? Does he wait for his turn in play and games or when the teacher is checking class work?

Listening: Is the child attentive? Does he listen to all of a story with evident enjoyment so that he can re-tell it or part of it? Does he listen to others without interrupting? Can he follow two or three simple directions?

Adjustments: Can the child see a task completed without being discouraged? Does he accept changes in school routine quietly? Can he accept a certain amount of opposition or defeat without crying and sulking? Does he appear to be happy and well adjusted in his school work? Can he meet strangers without unusual shyness?

Psychological readiness

Mental set: Does the child appear interested in books and reading? Does he inquire about words or signs? Is he curious about the shapes or unusual words?

Language: Does he speak clearly? Does he speak correctly after being helped with a difficulty by his teacher? Does he speak in sentences? Does he know the meanings of words that occur in pre-primers and primers? Does he know certain relational words such as up and down, big and little, top and bottom?

Appendix B

SOME RESERVATIONS ABOUT THE READING READINESS CONCEPT

Educational Research 1963

In this country, in a symposium on Reading Readiness published in *Educational Research*, A. E. Sanderson, R. Lynn and J. Downing[1] raised a series of objections to the concept of Reading Readiness which are briefly summarised below.

A. *Sanderson—The idea of reading readiness—a re-examination*

Sanderson's chief criticisms are levelled at the administration of R-r tests and run as follows:

1 The character of any tests or other measures used will depend on the view taken of readiness itself. (cf. Ronald Morris: 'It must never be forgotten by the user of a test that standardisation can do no more than establish a careful statistical description of the results obtained with a test constructed from items selected with certain assumptions in mind. It follows then that no test can be better than its basic assumptions.')

2 If R-r depends on mental age, an intelligence test should clearly be administered, *but* the most effective tests (e.g. The Wechsler Intelligence Scale for Children) must be given individually and by a trained examiner.

3 The suitability for use in Great Britain of many R-r tests is open to doubt (cf. Standish, 1959); since most of them are designed for America some of the items and the content are liable to be more familiar in that culture; the norms established in American school populations rarely go as low as the age level required in this country.

4 R-r tests without exception are group tests, therefore possibly unsuitable for children below seven years.

5 The correlation between scores on R-r tests and measures of subsequent success in reading (Robertson and Hall, 1942) does not seem sufficiently high to warrant exclusive reliance on test results in any individual case.

6 Sanderson cites Witty and Kepel (1939)—'the best index of readiness is the child's actual ability to read letters and words in meaningful units and sequence'—i.e. the child demonstrates his readiness to read by getting on with it!

[1] *Educational Research* vol. 6 (1963), 3–28.

7   The immediate response of most teachers in the Kent Survey was that they recognised R-r by intuition—when pressed, indications of R-r were: the child's interest in books coupled with a request for and interest in words.

8   The child's *desire* to read is the only factor which no test can measure and it has been comparatively neglected by research studies.

Sanderson concludes that a reassessment of the harmful effects of 'forced' early reading would be useful at the present stage.

B. *Lynn—R-r and the perceptual abilities of your children*

Dr Lynn first reminds the reader that according to maturation theory, a child is unable to perceive words or letters accurately before a mental age of six, seven or even eight. He quotes Vernon (1957) as saying: 'The normal child of mental age five to six can perceive simple forms without great difficulty. What is less certain is the extent to which he can remember accurately the small differences between a number of similar shapes like those of the letters of the alphabet.' Lynn suggests that when naming or pointing is used instead of drawing as an index of perceptual ability, it is evident that children can make perceptual differences at a considerably lower mental age (Hunter Diack (1960) had also recorded evidence in his book *Reading and the Psychology of Perception* of the ability of young children to perceive differences in letter shapes).

Young children who have learnt to read: Lynn cites examples of young children, some as young as 17 or 18 months, who were 'taught' successfully to read—there is plenty of evidence and more, since Lynn wrote his article, from researchers such as Doman in the United States, to demonstrate that very young children *can* learn to read. The evidence suggests that accurate perception and learning of whole words is readily accomplished at a mental age of $2\frac{1}{2}$–$3\frac{1}{2}$ years and probably earlier.

Lynn concludes his outline by reminding the reader of three popularly misunderstood theories:

1   The maturation theory of delayed perceptual powers in infants.

2   The widely held belief that early cognitive stimulation has undesirable emotional effects.

3   The belief that intelligence is largely determined by inheritance.

C. *Downing—Is a mental age of six essential for R-r?*

Downing quotes further evidence of children who have learnt to read successfully before they were six. Of particular interest perhaps are three studies in the 1960s:

1 Durkin (1961) studied 49 children who had started to learn to read between three and five. Their median Binet IQ was 121—one-third of the subjects had IQs of less than 110. The help of parents and siblings appeared to have been an important factor in their early development of reading ability.

2 Denver (1962) reported on an experiment in which parents were shown how to teach their children basic reading skills—through the use of a guidebook and TV lessons. It was found that most children with mental ages of 4½ + profited from this approach.

3 Holmes (1962) surveyed the scattered investigations in which normal children are successfully taught to read before six, and concluded that the necessary mental age for beginning to learn to read is *relative to the conditions under which the child must work at this task.*

Downing then turns his attention to the part played by problem solving in the learning-to-read process, and takes as his standpoint the two premises that 'the vital element in learning to read is its *decoding* operation' and that 'the child's task is to break the code of the printed medium of the language'. He maintains in this article that four-year-olds who would experience difficulty in tackling traditional orthography can handle words written in a simplified and regularised system such as the initial teaching alphabet.

In a more recent paper published in the Third International Reading Symposium, Downing (1968a) reconsiders the whole age controversy under the two headings: (a) Can children? and (b) Should children?

Can children? He concludes that there is now general agreement that children *can* read before they reach a mental age of six and cites the following researchers, in addition to those cited in his earlier paper, to confirm this view: Shaw (1964), Sutton (1966), Mason and Prater (1966). He continues with the following quotation, however:

All this does not mean that *all* children can begin reading at an earlier age—only some children . . . probably the majority—but there will still be a significant minority who cannot, e.g. children with a low level of intelligence, or impoverished linguistic experiences.

He suggests that the following conditions must exist if early reading is to be successfully accomplished:

1 Children's innate capacities have to be sufficient.

2 The necessary abilities must have been derived from their experiences in the pre-school environment.

3 The circumstances in which the child is learning must be favourable (cf. Gates, 1937 and Morris, 1959 and 1966).

Should children? To this second question Downing gives a qualified 'yes' and suggests the following IFs which should in his view condition teachers' support of early reading:

1 *IF individual differences in the pupils determine their early reading activities.* Forcing all children to follow *the same mass methods* is bad practice at the age of 5 or 6, but it becomes worse if one applies it to younger children. In introducing reading at earlier ages, the approach *needs to be more and more an individual one.* Each pupil should be encouraged to progress at his own pace and no pupil should be made to feel inadequate if his individual needs suggest a later start or slower progress.

Downing demonstrates 'the very real danger of introducing early reading without thought for these important individual differences' by citing a recent early reading experiment reported by Kelley (1966). In the original pilot programme no child read who didn't want to, and no child was kept out who wanted to be in the early reading group. The preliminary evaluation of the programme showed that the children who had learned to read in kindergarten were by second grade not only significantly advanced in reading skills but also in their attitude towards reading. These results encouraged the undertaking of a more rigorously controlled experiment which meant that 'some bright children in the control group who wished to read and some others in the experimental group who did not wish to read had to be frustrated'. It proved to be *virtually impossible* to teach some children in the experimental group to read and when attitudes were measured on a self-reporting inventory at the end of the kindergarten year. 'It was found that the *control* group had more favourable attitudes towards school than the *experimental* group.' Downing concludes: 'The policy for teaching early reading should be determined by the needs of young children and not vice versa.'

2 *Early reading should only be considered IF the early reading activities are enjoyable and satisfy basic needs of young children.* Imposing 'daily pen-pushing activities' on young children will only put them against reading.

3 *Early reading should only be considered IF school conditions are adequate.* If teachers are not properly trained in the teaching of reading and an understanding of the individual needs of young children, if the classroom does not have a rich variety of books, if there are too many pupils in the class, then an earlier beginning had better not be attempted.

Downing states firmly that these three conditions are *essential* conditions 'which must be satisfied before introducing reading at an earlier age than six'. If they are satisfied Downing suggests that the following considerations be borne in mind:

1 Parents could be given a briefing on the part they can play in helping their children to read earlier. He cites Brzeinski (1964 and 1965) who has described how parents have been trained to help their children to learn to read earlier in the Denver project, and also McManus who confirmed Brzeinski's findings and Durkin who 'found that help from parents and siblings was an important factor in earlier reading'. At the same time Downing points out: 'It is important to recognise the danger in involving parents in attempts at getting their children to read at an earlier age—it would be a worse then retrograde step to allow a child to become subject to pressures arising out of their parents' wishes for them to "keep up with the Joneses" in their progress in reading'.

2 'The language and the way in which that language is written influences our decision on when to begin reading.' Hildreth (1966), for instance, reports that Armenian children 'make rapid progress in learning to read, write and spell—even when they begin at the early age of five'. She attributes this to the Armenian language which 'employs a phonetically consistent alphabet which unquestionably eases the learning task'. Downing also refers to his own research with the Initial Teaching Alphabet which yielded similar results.

Appendix C

DIAGNOSTIC TESTS FOR READING READINESS

A list of tests compiled and catalogued by the National Foundation for Educational Research[1]

A. *List of reading readiness tests compiled by the NFER in 1958*

1 *American School Reading Readiness Test* (1955): For use with groups of 10–15 children in the first grade (6 year olds). No time limit. Separate norms for kindergarten and non-kindergarten children. Specimen set available.

2 *Reading Aptitude Tests. Primary Form* (1935) by M. Monroe: Groups of 10–12 children in the beginning of the first grade (6 year olds) taking 30–40 minutes, but includes individual items which take 10–15 minutes. Meant to be used as a diagnostic test as well as readiness test. Norms standardised for children $5\frac{1}{2}$–$8\frac{1}{2}$ years. Specimen set available.

3 *Lee-Clark Reading Readiness Test* (1951 revision): Groups of 10–15 children in kindergarten or first grade (5–6 year olds) taking about 15 minutes. Specimen set available.

4 *Murphy-Durrell Diagnostic Reading Readiness Test* (1949): Group test to measure auditory and visual discrimination and 'improper adjustment of instruction to learning rate' of first grade pupils (6 year olds). Test of auditory and visual discrimination takes approximately an hour, but the third test has important time specifications and involves individual testing. No indication of size of group. Specimen set available.

5 *Diagnostic Reading Tests. Survey Section: Kindergarten—Fourth Grade* (1957): Comprises two booklets (a) Reading Readiness Booklet Form B and (b) Booklet I: Grade I, Form A. Published by the Committee on Diagnostic Reading Tests, Inc. Group Tests for use with children in kindergarten and end of first grade (5–7 year olds). Research still in progress. Specimen set available.

6 *The Harrison–Stroud Reading Readiness Profiles* (1956): Groups of 12–15 children of the first grade (6 year olds) with no time limits but takes about $1\frac{1}{4}$ hours for complete test. Specimen set available.

[1] Available on application to the NFER.

7 *Metropolitan Readiness Tests—Forms R and S* (1949) (Available Test Agency): Groups, of unspecified size, of children at the end of kindergarten or beginning first grade (5–6 year olds) taking 1 hour. Specimen set available in two forms.

8 *Gates Reading Readiness Tests* (1939) (Available Test Agency): Groups of unspecified size (depends on teacher's experience) of children beginning the first grade. Some items may have to be given individually. Tests may be repeated after an interval of a month as a means of measuring progress and adjusting instruction to individual needs. Specimen set available.

B. *Reading readiness tests which are specified in the NFER
'Test Agency Catalogue'*

1 *Metropolitan Readiness Tests* formulated by Gertrude H. Hildreth, Nellie L. Griffiths, Mary E. McGanvran: Group tests that assess important aspects of readiness for formal first grade instruction: linguistic maturity, perceptual abilities, muscular co-ordination and motor skills, number and letter knowledge, ability to follow directions, attention span. Forms A and B.
Range: grades Kindergarten—1st Grade (5–6 years)
Norms: five level readiness status ratings and percentile ranks
Time: three sittings totalling approximately 60 minutes working time

2 *Marianne Frosting Developmental Test of Visual Perception* formulated by Marianne Frosting and Associates: An aid to evaluating perceptual skills of young children. Test yields scales scores in five different perceptual areas, enabling examiner to identify both strengths and handicaps. These areas are (a) eye motor co-ordination (b) figure ground (c) constancy of shape (d) position in space (e) spatial relationships. A paper and pencil test requiring no expensive equipment. May be administered to small groups as well as to individual children. Normative data based on 2116 normal children between the ages of 4 and 8 reported in quarter-year intervals. Overall results may be recorded in 'Perceptual Quotients' which readily reveal child's deviation from expected perceptual development for his age level. Test developed at the Marianne Frosting School of Education Therapy, Los Angeles, where it has been used in evaluating children referred for learning difficulties or neurological handicaps. Useful set of training materials for children who show deficiencies on test has also been developed and published.

3 *The Illinois Test of Psycholinguistic Abilities—revised edition* formulated by Samuel A. Kirk, James J. McCarthy and Winifred D. Kirk: New, standardised edition of this test is an individually administered diagnostic test designed to tap significant abilities and disabilities in psycholinguistic functions in children aged 2–10. This comprehensive instrument evaluates abilities in three dimensions.

Channels of Communication: the auditory—vocal and visual motor
Psycholinguistic Processes: the receptive process, the organising process
                              and the expressive process
Levels of Organisation: the automatic level and the representational
                              level.

Contains 12 tests measuring performance in 10 separate and distinct areas. Sub-tests yield (a) composite psycholinguistic age which correlates highly with Stanford-Binet Mental Age; (b) estimated (Binet) Mental Age and IQ; (c) Scaled Scores on each of the 12 sub-tests which are profiled to determine discrepancies in growth, so that if specific disabilities are found, an appropriate programme may be prescribed.

Substantial improvements have been made over the earlier experimental edition in terms of clarity and durability of test components. One additional ability and two supplementary tests of clinical importance have been devised and the ceiling has been raised on most of the sub-tests to provide norms to ten years of age.

New ITPA materials are packaged in compact, durable and efficient carrying case. They consist of carefully elaborated directions for test administration and scoring; two picture books of test materials, newly-designed chips, tray, and pictured sequences for Visual Sequential Memory Test; dispensable picture strips and scoring tissues for new Visual Closure Test; six objects for Verbal and Manual Expression Test; and 33⅓ rpm instruction record and 25 record forms.

Experimental edition: Original edition still available and may be applied to all children to measure abilities and disabilities in the following nine areas:

1 Auditory Vocal Automatic Test

2 Visual Decoding Test

3 Motor Encoding Test

4 Auditory Vocal Association Test

5 Visual Motor Sequencing Test

6 Vocal Encoding Test

7 Auditory Vocal Sequencing Test

8 Visual Motor Association Test

9 Auditory Decoding Test

Results of tests reveal specific language abilities and disabilities and indicate remedial work necessary to overcome child's deficiencies in language development.

Appendix D

DENIS LAWTON'S SUMMARY OF BERNSTEIN'S 'TWO CODES HYPOTHESIS'

In *Social Class, Language and Education* Lawton (1968) summarises Bernstein's published work, theoretical and experimental, from 1958 to 1965. He divides his critique into three sections: (1) the early theoretical papers; (2) the report of experimental evidence; and (3) the later theoretical work, published in 1964–5, 'developing and modifying basic theory'.

Paper 1: '*Some sociological determinants of perception: an inquiry into sub-cultural differences*' (1958)

Lawton notes that Bernstein's first study was primarily concerned with 'the gap in the existing knowledge of the relations between social class and educational attainment', the specific aim of the paper being 'to indicate a relation between the mode of cognitive expression and certain social classes'. In this paper Bernstein postulated two types of 'ordering of relationships'— that arising out of sensitivity to the content of objects and that arising out of sensitivity to their structure. The hypothesis was that these two 'dispositions to perceive' were adopted by different social groups—the working class generally being characterised by 'a mode of perceiving and feeling arising out of sensitivity to content' and the middle class acquiring rather a sensitivity to structure. Sensitivity to structure was defined as a function of learned ability to respond to an object perceived and defined in terms of a matrix of relationships, whereas sensitivity to content was defined as a function of learned ability to respond to the boundareis of an object rather than to the matrix of relationships and interrelationships in which it stands with other objects.

Middle class children were further distinguished from working class children as follows:

1 Children in the middle class and associative levels were within a formally articulated structure.

2 Present decisions affecting the growing child were governed by their efficacy in attaining distant ends.

3 Behaviour was modified by and oriented to an explicit set of goals and values.

4 There was a stable set of rewards and punishments.

5 The future was conceived of in direct relation to the educational life of the child.

6 The child grew up in an ordered rational structure.

7 Direct expressions of feeling, especially hostility, were discouraged.

8 Value was placed on verbalisation of feeling.

Bernstein suggests that the different language forms involved constitute more than dialect difference. The middle class family recognises and responds to a child as an individual and makes use of language structure to express this individuation. In addition such a child's mother will reinforce and elaborate upon his own personal statements.

These different forms of language are described as 'public' (later 'restricted code') for the content-orientated variety, and 'formal' (later 'elaborated code') for the language that pays greater attention to structure.

In his discussion of the middle class controlled environment, Bernstein states 'here the critical factor is the mode of the relationship and this is a function of his [the child's] sensitivity to structure'. A dynamic interaction is set up: the pressure to verbalise feelings in a personally qualified way, the implications of the language learnt, combine to decide the nature of the cues to which he will respond—structural ones. This for the middle class child becomes part of his socialisation process and determines the level of conceptualisation possible.

This as Lawton points out now provides the link with education: for the middle class child, the school, which links the present to a distant future, does not clash with values of the home. Moreover, the child's level of curiosity is high and his ability to switch from public to formal language (restricted code to elaborated code) gives him sensitivity to role and status and enables him to behave appropriately in a wide range of social circumstances.

The working class child on the other hand comes from a less formally organised family structure with a less clear view of the universe in terms of space and time. Authority will often appear arbitrary; long-term goals are less likely than the desire for immediate gratification because the general notion of the future is vague and dominated by chance rather than planning.

This difference between structure and content was seen by Bernstein as 'degrees within a conceptual hierarchy'. Sensitivity to content implies that 'only the simplest logical implications or boundaries of the structure will be cognized. More definitely, certain aspects of our objects will not register as meaningful cues; or if they do, the verbal response will be inadequately determined.'

The working class environment is thus in conflict with formal education in the following ways:

1 There is a clash between the child's accustomed immediate responses and the 'mediate' responses required by the school.

2   There will be an inability to communicate with the teacher on the teacher's own level.

3   An inability to use language appropriate to the situation of inequality of status between pupil and teacher.

4   The working class child will resist extensions to his vocabulary and resist efforts to 'improve' his control over language.

5   He will experience difficulty in dealing with more abstract concepts in mathematics and other subjects.

6   This low level of curiosity and his tendency to detailed description rather than abstract analysis will be interpreted as poor application to work.

7   He will have little opportunity to enhance his self respect.

Paper 2: '*Public language: some sociological implications of a linguistic form*' (1959)

This paper sets out in greater detail the differences between public and formal language. The characteristics of public language were listed under ten headings:

1   Short, grammatically simple, often unfinished sentences, a poor syntactical construction with a verbal form stressing the active mood.

2   Simple and repetitive use of conjunctions (so, then, and, because).

3   Frequent use of short commands and questions.

4   Rigid and limited use of adjectives and adverbs.

5   Infrequent use of impersonal pronouns as subjects (one, it).

6   Statements formulated as implicit questions which get up a sympathetic circularity, e.g. 'Just fancy?' 'It's only natural, isn't it?' 'I wouldn't have believed it.'

7   A statement of fact is often used as both a reason and a conclusion, or more accurately, the reason and conclusion are confounded to produce a categoric statement, e.g. 'Do as I tell you', 'Hold on tight', 'You're not going out', 'Lay off that'.

8   Individual selection from a group of idiomatic phrases will frequently be found.

9   Symbolism is of a low order of generality.

10 The individual qualification is implicit in the sentence structure, therefore it is a language of implicit meaning. It is believed that this fact determines the form of the language.

Contrasted with the public language the characteristics of the formal language were:

1 Accurate grammatical order and syntax regulate what is said.

2 Logical modifications and stress are mediated through a grammatically complex sentence construction, especially through the use of a range of conjunctions and relative clauses.

3 Frequent use of prepositions which indicate logical relationships as well as prepositions which indicate temporal and spatial contiguity.

4 Frequent use of impersonal pronouns, 'it', 'one'.

5 A discriminative selection from a range of adjectives and adverbs.

6 Individual qualification is verbally mediated through the structure and relationships within and between sentences. That is, it is explicit.

7 Expressive symbolism conditioned by this linguistic form distributes affectual support rather than logical meaning to what is said.

8 A language use which points to the possibilities inherent in a complex hierarchy for the organising of experience.

In this paper Bernstein makes the point that 'language is considered one of the most important means of initiating, synthesising and reinforcing ways of thinking, feeling and behaviour which are functionally related to the social group. It does not of itself prevent the expression of specific ideas or confine the individual to a given level of conceptualisation, but certain ideas and generalisations are facilitated rather than others, that is, the language use facilitates development in a particular direction rather than inhibiting all other possible directions.'

In addition, Lawton comments that in this paper Bernstein makes the very important point that what distinguishes a middle class child from a working class child will not merely be size of vocabulary but sensitivity to a way of organising and responding to experience. It is worth stressing this point since so many studies have assumed that the provision of the right vocabulary would solve the linguistic problem.

In concluding this paper Bernstein suggested that the implications of a public language were (a) logical, (b) social, and (c) psychological. The psychological implications included not only the orienting and cognitive aspects already mentioned, but also the fact that many lower working class patients would be unable to benefit from psychotherapy because of the form of the social relation to the mode of its communication.

Paper 3: *Social structure, language and learning* (1961)

In this paper, intended to be read by teachers, Bernstein suggested that the problem for the lower working class pupil (using public language) becomes acute at the secondary level of education when the gap between what he *can* do and what he is *called upon* to do widens. The reason for this is that during the secondary stage the educational curriculum becomes more and more analytical and relies on what Piaget classified as formal operations, whereas the lower working class pupils are more likely to be restricted to concrete operations

Paper 4: *Social class and linguistic development: a theory of special learning* (*1961*)
In this paper Bernstein's theory is introduced by means of a survey of previous studies of language, environment and intelligence. Lawton comments on the usefulness of this setting, since it enables the reader to place Bernstein's work in some kind of historical context. It is in this paper that Bernstein uses the phrase 'linguistic determinism': 'It is proposed that two distinct forms of language use arise because the organisation of these two strata is such that different emphasis is placed on language potential. Once the emphasis or stress is placed, then the resulting forms of speech progressively orient the speakers to distinct types of relationships of objects and persons. The role intelligence plays is to enable the speaker to exploit more success-fully the possibilities symbolised by the socially conditioned linguistic forms.' There are exceptions to this 'linguistic determinism' which arise under special limiting physiological and psychological conditions. It is suggested that the typical and dominant mode of speech of the middle class is one where speech becomes an object of special perceptual activity and one where a theoretical attitude is developed towards the structural possibilities of sentence organisation. This speech mode is one where the structure and syntax are relatively difficult to predict for any one individual and where the formal possibilities of sentence organisation are used to clarify meaning and make it explicit. This mode of speech will be called a formal language.

If we now move on from the early theoretical papers to the later ones, Lawton notes that 'A socio-linguistic approach to social learning' (1965) 'presents no new evidence, but relates Bernstein's thesis to a wider framework —a socio-linguistic framework, which is explained historically as well as conceptually.'

Looking back over these published papers as a group, Lawton suggests that the 1962 experimental papers, which provide the objectively measure-able link between code and verbal planning, would seem to imply that at the linguistic level it ought to be possible to establish basic linguistic units which distinguish elaborated and restricted codes. In a restricted code the basic unit will tend to be a longer 'string' than in elaborated code: it will be a well-organised combination. In elaborated code on the other hand the basic unit will be shorter—i.e. in an utterance of a given length more choice points will occur. Moreover, in the elaborated code at every choice point in the syntactic system there is a greater element of discretion for the syntactic combinations created at such choice points. However, Lawton continues—in order to determine the location of such choice points it will be necessary not only for more texts to be examined but more texts *from a variety of contexts.*

Lawton concludes his critique by pointing out that 'A number of questions remain. First the empirical question—is it the case that restriction at the linguistic level is followed by restriction in the other three behavioural dimensions? Second, is it the case that an individual limited to a restricted code is different from an individual possessing elaborated code patterns because he possesses a much more limited knowledge of the linguistic rule system?' Bernstein's choice of words in the 1961 Paper: 'A theoretical attitude is developed towards the structural possibilities of sentence organisation' would seem to indicate his opinion that the working class have a nascent awareness of the rule system but that their social structure and culture does not lead them to explore it and develop it, nor to innovate within it to the same extent as elaborated code users.

Lawton notes finally that Bernstein's 'speech codes' hypothesis becomes increasingly complex; he represents the form into which it has evolved in the 1965 paper as follows.

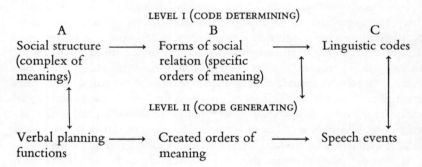

LEVEL I (CODE DETERMINING)

A   B   C

Social structure ⟶ Forms of social ⟶ Linguistic codes
(complex of   relation (specific
meanings)   orders of meaning)

LEVEL II (CODE GENERATING)

Verbal planning ⟶ Created orders of ⟶ Speech events
functions   meaning

'The arrows indicate reciprocal influence as it is possible for a verbal planning function to develop which creates novel orders of meaning and social relation.' Bernstein is essentially concerned with socialisation and the transmission of culture; therefore codes are seen as transformations of the critical roles in the socialisation process. On this basis the four critical roles are: (1) the kinship role, (2) age group roles, (3) educational roles, (4) work roles. It would therefore be theoretically possible to find linguistic evidence for four basic codes relating to the four critical roles; empirical work in this field has yet to be attempted.

Appendix E

STANDARDS AND PROGRESS IN READING[1]

by J. M. MORRIS

Summary and Conclusions

The complexity of the studies described in this volume and the later one has inevitably meant that information on many important topics is scattered over both reports. Here an attempt is made to bring together the main findings from each under broad headings corresponding to the principal areas of study covered by the programme as a whole, and arranged in a sequence which pays due regard to the type of data from which they were derived.[2]

Reading standards and progress according to test criteria

Comparisons of Kent with national norms: In 1954 and 1957, the standards of reading attainment reached by Kent children in the last year of their primary course were compared with those of children of the same age in the country as a whole. Before final results could be obtained, it was necessary to make adjustments to test scores which involved certain plausible assumptions. When they had been made it was concluded that in 1954 and 1957:

1 The reading attainment of Kent children in the final year of their primary course was above the average for the country as a whole.

2 Kent was above the national average with regard to the percentage of children classified as having 'superior' reading ability.

3 The percentage of Kent children defined as 'semi-literate' and 'illiterate' compared not unfavourably with national figures for this category.[3]

In line with a definite trend towards higher national standards in reading reported by the Ministry of Education (1957), it was also found that over the period 1954 to 1957 the average reading ability of fourth-year juniors in Kent significantly improved and the percentage of 'superior' readers amongst them increased markedly. Moreover, though not statistically significant, the

[1] Cross references in this Appendix are to *Standards and Progress in Reading*.
[2] For example, in cases where answers to a particular question have been sought in several ways, findings based on 'objective' assessments generally precede those on 'subjective' estimates, and those obtained from extensive studies of representative samples of schools and children come before those from intensive studies of selected schools and children.
[3] Tests of statistical significance could scarcely be applied here in view of the assumptions adopted and the fact that such small numbers of children fell into this class.

proportion of 'semi-literate' and 'illiterate' children at this stage decreased from 1.2 to 0.7 per cent.

There was no statistical evidence that the rate of improvement in Kent primary schools was better than the national average during these four years. But it was certainly as good, since the mean progress score for Kent on test SR 2 was actually greater, by one clear point, than that estimated for the country as a whole.

These findings indicate that *the county in which our studies of primary reading were conducted between 1954 and 1957 was one where, on the whole, good reading standards were not only achieved but maintained.* This relative superiority is of particular importance for the interpretation of many of the other results.

Comparisons within Kent: From January 1955 to July 1957, much of the research programme was carried out in ten schools selected for intensive study because the results of their junior pupils (born 1943–46) on Sentence Reading Test 1 (SR 1) in March 1954 deviated significantly from those of juniors in a random sample of Kent primary schools after the age, sex and non-verbal ability of the children concerned had been taken into account.

Observations in these schools suggested that, after the attributes of their child population and material circumstances had been considered, each school's success or failure in promoting good reading standards and/or progress depended mainly on the quality of its head and staff in that order. Some variables, particularly those concerning school conditions such as the contributions of teachers, were not assessed precisely enough to allow for statistical verification. Moreover, no distinction had been made between the reading standards of children at different stages of the junior course. Accordingly, an attempt was made to remedy these deficiencies and supply answers to other important questions by more detailed studies of 714 children in the 1946 age group who attended the selected schools during the last eight terms of their primary course.

Because their schools had been 'selected', there was a danger that only limited inferences could be drawn from some of the analyses of data for these children considered collectively, that is, ignoring school differences. To enable a wider interpretation to be placed upon them, therefore, their reading test results as second-, third- and fourth-year juniors were initially compared with those of children in the same age group who were attending the total sample of Kent schools and had been given the same annual tests.

On all the reading tests administered, the average scores of pupils in the selected schools were actually higher than those of the total sample, but, only on test SR 1 at the second-year junior stage was the difference in their favour statistically significant ($P < 0.05$). Moreover, there were no significant differences between the two samples with regard to the distributions of children classified according to this test as 'poor' and 'good' readers each year, or in the proportions of them falling into the Ministry's five categories of reading ability in the penultimate term of the primary course.

Thus, the reading standards of the 714 children as second-, third- and fourth-year juniors so closely correspond to those of the total Kent sample that they may be regarded as representative of junior standards in the country as a whole. It is reasonable to suppose, therefore, that some of the findings derived from detailed studies involving them are of general validity at least in Kent. They probably have even wider implications since the standards of these children towards the end of their primary schooling compared favourably with national norms.

Subsequent progress of children classed as poor readers at the age of eight: Various samples, groups and individual children were chosen for special study from the total 1946 age group in the ten schools selected in order to consider further aspects of reading ability and additional factors which might be related to it.

Special attention was given to the subsequent progress of 101 children who were either non-readers, or, in relation to the total Kent sample, extremely poor readers after five terms in junior classes. From this study, the following findings emerged:

1   On average, the reading attainment of the children significantly improved but only 13 achieved a standard equivalent to chronological age in the fourth year of their junior and secondary school course respectively.[1] Moreover, 65 per cent and 54 per cent at each successive stage of schooling could still be classed as 'backward' readers, 'semi-literate' or 'illiterate'.

2   The reading standards of the children relative to each other remained virtually the same as they had been when originally selected. In particular, those who had not made any real start with reading at the age of eight continued to have the severest difficulties, and, in the opinion of secondary school heads, their reading disability was such that it would probably be a major handicap in adult life.

These children represented a percentage of the total 1946 age group in the selected schools (14.1) which did not differ significantly from the percentage of the total Kent sample (15.5) classed as poor readers at the age of eight. It seems plausible therefore to regard the findings concerning their progress to the age of eleven as indicating what was generally happening in Kent and almost certainly elsewhere in this country. We can, however, only generalise in this manner about subsequent progress to the age of fifteen if we may assume that as much progress was made by these children during their secondary course in the 29 schools they attended as would have been made

[1] At the secondary stage of schooling, the sample was reduced to 98 for reasons stated on page 268, three children were in ESN schools and two in approved schools.

had they been scattered among schools selected to be representative of secondary schools in Kent. Such an assumption seems reasonable, though less sure than the first.

To avoid misinterpretation of our conclusions, one further point should be emphasised. Only one girl attended a remedial clinic during her secondary course—all the other children studied had their difficulties treated solely by teachers within the confines of their own schools. In other words, they were not given 'special' treatment in the strict sense of the term.

With the provisos outlined above we can conclude that, *at best, the chances of second year juniors with a reading problem eventually achieving average or normal competence is about one in eight, and at least half of them will remain very poor readers to the end of their school days.*[1]

Reading standards and progress according to a book criterion: A year before the research programme in Kent was initiated, an official report was reprinted (Board of Education, 1952) which suggested that the task for junior teachers is mainly one of developing reading comprehension, as only a few 'backward' children need systematic instruction in reading mechanics after the age of seven. Considering the wide range of initial abilities among infants and the shortness of the infant school course, this seemed somewhat optimistic. Accordingly, to test the validity of an assumption with important implications, especially in the training of prospective teachers, the level of attainment reached by 3022 children in the 1946 age group at the beginning of their junior course was ascertained.

Standards were assessed according to a criterion which transition teachers normally use, namely, the primer or book which pupils can read on entering their classes. This method naturally involves an element of subjectivity and is therefore not entirely reliable. However, the size and composition of the sample provided a reasonable check on any over- or under-estimates which may have been made.

This survey showed that, although estimated standards at seven vary from school to school and area to area, about 19 per cent of the children were still at the first primer stage or below it and therefore could be classed as non-readers, whilst a further 26 per cent, reading primers two and three, had some but not sufficient mastery of reading mechanics to enable them to make progress on their own.

Subsequent detailed studies of 714 children in the 1946 age group attending the selected schools indicated that approximately 16 per cent of these children were still struggling with infant primers after two years in junior classes and about a quarter of them were tackling books originally designed for first-year juniors. A year later, the percentage at the primer

---

[1] Since 'half' is equivalent to at least 7 per cent of the total Kent sample, this is probably the minimum percentage of children who left school in 1961 still experiencing considerable difficulty with reading.

stage had been reduced to 3, but, about 15 and 23 per cent were engaged on books normally considered suitable for first and second year juniors respectively. By the end of the primary course, out of every five children in this sample *three* had achieved a standard which was either commensurate with or above their chronological age, *one* could be classified as retarded by a year, and *one* by at least two years.

In the follow-up study of 98 poor readers, it was found that in the upper forms of secondary modern schools more than a quarter of the children were working from books specially designed for backward readers and approximately one in ten of them from books normally used by juniors. Moreover, the oral reading performance of about half of them was reported to be a mere 'barking at print'—about 17 per cent could not understand what they had read, and 9 per cent found difficulty in recognising words out of context.

The following conclusions were drawn about the task confronting teachers:

1 Except for 'A' classes in streamed schools, *few teachers of first-year junior pupils can concentrate mainly on the development of reading comprehension. The majority will be called upon either to teach reading from the beginning or to consolidate foundation skills imperfectly acquired.*

2 Although *teachers of second-, third- and fourth-year juniors* are decreasingly less likely to have to teach absolute beginners, they also *need to be equipped with the techniques of teaching the basic skills of reading.*

3 *Teachers responsible for the lower forms and lower streams in secondary modern schools require a knowledge of remedial reading methods.*

Reading attainment and related skills

In seeking reasons for the different levels of reading attainment among children beyond the infant stage, the possibility was explored that these levels were due fundamentally to differences in the extent to which the basic mechanical skills had been acquired. Two groups of children were studied in this connection—101 'poor' readers and 98 'good' readers. These children were not individually tested until their third junior year, by which time the attainment of a small proportion was such that their original classification as 'poor' and 'good' readers was no longer justified in relation to the total Kent sample. Consequently, because the groups did not represent so clearly the extremes of reading comprehension ability as hitherto, it was anticipated that differences for the other aspects of reading skill under investigation would be less than expected.

For pupils in their third junior year, the results were as follows:

1 *Recognition of isolated words*: There was a highly significant difference in favour of the 'good' readers who had an average reading age (13.7) six

years in advance of the 'poor' readers. Among the latter, those with the poorest powers of word recognition usually had the lowest scores for reading comprehension and vice versa. The relationship was not so close for the 'good' readers.[1] 'Good' readers broke down unknown words from test R 1 into syllables, sounded each part in sequence and then synthesised the sounds to form a word which sounded 'right' from their previous experience. In contrast, the majority of 'poor' readers either did not attempt words or made wild guesses.

2　*Knowledge of alphabet names*: Almost a quarter of the 'poor' readers could not name all letters of the alphabet. Fewer errors were made in naming capital letters than lower-case letters.

3　*Knowledge of alphabet sounds*: Most of the 'poor' readers had an imperfect knowledge of alphabet sounds, and, for nearly half of them, this could be regarded as one of the main causes of their unsatisfactory progress. Many did not clearly understand the difference between letter names and letter sounds. Both 'poor' and 'good' readers made markedly fewer mistakes in sounding letters presented as capitals.

4　*Analysis and synthesis of words containing common phonic units*: Only 'poor' readers were given test R 5. Results showed that these children either had a limited ability or, in a few cases, no ability at all to analyse and synthesise words containing common phonic units. There was a relatively high correlation (0.81) between their scores on this test and test R 1 (Word Recognition).

5　*Directional attack on words*: About 38 per cent of the 'poor' readers had such a scanty knowledge of words and their constituent parts that they did not attempt or merely guessed the items in test R 6. Although faulty habits of directional attack were detected in all but eight of the remaining children, in only three of them were they sufficiently pronounced to be considered a major cause of their retarded reading development.

6　*Visual word discrimination*: Test R 7 was completed by 99 'poor' readers. A total of over 11000 errors was recorded of which 42 per cent were due to the transposition of letters, 30 per cent to letter substitutions and 14 per cent to omissions and additions of letters respectively.[2]

7　*Methods of memorising words*: The percentage of 'good' readers using an eclectic method was more than three times greater than that of the 'poor' readers, and the percentage relying on total word shapes less than half.

[1] This could be explained by the fact that, relative to each other, the 'good' readers were less likely to gain the same scores on test SR1 and test R1 since much depended on whether they had been introduced to the particular difficult words comprising the final items of the tests.
[2] These findings suggest that poor readers are more aware of differences in the length of words than differences in their letter content and order. Thus, they would be greatly encouraged if systematic training in word analysis was not confined to illustrative words containing the same number of letters.

Twelve months later the testing programme was repeated. In general, a marked improvement had occurred in the basic reading skills of the 'poor' readers during their fourth junior year. Pupils with the lowest reading standards according to test criteria and in functional terms still had the least mastery of reading mechanics. However, even the twelve worst readers had made considerable progress as illustrated by the fact that, with one exception, they were pupils in the school where the amount of improvement in phonic knowledge amongst the 'poor' readers reached the highest level of statistical significance. Admittedly, the previous reading skills of these children had been so inadequate that the efforts at word-building initiated by their teachers, in common with most of those responsible for the poorest readers attending the other selected schools, were likely to effect a more startling improvement. Nevertheless, it is unlikely that this could have been achieved within a year and without the benefit of clinical diagnosis and treatment had the greater initial retardation of their pupils been due to organic brain defects. It was concluded, therefore, that the poorest readers were not in any reasonable interpretation of the term a neurological problem, and that the study as a whole lends little support to the idea that 'specific developmental dyslexia' is an identifiable syndrone distinct from 'reading backwardness'. In other words, *if 'wordblindness' exists as a condition which cannot be treated by good teaching within the state educational system it must be a rare condition indeed.*

Reading achievement in relation to children's individual attributes

The duties imposed on local authorities by the 1944 Act include the provision of special educational environments for children severely disabled in mind or body, and special treatment for those retained in ordinary schools because their handicaps are relatively less severe. Retarded readers usually fall into the last category if their intelligence quotients are not less than 70. Hence, there should be no pupils, or at most only a tiny minority, following the normal course in state schools who cannot eventually learn to read effectively.

That this was not the case five years ago even for children in the care of an education authority whose primary schools achieved and maintained reading standards above the national average is suggested by the evidence summarised above. What then could be the reasons for this situation?[1] Are a considerable number of 'educationally subnormal children' retained in ordinary schools through a lack of special provision? Has the proportion of children requiring special treatment in clinics and remedial classes been underestimated and, if not, are some not receiving it owing to a shortage of educational psychologists, teachers and accommodation? Are the individual attributes and home circumstances of some 'technically educable' pupils so adverse that it is virtually impossible for them to learn to read effectively in ordinary classes? Finally, are the conditions under which they are taught in schools partly responsible for their lack of achievement?

[1] The situation before the Kent inquiries began is discussed in the Introduction.

In seeking answers to these and related questions, we carried out a series of studies in which the reading standards and progress of a decreasing number of Kent children were examined in increasing detail in relation to an increasing number of factors classed broadly as centred in the child, in the home and in the school. Our choice of variables within each category was guided by the opinions voiced by heads of the 60 primary schools involved in the survey as to the main causes of reading retardation, by the findings of previous investigators, and by the suggestions of local inspectors and other experienced educators.

MENTAL ATTRIBUTES

Educational subnormality: A few 'educationally subnormal' children followed the normal school course for a time but they amounted to less than 1 per cent of the total sample. Consequently, though their presence in ordinary classes did not make the task of teachers any easier, the inclusion of data for them made no significant difference to the size of the problem in Kent already stated.

Reading and non-verbal ability: In our studies, 'intelligence' was defined solely in terms of children's scores on non-verbal tests since they indicate a capacity for 'intelligent' behaviour in a novel situation which is not dependent on the ability to read. They are also used in the preliminary selection of children for remedial treatment in some areas and as a guide to methods of dealing with backward readers in some schools, and we wished to find out if the assumptions underlying these practices were valid.

The main results obtained from statistical analyses of data on (a) representative samples of children; (b) selected samples of 'poor' and 'good' readers; and (c) sub-groups of a selected sample of 'poor' readers were as follows:

1　Junior reading standards were associated with non-verbal ability, the closest association being at the age of nine ($r = 0.57$).

2　Reading progress between the ages of eight and eleven was not related to non-verbal ability at the age of eight.

3　Progress in reading between the ages of eight and ten was not associated with improvement in non-verbal ability over the same period.[1]

4　Reading tests forecast later attainment better than tests of non-verbal ability, and the best single predictor of the reading ability of children aged eleven was the same reading test given in the preceding year ($r = 0.82$).

5　On average, the non-verbal ability of second-year juniors classed as 'good' readers was consistently better than that of 'poor' readers during

[1] It was only possible to examine this relationship over a twelve-month period as a different non-verbal test was administered in the final year of the primary course.

the last three years of the primary course (P<0.01). But, considerable overlapping in the distribution of test scores each year indicated that *the reading difficulties of some children and the superior standards of others could not be attributed to their capacity for 'intelligent' behaviour as measured by non-verbal tests.*

6   Differences between the reading standards of groups of fourth-year juniors classed as 'poor' readers at the age of eight could be explained largely in terms of their current mastery of the basic reading skills, but only to a limited extent, if at all, in terms of their non-verbal ability.

7   Among children classed as 'poor' readers at the age of eight, those, who as potential school leavers six years later achieved 'just below average' to 'superior' reading standards, began their secondary school course with a greater mastery of reading mechanics, and on average better non-verbal ability than those who were still 'backward' readers or 'semi-literate' at the age of 14.[1]

Considered together, these findings support the conclusion that *it is a doubtful procedure to base the preliminary selection of children for special treatment and the methods of dealing with backward readers in schools, on the results of non-verbal ability tests alone.* This does not mean that a child's non-verbal score has no diagnostic value, for the Foundation's studies, and almost without exception those of previous investigators, show a positive correlation between reading and non-verbal ability. But it should be equated with reading potentiality. In other words, all children still experiencing reading difficulties at the age of eight, irrespective of their non-verbal IQs, should be regarded as likely to benefit from remedial tuition whether it be given by good class teachers or by reading specialists in schools or clinics.[2]

Reading as a specific ability: Analyses were carried out of the scores gained on tests of mechanical arithmetic by 'poor' and 'good' readers attending the selected schools in their second and fourth junior years, and, in the latter, on a test containing problem items also. The main object was to find out whether, and to what extent, they had correspondingly low and high standards in this basic subject. In the event of a close correspondence not

---

[1] The finding with regard to non-verbal ability differs from that in (c) partly because the latter was based on analyses of data for five sub-groups within the sample of children initially classed as 'poor' readers. Moreover, there was a certain amount of overlapping in the distribution of non-verbal scores for the two groups in (c) 2.

[2] Of course, 'all' does not necessarily include severely 'educationally sub-normal' children who may be retained in ordinary schools because parents refuse to allow their transfer to special schools, or whose sub-normality is not verified at an early age. However, such children probably constitute only a minute proportion of the 'normal' school population, as illustrated by the fact that there were only four of them in our selected sample of 'poor' readers representing about 0.5 per cent of their age group. Moreover, remedial tuition would certainly be of value to such children though it is doubtful whether it alone would meet all their needs.

being established, there would be support for the conclusions of previous research that specific abilities are involved in reading and arithmetic, though it was realised that discrepancies might be due, among other things, to differences in the skill with which either subject had been taught and the emphasis placed on each by the opportunities afforded for practice.

It was found that, on average, the 'good' readers had much greater facility in mechanical arithmetic than 'poor' readers at the age of eight or ten. Not surprisingly, in view of the reading ability involved, they were also much better, on the whole, at problem arithmetic in their final junior year. However, the score distributions of both groups and the low correlations between reading and arithmetic test results showed that the 'poor' readers did not necessarily find *mechanical* arithmetic particularly difficult, nor was the converse true of 'good' readers. This is demonstrated by the fact that, had the criteria for the selection of children for special study been inferior and superior arithmetic ability, less than half the 'poor' readers would have again been chosen and about 60 per cent of the 'good' readers.

Thus, considered in conjunction with the observations of class teachers responsible for the selected children, and the findings regarding relationships between reading and non-verbal ability, these results indicate that the possibility of reading (and arithmetic) being a specific ability or disability in some cases cannot be ruled out.[1] But even if cases of non-agreement were found to be adequately explained in terms of differences in individual attitudes to reading and arithmetic and/or in conditions of acquiring each skill, the fact that this study has shown they exist is of educational significance. It is frequently assumed, for example, by the majority of heads in the Kent survey, that reading retardation is due to lack of intelligence and is therefore synonymous with general backwardness. Consequently, there is a danger that poor readers allocated to backward classes will have their potential for success in mechanical arithmetic overlooked. Moreover, those who maintain a low level of arithmetic attainment in accordance with expectation may do so not necessarily because the common factor in both subjects is general intelligence, but because, as some of the findings summarised under school conditions show, 'poor' readers tend to be less fortunate than other pupils, especially 'good' readers, in certain aspects of their primary schooling.

PHYSICAL ATTRIBUTES

As all data obtained in the Kent inquiries were examined for possible sex differences, the findings summarised immediately below are based on representative as well as selected samples of children. In context, those given

[1] Here, specific ability/disability means low/high achievement in reading not accompanied by low/high attainment in mechanical arithmetic. The earlier finding that none of the 'poor' readers suffered from 'specific developmental dyslexia' is not contradicted, therefore, because it was based on a strict definition of this concept: 'reading disability due to organic brain defects'. Children with this disability could not be expected to respond to tuition given by class teachers over a short period as actually happened.

under the subsequent sub-heading regarding relationships between other 'physical' attributes and reading ability derive only from comparative studies of 'poor' and 'good' readers attending the selected schools.

Sex differences in reading ability: With one exception[1] which suggested that any sex differences observed in reading surveys should be interpreted cautiously, the results were as follows:

1 On average, the reading attainment of girls was better than that of boys at the age of eight, but the difference in their favour decreased with age and was not statistically significant at the upper junior stage.

2 In each of the last three years of the primary course, the percentage of boys and girls who were 'good' readers was not significantly different.

3 The percentage of girls with 'poor' reading ability was consistently lower than that of boys during the last three years of the primary course, but the difference decreased over this period ($P = 0.001$ at $8+$, 0.01 at $9+$ and 0.05 at $10+$).

There was no evidence that the apparently slower development of reading ability among boys in general could be attributed to sex differences in 'intelligence' as measured by non-verbal tests for these were negligible in all comparisons made. But there was some indication that it might be due, in part at least, to sex differences in adjustment to the school situation, as boys, on the whole, were found to be markedly less well adjusted in this respect than girls between the ages of eight and ten. Interviews with the selected 'poor' readers also suggested that differential behaviour traits may partly explain sex discrepancies in reading growth in so far as reading requires careful attention to detail and the boys tended to be far more impetuous and careless when tackling test items than girls. In fact, it was this dissimilarity of approach which accounts for the markedly inferior average score for visual word discrimination gained by the boys. Reasons for differences in the reading development of boys and girls may lie, too, in other factors distinguishing them of a maturational, motivational and environmental nature.

Physical characteristics of poor and good readers compared: No statistically significant differences were found between the selected samples of 'poor' and 'good' readers with regard to general physical condition, physical build, handedness, month of birth, and the incidence of visual defects, other physical handicaps (hernias, abnormal heart conditions, orthopaedic defects),

[1] A result in favour of the boys aged ten plus in the 1954 survey contradicted all others obtained in the research programme, although it agreed with the Ministry of Education's findings for fourth-year juniors using the same test (SR 2). This confirmed a suggestion made by the Ministry that the content of the particular reading tests administered in surveys may determine any sex differences in reading ability disclosed.

nervous conditions, respiratory diseases and diseases of the skin, lymphatic glands or abdomen.

Hearing defects appeared to be more common among the 'good' readers. But no educational significance can be attached to this because a sizable proportion of them, and relatively few of the 'poor' readers, attended a school where an audiometric examination conducted in addition to the usual whisper test ensured that all hearing losses would be detected.

In contrast, comparisons of the two samples for the only other characteristic which was considered, loosely termed 'physical', left no doubt that *speech defects and unsatisfactory language development are associated with inferior reading ability*. It is also interesting to note that, according to the medical records of the poor readers with defective speech, symptoms were usually manifested before the age of seven and arose either from early childhood diseases or from emotional problems connected with unfavourable home circumstances. Therefore, if the treatment of speech difficulties can begin sufficiently early in children's lives it may remove, or at least mitigate, a potential hindrance to reading progress.

EMOTIONAL ATTRIBUTES

Of those individual attributes of children broadly classed as 'emotional' which were studied in relation to differential achievement, three were motivational in character in that they concerned the attitudes of 'poor' and 'good' readers to reading itself, the place occupied by reading in their lesson preferences and in their aspirations towards attaining higher standards in school subjects generally. The rest were the social and emotional characteristics of children reflected by their behaviour in school, which, from previous research and on commonsense grounds, might be expected to be associated with scholastic progress generally, and especially with reading, because of its fundamental role.

Some information on the selected children's 'emotional' attributes during their early school years was obtained and has been incorporated in the case studies described in Chapter XV. The main data, most of which were subjected to statistical analysis, referred to their characteristics after the age of eight, that is, subsequent to their being chosen for special study. This means that the results produced are difficult to interpret in terms of cause and effect because any significant differences between the 'poor' and 'good' readers disclosed were at least as likely to be the consequences of failure or success as to be the original reasons for it. Moreover, any changes in the attributes of the 'poor' readers from year to year may be attributed not only to the significant improvement in their reading skills already discussed, and vice versa, but also to the natural course of maturation. In view of these difficulties of interpretation, which, incidentally, have been experienced by many other investigators seeking to establish the causes and effects of reading retardation, the main value of the following findings probably lies in their confirmation of some concomitant factors in differential reading achievement, particularly in persistent failure, and of some of the unfavourable attributes of backward readers which need to be overcome if they are to make progress.

Motivational factors in differential reading achievement: Not unexpectedly, a close association was found between attitudes to reading and levels of ability. The majority of 'good' readers were self-confessed 'bookworms', and the rest were 'moderately' enthusiastic about reading only because it took second place among their many other interests. Just over a third of the 'poor' readers also expressed enthusiasm for reading, but this was largely confined to school time, whereas it pervaded the leisure hours of the 'good' readers. The findings of greatest importance were that *approximately 16 per cent of the 'poor' readers hated reading in their third junior year, and 9 per cent had abandoned all interest in books by the end of the primary course and were already planning future occupations for which they believed reading skill to be unnecessary.* Even among the rest of this group the liking for reading was so lukewarm as to make it likely that they would adopt the same attitude unless greatly encouraged by their teachers in secondary modern schools.

A tendency for children of inferior and superior reading ability to prefer the same lessons was revealed, the most popular being arithmetic and reading in that order. But the reasons for their preferences were usually different because lessons varied in content and scope according to children's abilities despite bearing identical names on the timetable.

In general, the 'good' readers manifested greater awareness of their deficiencies than the 'poor' readers. The majority keenly desired academic success in the shape of a grammar-school place, and so their predilection for arithmetic lessons was also dictated by a realisation that if they did not make progress in this subject their ambitions might be frustrated. *None of the 'poor' readers, on the other hand, mentioned the eleven-plus selection procedures, and about half of them confined their aspirations to higher achievement in one subject only, which, for a considerable number, was not reading.* Moreover, although approximately 50 per cent wanted to solve their reading problems, more than a quarter appeared to be complacent about them.

As it was the children most highly motivated to improve their reading standards who eventually succeeded in doing so, it would seem that the apathetic attitudes of backward readers, and in some cases their hatred of books, are included in the principal factors contributing to persistent failure. In a sense, research is not necessary to reach this conclusion as it is self-evident. It is necessary, however, to show the incidence of weak motivation amongst retarded readers and to provide a basis for hypotheses regarding its causes. Because of the feelings of inferiority engendered by continued failure, a vicious circle is created which can be broken only by providing plenty of encouragement and opportunities for success. As studies of the home circumstances and school conditions of the 'poor' readers showed that these were not satisfactory for a large proportion, the lack of motivation and its consequences for these children are understandable.

Social and emotional adjustment in relation to differential reading achievement: During the two terms following their selection for special study, the 'poor' readers, in general, adapted themselves to the school situation far less well than the 'good' readers. On the whole their behaviour was also markedly inferior to that of children in the total 1946 age group, whilst that of the 'good' readers was greatly superior. Between the ages of eight and ten, therefore, the two samples largely represented what are often described as 'problem' and 'model' pupils respectively.

More detailed data on the behavioural characteristics of the selected children in their third and fourth junior years were obtained by means of the 'Bristol Social Adjustment Guides'. The main results derived from statistical analyses of these are briefly as follows:

1 On average 'poor' readers manifested a larger number of signs of maladjustment and unsettledness than 'good' readers during the last two years of the primary course.

2 There was a greater incidence among 'poor' readers than among 'good' readers in their upper-junior years of:
   (a) 'inhibited' characteristics (withdrawal; depression);
   (b) characteristics of a 'demonstrative' or 'aggressive' nature (anxiety for adult attention and affection; hostility to adults; indifference to the adult figure; anxiety to gain acceptance and prestige among other children; hostility to other children;[1] restlessness);
   (c) miscellaneous symptoms of emotional tension, strain or disturbance;[2]
   (d) miscellaneous nervous symptoms.

On the whole, the adjustment of the 'poor' readers as fourth year juniors was better than it had been in the previous year. For example, there were statistically significant decreases with regard to the average number of signs of unsettledness and miscellaneous symptoms of emotional disturbance recorded, as well as in the characteristic of withdrawal. As already pointed out, this improvement could be attributed to their maturer age, but it is reasonable to suppose that it was also due to their increased reading ability and more favourable school conditions generally.

Despite these satisfactory changes, however, there was a remarkable degree of consistency in the behaviour of the 'poor' readers and that of the 'good' readers over the two-year period and in so far as the same children tended to have the greatest number of unfavourable traits of a similar type each year and vice versa. This finding might reflect the constancy of teachers'

[1,2] Statistically significant in the third junior year only.

attitudes to particular pupils if those responsible for the selected children had been the same in both years. But as over half the children had different teachers completing Stott's guides, support is lent to his contention that the guides provide a reasonably reliable assessment of children's social and emotional adjustment in school. In doing so, they provide a valid basis for the differences found in favour of 'good' readers.

Relationships within each sample between the behavioural characteristics of boys and girls and their reading test scores as third- and fourth-year juniors were also examined. The results for the 'good' readers are interesting but not perhaps educationally significant,[1] whereas those for the 'poor' readers which follow supply further evidence of the link between adjustment in school and reading ability:

1 Among girls classed as 'poor' readers at the age of nine, miscellaneous symptoms of emotional disturbance were most frequently observed in those who had the severest reading difficulties.

2 Among boys classed as 'poor' readers at the age of nine, those with the severest reading problems tended to be the most unsettled, maladjusted, unforthcoming and depressed. They also manifested the greatest number of miscellaneous symptoms of emotional disturbance.

3 Among boys classed as 'poor' readers at the age of ten, those with the severest reading problems tended to be the most unsettled, maladjusted, hostile to adults, hostile to other children and yet anxious to be accepted by them. They also manifested the greatest number of miscellaneous symptoms of emotional disturbance.

Additionally it was found that, among the 'poor' readers, the boys were markedly more depressed and anxious for the approval of other children, than the girls in their third junior year and more restless during the final year of their primary course. By their behaviour in school, therefore, backward boys tend to focus greater attention upon themselves than girls, and it is probably for this reason, in part, that they figure more frequently in the literature concerning cases of reading disability referred for special remedial treatment. Moreover, as three of the boys in this sample, and none of the girls, were eventually transferred to approved schools because of delinquency, there is some indication that this sex difference in overt reaction to failure is not confined to school hours.

ATTENDANCE AND MIGRATION

Differences in the average attendance of 'poor' and 'good' readers at the infant stage and in the mean number of school changes experienced between the ages of five and eight were not statistically significant. Thus, *there was no evidence that, in general, the low reading standards of juniors are attributable to the*

[1] See Chapter X, pp. 191–192.

disruptive effects of absence and changes of school during the early years of the primary course, although they can be regarded as contributory factors in the case of individual children.

In their lower and upper junior years, however, the 'good' readers had a far more satisfactory record of attendance on average than the 'poor' readers. The reason for this difference probably lies in some of the findings already discussed. For example, according to their medical records the 'good' readers did not enjoy better health on the whole, but they were more enthusiastic about reading and school work generally which would induce them to make every effort to attend regularly. Contrastingly, as the attitudes and environmental circumstances of the 'poor' readers were less conducive to success, they would naturally find excuses to escape from a situation in which their inadequacies were all too obvious. Whatever the reasons for their comparatively poor attendance, however, it is reasonable to suppose that it contributed to their slow progress during the junior course.

Reading achievement in relation to children's home circumstances

Visits to the 60 primary schools taking part in the survey indicated that the responsibility for teaching the majority of pupils to read effectively rested entirely with the teachers in 55 of them. But the task in some schools, situated in certain rural and poor urban areas, was initially more difficult because the home circumstances of most of their new entrants had not fostered a command of the spoken language, or provided experiences on which the foundations of reading ability could be built. Contrastingly, the remaining five schools enrolled a high proportion of children in their reception classes whose parents had introduced them to reading, and, in the school whose catchment area was given the highest rating for socio-economic status in the total Kent sample,[1] many had already mastered its mechanics.

In view of these differences at the beginning of the primary course, and the fact that the circumstances which contributed to them naturally tended to continue operating, one could hardly expect schools drawing their child populations from such varied backgrounds to achieve equally satisfactory results by the time their pupils reached the age of seven. One would consider this even if, in general, the 'innate' abilities of the children and their conditions of learning and teaching reading were equally favourable. It is not surprising, therefore, that an association was found between the reading standards of 2906 first-year juniors and the socio-economic status of their school catchment areas ($r = 0.57$), or that the school with the highest average attainment at this stage was the one situated in the 'best' neighbourhood. Moreover, as the 'intelligence' of the children according to non-verbal ability tests was significantly related to their socio-economic status as a school group ($r = 0.45$), it would seem that the schools in good districts had

[1] Based on the Juror Index for the village or ward(s) in which each school was situated plus assessments made by the Kent Inspectorate, Divisional Education Officers and the writer.

an additional advantage to explain their reading results, although this finding must be treated with reservation for reasons given earlier.

The relationship between the reading standards of 7409 children aged seven to eleven and the socio-economic status of their school catchment areas was closer ($r = 0.68$). For the same sample, the correlation between this variable and non-verbal ability was also greater ($r = 0.71$).[1] These findings suggest that the schools in the poorer neighbourhoods were unable to compensate for the initial disadvantages of the majority of their pupils as they grew older in so far as they continued to lag behind those attending schools with a more favourable background. Again, this is scarely surprising, for without taking into account the heads' assertions that they generally lacked parental support for their endeavours, and the lower average non-verbal IQs of their child populations, the slower start and subsequent slow progress of their pupils would naturally engender less enthusiasm for reading than if they had experienced early success.

Answers to two questions arising from these findings were sought. First, we examined the possibility that the schools in good districts had other favourable characteristics which might explain the better average attainment of their pupils aged seven to eleven. It was found that they were generally separate junior schools, and this type of organisation was closely associated with good reading standards both before and after making an allowance for the non-verbal ability of the children concerned. Moreover, interviews with their heads indicated that they experienced comparatively greater ease in recruiting suitably qualified staff.

Our second question was whether there were any schools whose reading test results diverged from expectation, considering the socio-economic status of their catchment areas. We looked for an answer only in the ten selected schools for the obvious reason that our intensive studies of them provided more detailed information.[2] Seven of these schools reflected the findings of the broad survey summarised above. But, in 'Deteriorator' School (1) the reading progress of children over the junior course was worse and that of pupils attending 'Improver' Schools (1) and (2) better than expected in relation to the socio-economic status of their backgrounds as school groups. Observations in these schools suggested that these differences could be explained largely in terms of the qualities of their heads and staffs.

One of the outstanding qualities of the heads of both 'improver' schools, which was echoed by most of their colleagues, was their determination to compensate the majority of their pupils for the fact that they came from underprivileged homes. In general, heads of schools with the most satisfactory

[1] Although ignoring school differences, the highest correlation obtained between reading and non-verbal ability in the whole research programme was 0.57, all inter-school correlations were of higher value, and one, in fact, reached 0.84. This increased correlation is probably due, therefore, to the same environmental circumstances acting upon children's non-verbal ability as on their reading attainment.
[2] Salient characteristics of the selected schools are described in Chapter IV.

results in the survey also believed that, though children's home circumstances undoubtedly influence their reading progress, the contribution of their schooling should be infinitely greater. The head of 'Good' School (2) went further and asserted that, in the unlikely event of any pupils finishing the primary course in his school unable to read, he would consider the fault lay with their teachers despite all other handicaps the children might have, save one, namely 'educational sub-normality'.[1] However, it is obviously easier to be optimistic about the efficacy of primary schooling in promoting satisfactory reading standards regardless of children's home circumstances, in schools where the proportion of pupils receiving little or no parental support for their efforts is comparatively small. The fact that it was the heads of schools in the poorer neighbourhoods who more frequently attributed reading failure to adverse home influences is therefore understandable.

Although only one aspect of children's home backgrounds was considered in the initial survey, almost all those mentioned by heads were included in the subsequent comparative studies of 101 'poor' and 98 'good' readers attending the selected schools, as well as others regarded as important from previous research. These studies revealed that *the home circumstances of the 'poor' readers as a group were clearly inferior to those of the 'good' readers in the following respects. Most of their fathers' occupations were of lower socio-economic status, and a higher proportion of their mothers had full-time jobs outside the home when the children were in third-year junior classes. A much lower percentage of their parents belonged to public libraries, and, in the comparatively few homes where there was a permanent collection of books, these were not generally of literary merit. The majority of 'poor' readers were also less fortunate in the amount of direct encouragement to read and make progress in school which they received from their parents. Furthermore, their families tended to be larger than those of the 'good' readers.[2]*

These results support the survey findings, and the broad inferences drawn from them, in so far as they show that juniors with poor reading standards tend to have lower working-class parents, and this characteristic is associated with lack of parental support and other home circumstances unlikely to encourage reading progress. *However, there was no evidence to include 'broken' or 'difficult' homes among the latter circumstances since the number of 'poor' and 'good' readers whose homes could be so described was not significantly different.* This may seem surprising in view of the frequent references to this unfor-

[1] Two children belonging to the 1946 age group did in fact leave this school with their reading problems largely unsolved, but shortly afterwards they were classed as 'educationally sub-normal' and transferred to special schools. Thus this head's confidence in his staff, which he expressed at the beginning of the research programme and maintained throughout the four years he took part in it, was vindicated.

[2] In addition to these main findings, several subsidiary results are of some interest (details are given in Chapter XI). For example, the amount of encouragement given to both 'poor' and 'good' readers by their fathers was not related to the size of their families or to their occupational status. There was also no evidence that the mothers of children in either sample who were housewives only gave them more encouragement than those in full- or part-time employment outside the home, but the larger their families the less concerned they tended to be about their children's educational progress.

tunate circumstance in the literature on reading backwardness. But, apart from the possibility that our data might not be entirely reliable, it is probably due to the fact that we raised the question of how many 'good' readers come from such homes, which for obvious reasons, is rarely considered even by research workers.[1]

Though not strictly home 'circumstances', information was obtained about the out-of-school activities of the selected children. *Highly significant differences in favour of the 'good' readers were found with regard to their membership of public libraries during the last three years of the junior course, and the amount of reading they did at home. On average, the 'good' readers also read fewer comics,*[2] mainly because they preferred and could read books of varied content including non-fictional material. Moreover, *although approximately the same percentage of children in each sample were regular television-viewers and radio-listeners, the 'good' readers, unlike the 'poor' readers, exercised discrimination in their choice of programmes* usually with parental assistance and because they had several other absorbing hobbies competing for their attention.

Thus, in so far as reading progress is fostered by reading and by experiences arising from a rich and full life out of school hours, these findings provide a further explanation for the different reading achievements of juniors.

Reading achievement in relation to children's school conditions

The major part of the research programme was devoted to studying reading in the school setting and relations between some salient features of children's schooling and their reading achievement.

During the first year, data were collected on the conditions of learning and teaching reading in a random sample of 60 Kent primary schools, and nine characteristics of these schools were studied in relation to each other and to the reading comprehension and non-verbal test scores of over 8000 children aged seven to eleven (1943–46 year groups) attending them. The results of this inquiry raised questions which we subsequently tried to answer by extensive and intensive studies of a sequential nature all of which involved schools drawn from the original sample and children born in 1946. Findings concerning each of the main aspects of children's schooling considered are summarised below.

SIZE AND LOCATION OF SCHOOL

1 In schools with the larger numbers of pupils on roll, the average reading attainment of first-year juniors was superior to that in small schools (P < 0.001). It was also better when the reading standards of children aged seven to eleven were considered together (P < 0.01).

[1] Amongst those who have considered this question in recent years Malmquist (1958) also found no significant association between poor reading ability and 'broken' homes.
[2] No 'horror' comics were taken regularly by any of the selected children, and only one 'poor' reader took a comic classed as 'objectionable'.

2 On the whole, the reading standards of children aged seven to eleven attending urban schools tended to be higher than those of juniors in rural schools (P = 0.01). Urban schools also had a greater proportion of fourth-year junior pupils whose reading ability was above average (P<0.05).

With few exceptions, large schools are situated in urban districts and so associations between reading achievement and each characteristic naturally lie in the same direction, though in different degrees. However, as large schools tend to have large classes (P<0.001), reasons for the relatively good standards of their junior pupils were sought by considering other factors connected with their size and location. A high level of non-verbal ability among juniors was found to be associated with large schools (P<0.01), but, as already pointed out in the previous section of this Appendix, this apparent advantage may be due to the same environmental circumstances acting upon children's reading and non-verbal test scores. Large schools in Kent usually have superior buildings (P<0.001), and they (or their contributory infant schools if organised for juniors only) are inclined to adopt a formal approach to reading in their reception classes (P<0.001), both characteristics being favourably associated with reading attainment (P<0.01). Moreover, large urban schools have sufficient pupils to organise homogeneous classes which, from our subsequent intensive studies, appear to mitigate any disadvantage in their large numbers. Their heads can and do allot a greater proportion of their capitation allowance for the purchase of library books, and generally find it easier to recruit suitably qualified staff. Furthermore, the fact that there is particularly strong competition for headships of this type of school suggests that those who obtain them are successful teachers and possess additional outstanding qualities, the importance of which in raising reading standards was outlined by our studies in the selected schools.

SCHOOL AND CLASS ORGANISATION

Junior with/without infant schools: Because junior/infant schools can ensure continuity of reading development more readily than schools catering for juniors only, one might expect this advantage to be reflected in the attainment of their junior pupils. However, considering the standards of seven- to eleven-year-olds together, the initial inquiry refuted this expectation in so far as good attainment was found to be closely associated with separate junior schools, both before and after making a statistical allowance for the non-verbal ability of the children concerned (P<0.001). Moreover, reading standards were better in schools with this type of organisation even when, in addition to the higher average non-verbal ability of their pupils, the fact that they tend to be of large size and to be situated in urban districts of relatively superior socio-economic status had been taken into account (P<0.01).

A separate analysis based on test scores gained by 2906 children in the

1946 age group who had been 'juniors' for only six months at the time of the first survey produced similar results. These suggested that education in an infant 'school', as distinct from an infant 'department', might be a more important factor contributing to satisfactory reading achievement than later attendance at a school for juniors only. Accordingly, further evidence that the latter is a favourable circumstance in learning to read was sought in our sequential study of 1848 children in the same age group attending 52 schools.[1] From this, the following results were obtained:

1   On average, the reading attainment of second-, third- and fourth-year juniors attending separate junior schools was better than that of pupils at the same stages of their primary course in junior with infant schools ($P < 0.01$).

2   Over the last three years of the primary course, children attending junior with infant schools made greater progress in reading, on the whole, than pupils in schools catering for juniors only ($P < 0.01$). But it was not sufficient to reach the general level of reading ability achieved by the latter in their final primary year.

Before drawing conclusions from the findings of this study, it must be pointed out that test SR 1, which was used to assess the reading comprehension ability of the children involved, does not have enough final items of increasing difficulty to allow second-year juniors who are already 'good' readers to demonstrate their subsequent progress adequately.[2] Consequently, as separate junior schools have a larger proportion of pupils with above-average reading ability at this stage, it is not surprising that the overall rate of improvement of those attending junior with infant schools appears to be more satisfactory. On the other hand, there is no doubt that the latter type of organisation is an unfavourable school characteristic as far as the reading standards of juniors are concerned; though this may be partly due to the fact that, in Kent, schools catering for the full primary age range tend to have the previously confirmed disadvantages of comparatively small child populations drawn from catchment areas of relatively poor socio-economic status. Moreover, despite the fact that no statistical allowance for non-verbal ability was made in the later study because the initial inquiry raised doubts about the validity of such a procedure, the possibility cannot be ruled out that schools of this type have an additional handicap in that their pupils are generally less 'able' in this respect.

Considered together our studies clearly show that *good reading standards*

[1] Eight schools belonging to the original sample had to be excluded from this study because they did not cater for children beyond the first-year junior stage.
[2] This is shown by the fact that some of the children chosen for special study because they were 'good' readers at the age of eight, subsequently gained reduced standardised scores on test SR 1, although, in functional terms, their reading ability continued notably to improve.

are associated with separate junior schools[1] *even after allowing for their propitious concomitant circumstances.* Nevertheless, they do not justify the conclusion that this type of organisation is in itself an important factor contributing to satisfactory reading achievement, for this would require proof that the segregation of infants and juniors directly and favourably influences the instruction they receive. Though this hypothesis was not tested, observations in Kent schools suggest that in future research it might be particularly fruitful to compare heads of infant schools and teachers responsible for infant departments with regard to (a) their acceptance of the doctrine that infants should be allowed to proceed at their own speed, and (b) its consequences in terms of the drive made by them and their colleagues to ensure that children can read, at least mechanically, when transferred to parent junior schools and transition classes in the same schools respectively.[2]

Size and composition of classes: In the first survey, schools with an unfavourable pupil–teacher ratio returned higher reading scores, on the whole, than those with small classes. However, as large classes were found to be closely associated with large schools and other circumstances tending to raise scores, judgement on this controversial issue was suspended until results of further study, including an examination of relations between the composition of classes and reading achievement, were available. Those obtained are briefly as follows:

1 (a) In general, the reading standards of second-, third- and fourth-year juniors in large classes were superior to those of children in small classes (P < 0.001).

(b) On average, the reading attainment of second-, third- and fourth-year juniors in homogeneous classes with regard to age and ability was superior to that of pupils in heterogeneous classes (P < 0.001).

2 (a) The average size of class in which children classed as 'good' readers at the age of eight were taught as infants, lower and upper juniors tended to be larger than that of 'poor' readers (P < 0.01).

(b) A much higher proportion of 'good' readers in comparison with 'poor' readers spent the last three years of their primary course in classes which were homogeneous with regard to age and ability (P < 0.001).

3 Below-average readers at the age of eight taught in large and/or homogeneous classes for the remainder of their primary course made approximately the same amount of progress in reading on average as those in small and/or heterogeneous classes.

These findings support those of the initial survey in so far as large classes do

1 'Good' Schools (1), (2) and (3), that is, the schools where the reading standards of juniors were the highest in the total Kent sample, catered only for children aged seven to eleven.
2 Heads of infant schools generally felt that it would reflect badly on their school's reputation, themselves and colleagues if children entered parent junior schools unable to read.

not appear to be an unfavourable characteristic for reading. Particularly surprising is the fact that second-year juniors with serious reading difficulties tended to have been fortunate in the size of their previous classes. From this stage they were also taught in relatively small classes yet, as already stated elsewhere, only one in eight achieved normal competence in the final year of primary schooling. Moreover, when they and all below-average readers were considered together, there was no evidence that small classes are an advantage for subsequent progress. It would seem, therefore, that either the size of classes for such children was not small enough (and here further research is needed to establish the optimum size for backward readers) or other factors more important than class size were involved. Though composition of classes for all below-average readers did not bear any significant relationship to their subsequent progress, the fact that, during the last three years of the junior course, 'poor' readers tended to be in heterogeneous classes whilst 'good' readers were in homogeneous classes, suggests that this may be one of the reasons why their reading difficulties tended to persist. At first sight, finding 1(b) above, which is based on data for 714 children comprising the total 1946 age group in the selected schools, seems to support this hypothesis. However, both this and the previous one relating to class size, derived from the same sample, arise mainly because of the following concomitant circumstances. Heads of large schools, which, *ipso facto*, had an unfavourable pupil-teacher ratio, had sufficient pupils to stream them rigidly for age and ability. Furthermore, they not only had a high proportion of above-average readers, but generally assigned them to large classes in order to give greater opportunities for individual attention to backward pupils in relatively small bottom 'streams'. It cannot be said, therefore, that large homogeneous junior classes 'promoted' good reading standards because the children allocated to them were usually competent readers already. Nor, incidentally, do our studies establish the merits of streaming *per se*, for this would imply that heads of the selected schools had equal opportunities to choose this form of class organisation. We must conclude, therefore, that *our inquiries do not provide sufficient evidence to suggest that, in themselves, class size and composition are important contributory factors to reading achievement*. But, because they show that backward readers were generally taught in relatively small classes, which were more frequently heterogeneous than homogeneous, it seemed likely that these characteristics are associated with others of an adverse kind. Accordingly, an attempt to identify the latter was made with results as summarised in later sections.

Staff changes: We considered the possibility that reading failure is associated with an abnormal number of teachers over the primary course.

It was found that *the slower start of the 'poor' readers* in our selected sample *could not be attributed to frequent staff changes*. The 'poor' readers had in fact had significantly fewer changes of infant teachers than the 'good' readers.

But there was reason to believe that this factor contributed to their subsequent unsatisfactory progress in general, since the average number of teachers responsible for them as lower juniors, and particularly as upper juniors, was markedly higher than that of the 'good' readers.

Interviews with heads in the initial survey indicated that staffing difficulties were generally more acute in rural than urban schools on account of their location and associated characteristics. However, intensive studies revealed that the head of the urban school with the highest reading standards in Kent also had to cope with this problem, due in his case either to the promotion of colleagues to headships or the fact that some could not stand the pace expected of them. He reduced its ill effects by having a detailed scheme of work in reading and all subjects for each class. From their predecessors' records, newly-appointed teachers could ascertain exactly the stage reached by their pupils, and they were constantly supervised and helped with suggestions by the head during their first few weeks in school. This may seem an autocratic solution to the problem, but it appeared to be satisfactory, probably because all teachers, new and old, felt it gave direction, shape and continuity to their work and that of their pupils. The problem of turnover in staff might therefore be solved in other schools, at least partially, if similar methods were adopted.

SCHOOL BUILDINGS AND MATERIAL CLASSROOM CONDITIONS

Reading achievement was studied in relation to classroom conditions to determine whether the survey finding that superior school buildings were associated with good reading standards was concerned with a general amenity having no direct bearing on learning and teaching reading. Assessments were made of various aspects of the accommodation and basic equipment provided in 91 classrooms where the total 1946 age group in the selected schools was to be found during the last three years of their primary course.

The first analysis using these assessments showed that, in general, the children attending schools classed as 'good' on the basis of their reading test results in the survey, had much better classroom conditions than the rest of the sample, whereas the converse was true of those in the 'bad' schools. Moreover, when pupils in the 'good' and 'improver' schools were considered together, there was no doubt that their classroom facilities were markedly superior to those of children in the 'bad' and 'deteriorator' schools.

Subsequent analyses, ignoring school differences, and using data for the whole sample and for the selected 'poor' and 'good' readers produced the following results:

1   On the whole, the higher the reading standards of second-, third- and fourth-year juniors, the more satisfactory their classroom conditions tended to be ($P < 0.001$).

2 (a) 'Good' readers tended to have much better classroom conditions than 'poor' readers during their last three years of primary schooling (P < 0.001). (b) Compared with the classroom conditions of other second-, third- and fourth-year juniors those of 'good' and 'poor' readers were generally more favourable (P = 0.001) and much worse (P < 0.001) respectively.

Thus, there is evidence from all our studies that *juniors who need the most encouragement to improve their reading standards were generally given the least in terms of the material conditions of learning and teaching provided for them at school and classroom level.* Obviously the building of new, well-equipped schools and improvements in existing ones were urgently required, for although they would not solve the reading problem, they would ensure that, in their school environment, backward children, who usually come from underprivileged homes, are not at a further disadvantage compared with others more fortunate in this respect and in their ability to read.

LIBRARY FACILITIES AND READING MATERIALS

From information obtained in the survey, it seemed likely that, with regard to library and other books, the needs of backward readers might not be catered for as well as those of other children. To test this hypothesis scores were given for (a) the content and general condition of libraries, and (b) the quantity and quality of books additionally available in classrooms of the selected schools where 714 children in the 1946 age group spent their last three years as juniors. The combined score, representing the total reading environment for each class, was then used in analyses, considering school differences and ignoring them.

Both types of analysis indicated that class reading environment is closely associated with attainment, but, for reasons given elsewhere,[1] the second provided more substantial evidence of this association. In other words, it confirmed the hypothesis that the lower the reading standards of second-, third- and fourth-year juniors, the more unsatisfactory their class reading environment tended to be (P < 0.001).

In comparative studies of the selected 'poor' and 'good' readers, aspects (a) and (b) of their reading environment were considered separately, mainly because it was reasonable to suppose that, in the case of retarded pupils, the building up of a stock of simple books for their instruction and practice in reading lessons would take precedence over supplying them with library books. However, not only were the 'poor' readers found to be at a distinct disadvantage with regard to class libraries, but the books generally available to a sizable proportion were both insufficient in number and unsuitable in content. Moreover, closer inspection of the books on which the children were actually engaged as upper juniors indicated that those given to the most

[1] Chapter VI, p. 112.

retarded, in particular, were more likely to hinder progress than promote it. Besides being too difficult, they were not always selected with the previous experiences and current interests of the children in mind, nor were they changed frequently enough to prevent boredom.

Reading apparatus might have helped to fill the gap created by inadequate books for the worst readers. But, in accord with the belief expressed by heads in the survey that it is inappropriate for juniors because they regard it as 'babyish', little was used. The amount of published apparatus purchased was not sufficient for it to be employed in a systematic manner, neither was that made by a few teachers since they felt unsure of its value as an encouragement to progress.

The results of all these studies, therefore, suggest *that in the selection and supply of materials for backward readers in junior classes lies one of the reasons why their difficulties tend to persist.* By its very nature, this is one of the potential causes of unsatisfactory reading development which can be removed most easily.

APPROACH AND READING METHODS IN INFANT CLASSES

Formal/informal approach in the reception class: New entrants in 12 of the 60 schools taking part in the survey were expected to settle down quickly, systematic instruction using a primer was undertaken straight away, and a strictly formal approach to learning was maintained thereafter. In contrast, the atmosphere in the remaining schools was more permissive, though it became less so during the junior course, and pupils were not usually introduced to a primer until they had acquired a small sight vocabulary and become familiar with the characters they were going to read about. Accordingly, we examined the possibility that this difference of approach might be related to the reading standards subsequently achieved.

From the main analysis, based on a combination of test results from 7409 children aged seven to eleven, good reading attainment was found to be associated with a formal approach to reading in the reception class ($P < 0.01$). However, the association was not so close when the standards of first-year juniors were considered separately, which suggested that the initial finding might have risen partly from differences in junior practice. Unfortunately, our data on the latter were not sufficiently formalised to prove or disprove this point. But we were able to study the question of whether the type of infant approach adopted is an important factor in itself, or merely appears to be so because of other concomitant circumstances. This entailed eliminating the effects of school size, urban/rural location and socio-economic status, and making adjustments for the non-verbal ability of the children concerned.

Neither analysis using data for the total sample, nor for pupils in transition classes alone revealed any statistically significant relationships. Consequently, there are some grounds for believing our second hypothesis to be correct, and for concluding that *our findings lend little support to the advocates either of a formal or an informal approach for infants*—at least as far as reading is concerned.

Phonic/whole-word methods for teaching beginning reading. Current educational theory and majority opinion favours delaying systematic phonic instruction until beginners have made some headway with whole-word methods, mainly because it is believed that a too early introduction to sounds impedes reading comprehension and speed later on. As this principle was disregarded in 13 of the initial survey schools, an opportunity was presented of comparing its after-effects on their pupils with those on children attending the remaining schools where it was followed.

Results of the main analysis using the reading test scores of all juniors in combination, and of a subsidiary one based only on data for children aged seven plus (1946 age-group), were not statistically significant. But relationships were established when adjustments had been made for the non-verbal ability of the children concerned both before and after eliminating the effects of school size, urban/rural location and socio-economic status. These indicated that there might be something to be said for introducing infants to reading by phonic methods. However, they did not warrant a more definite verdict supporting minority practice, because significant associations emerged only in consequence of the rather questionable procedure of artificially raising the reading test scores of some schools to compensate for their lower intelligence test scores.[1]

In seeking further evidence on the merits of each introductory method, we examined data for 1848 children (1946 age group) attending 52 schools during the last three years of the junior course. The principal results of various analyses may be summarised as follows:

1   There was no significant difference between the average level of attainment achieved by second-, third- and fourth-year juniors introduced to reading phonic and whole-word methods respectively.

2   On average, reading *progress* (and improvement in non-verbal ability) during the last three years of the junior course was greater for pupils whose introduction to reading had been by whole-word rather than phonic methods.

It must be pointed out that the two groups were evenly matched for non-verbal ability, and so, had it been considered desirable, a statistical allowance for this variable would not have altered the first result. Moreover, though the second and subsidiary findings[2] appear to favour teaching

[1] This procedure cannot reproduce the real situation of groups matched for either reading attainment or non-verbal ability. Moreover, it may well 'reward' some schools for failing to teach their pupils to read and to take tests generally.

[2] For example, junior schools whose contributory infant schools introduced reading by whole-word methods yielded the highest mean scores on reading tests in two years, and on non-verbal

beginning reading by whole-word methods, they may not represent the consequences of infant training any more than the more immediate effects of junior practice. Details of the latter in the selected schools were obtained, but differences in the use of synthetic and analytic methods were not sufficiently distinct to allow statistical verification of this point. In any case, as will be subsequently suggested, the actual reading methods used appeared to matter far less than the manner and skill with which they were employed and other attributes of the teachers concerned.

Probably, the same might be said of infant practice if similar classroom observations had been carried out. Consequently, it would be unwise to say more than that the Kent inquiries *do not provide sufficient evidence to support advocates of either phonic or whole-word methods for introducing infants to reading.* Beyond declaring a kind of truce, therefore, they do not help to settle controversy on this issue, and it is likely to remain a source of contention among educationists until resources are available to mount a large-scale experiment in which methods are clearly distinguished and all-important variables are rigorously controlled. Studies of practice in Kent schools suggest that it might be even more worth while for future investigators to consider an extension of the original question, that is, 'How appropriate and effective are phonic and whole-word methods for particular types of beginners when employed by different kinds of teachers?'

READING PRACTICES WITH JUNIORS

The survey yielded a good deal of information on junior practices and problems, a subject which had received little attention from previous investigators compared with that focused on work with infants. This provided a reference for more detailed studies of the ways in which the reading needs of 714 pupils in the selected schools were catered for during the last three years of their primary course. For reasons given in Chapter VII, where these are initially described, no attempt was made to relate them by precise statistical analysis to the reading standards of all the children concerned, though the data were used in assessments of their teachers' contributions to progress. However, as findings on practices for the total sample, *per se*, indicated that some of those for the less able pupils were unsatisfactory, confirmation was sought and obtained in comparative studies of the selected 'poor' and 'good' readers.

Obviously the main value of our inquiries lies in results suggesting improvements which might be made in dealing with the problem of backward readers. These were as follows:

1   In none of the selected schools, and in only one of the total sample were

---

tests in three years. Whereas, junior mixed and infant schools employing whole-word methods for beginners had the best rate of improvement in reading and non-verbal ability over the three year period.

diagnostic reading tests used because it was generally believed that time given to testing could be spent more profitably in teaching. Moreover, our intensive studies revealed that most teachers did not accurately ascertain the particular difficulties of their retarded pupils by other methods. Consequently, because much of the instruction given was not directed towards specific objectives it was not as effective as it might have been. It would seem advisable, therefore, that *all teachers should be trained to diagnose before giving treatment*, especially as the number of educational psychologists may long remain insufficient to allow 'regular' visits to 'every' school for this purpose.[1]

2   The majority of backward readers received only 'spontaneous' assistance from their teachers, that is, they were prompted whilst trying to read unknown words and shown how to build up those which happened to be regular from their component parts. Also, beyond being told to practise the passages recently gone over, they were not set follow-up activities to help reinforce what had been learned. Not surprisingly, the children asked to re-read these passages made the same errors and omissions as they had done during the lesson and so had gained virtually nothing from it. Thus, our studies suggest that *'prepared' reading lessons followed by the setting of activities based upon them should be the general rule for retarded juniors instead of minority practice.*

3   From observations of several forms of group reading practised, it was clear that further research into the value of this activity is necessary. For backward readers, the kind in which the teacher is engaged with one group whilst the remaining groups work under the supervision of child leaders appeared to be singularly unproductive. This was largely because they generally disliked it and a crescendo of noise and unruly behaviour tended to ensue. Accordingly, *a better solution to the problem of backward readers in a class of mixed abilities may be to follow the example of the few teachers who gave a 'prepared' lesson to one group after settling the rest of their pupils down to some other task.*

4   Providing backward readers with regular individual tuition is the biggest problem, and it is significant that less than half the selected sample received it as second-year juniors. Heads in the 1954 survey recommended the formation of a part-time class in each school as the best solution but, with one exception, they had been unable to do this because no extra teachers or spare rooms were available. Subsequently, heads of two selected

[1] It was the general opinion of heads that such visits were highly desirable, but none of the survey schools (1954) or the selected schools (1955–57) received them. Since then, the number of personnel employed in the Kent Psychological Service has increased and a different situation would probably be revealed if the Foundation's inquiries were repeated today. Nevertheless, the current shortage of educational psychologists in the country as a whole suggests that, except for the most difficult cases, the diagnosis of individual reading difficulties and their treatment remains the responsibility of teachers.

schools managed it by encouraging local retired and married women teachers to return to part-time teaching.

The reading standards and progress of 15 pupils coached daily for an hour by these teachers over a two-year period were found to be significantly better than those of 86 'poor' readers for whom provision of of this kind could not be made.[1] Thus, the results of this small comparative study suggest that *part-time remedial classes for all backward readers in junior schools would be well worth while.*

CONTRIBUTIONS OF TEACHERS

Findings of the survey indicated that the reading standards of seven-year-olds were such that nearly half of them still needed the kind of teaching associated with the infant school. Yet approximately 75 per cent of the teachers responsible for their first year junior classes had received no training in infant methods, 52 per cent had no experience in an infant school and about 18 per cent were neither familiar with infant methods nor had any knowledge of how to teach beginning reading. It was also found that first year junior teachers without infant training or experience were in charge of poor readers in half the sample schools. Moreover, in one in ten of the schools, those responsible for ensuring the progress of backward readers were not, in the opinion of their respective head teachers, well equipped for the task.[2]

Subsequent interviews with junior teachers suggested that the discrepancy between their task and their equipment for it lay partly in the fact that, in college, they were not usually made sufficiently aware of their rôle as potential teachers of reading and given instruction and practice accordingly.[3] Many began their careers imagining they would rarely have to cope with pupils who could not read, and were shocked to discover that this was not so. As only a minute proportion continued their studies by attending courses, etc.[4] their learning to deal with the problem was largely by trial and error which is time-consuming and not, meanwhile, conducive to the progress of the children involved.

Of course, if the progress of late beginners was in fact entrusted to experienced and/or gifted teachers we should have to conclude that the teaching factor plays little part in the persistence of reading difficulties. To find out, therefore, whether this conclusion was tenable, data from classroom observations and other sources were collected on the 91 teachers responsible for 714 children whose reading achievements and school conditions during the last three years of the junior course have already been summarised.

---

[1] Since data for this study were obtained, the number of remedial schools in Kent and other areas has increased, but it is still difficult for local education authorities to fully implement the 1944 Act because of the shortage of teachers and accommodation.

[2] A subsidiary finding of some interest in view of the sex differences in children's reading development summarised on p. 308 is that only 10 per cent of the teachers staffing transition classes were men, and the problem of persuading more of them to take on this important work was particularly acute.

[3] Cf. p. 301.   [4] Op. cit. Morris (1959), p. 111.

The final assessment for each teacher, expressed as a grade on a nine-point scale, was obtained by adding separate scores for a number of qualities which included a few not directly connected with the teaching of reading, but indicative of attitudes and abilities having repercussions in this sphere.

No association was found between the teachers' grades and their sex, age or marital status. There was no difference in the distribution of grades among the male teachers who had taken an 'emergency' one year course of training and those whose college course lasted at least two years. However, for both sexes together, high teachers' grades were associated with:

1   long training ($P < 0.05$);

2   additional experience with infants and/or secondary school children ($P < 0.05$);

3   longer teaching experience ($P < 0.001$).

An independent examination of associations between the teachers' grades and their assignments was carried out although, as far as possible, the relative difficulty of the latter had been taken into account when rating the qualities making up their final assessment. The assessments were not found to be related to the assistance given by head teachers, and there was not sufficient evidence to establish that the larger classes were taught by better teachers. But the teachers with the higher grades tended to have:

1   responsibility for classes 'streamed' for ability ($P < 0.05$);

2   responsibility for classes composed of one age group ($P < 0.001$);

3   good classroom facilities and reading materials ($P < 0.001$).

Analyses considering school differences showed clearly that *pupils attending schools with outstandingly good reading attainment had considerably better teachers each year than those in other schools.* The difference was not quite so marked when the children were fourth-year juniors, probably because in some of the schools with the lower levels of attainment their best teachers were given the task of ensuring as many '11 + successes' as possible. Nevertheless, in all years, compared with other schools, a very much larger proportion of children attending schools with poor reading standards were taught by teachers whose assessments were low.

Results of analyses ignoring school differences may be summarised as follows:

1   On the whole, the higher the reading standards of second-, third- and and fourth-year juniors the more outstanding their teachers tended to be ($P < 0.001$).

2 (a) 'Good' readers tended to have much better teachers than 'poor' readers during their last three years of primary schooling (P < 0.001).

(b) Compared with the teachers of other children aged eight plus, nine plus and ten plus, those of 'good' and 'poor' readers were generally of much higher and lower calibre respectively (P < 0.001).

Thus, there is a marked tendency for juniors with low reading standards to be under-privileged as regards their teachers, and, with the exception of class size, for both backward readers and poor teachers to receive the least encouragement to succeed in their respective tasks by the conditions of learning and teaching provided for them at school and classroom level. In other words, our findings about junior teachers form the last and most vital link in a chain of circumstances which suggest that *in the subsequent schooling in reading of late beginners lies one of the main reasons why their diffiulties tend to persist.*

Multiplicity of factors in differential reading achievement

After comparing the selected samples of 'poor' and 'good' readers for variables in isolation, we carried out further analyses of the data on their individual attributes, home circumstances and school conditions to find out initially whether, on average, the 'poor' readers had a significantly greater number of 'unfavourable' characteristics in each area and overall.[1] As this proved to be the case an explanation of the inferior and superior reading standards of the majority of children in both samples was obtained in terms of the multiplicity of their additional handicaps, and, by inference, their advantages respectively. However, the fact that a small proportion of the 'poor' readers had relatively few adverse characteristics and a similar proportion of the 'good' readers had many[2] suggested that, in some instances, differential achievement is determined more by the nature of children's disadvantages and advantages than by their number. Accordingly, profiles of these exceptional children were examined for common distinctive features such as low intelligence and a dislike of reading on the one hand and high intelligence and a love of reading on the other. This examination revealed some differences in this direction, but they were insufficiently marked to explain adequately the comparative failure and success of each group. It was concluded, therefore, that this was an unfruitful line of inquiry to pursue as, for these children, the reasons lay in the complex interacting pattern of their individual attributes and environmental circumstances which could only be shown by descriptions of their case histories.[3]

Data for the latter were included, however, in analyses to disclose relationships between the unfavourable individual attributes, home circumstances and school conditions of the children within each sample. Findings for the

[1] The criteria of 'unfavourability' established for children's individual attributes, home circumstances and school conditions, respectively, are given on pages 200, 220–221, and 243–244.
[2] This is illustrated in Figure 7, p. 246.
[3] The history of one of these children is summarily described as Case 2 in Chapter XV.

'good' readers have little educational significance,[1] whereas those for the 'poor' readers have important implications. Briefly, *they implied that poor readers with the greatest number of personal handicaps not only come from the least propitious homes but also have the most unsatisfactory primary schooling.*

It was reasonable to suppose that the late beginners who were most clearly caught in the kind of vicious circle indicated by this last finding would be the children whose reading difficulties persisted in the acutest form. This proved to be the case in so far as, on average, the total number of unfavourable characteristics of the children still engaged on infant primers at the end of the primary course was far greater than that of the sample remainder (P > 0.001). Moreover, when these 'worst' readers were grouped with the children who were also 'poor' readers at this stage according to the original test criterion,[2] their mean number of adverse characteristics was markedly higher than that of the rest of the sample (P < 0.01).

Additional results for these and other groups in the sample support the conclusion that, in varying degree, persistent reading failure is attributable to the cumulative effect of handicaps centred in the child, home and school. In accord with commonsense expectation, they indicate, too, that unsatisfactory primary school conditions constitute the 'last straw which breaks the camel's back' for late beginners handicapped both personally and by their home circumstances. Whereas, as far as reading *progress* is concerned, they do not have such a deleterious effect on those more fortunate in either respect. This is illustrated by the fact that, compared with the children who remained 'backward' readers or 'semi-literate' to the end of their school days, those who achieved normal competence did not, on the whole, have better school conditions at the primary stage, but they came from comparatively good homes (P < 0.001) and/or had greater resources within themselves (P < 0.001).[3]

Reading achievement in relation to secondary school selection and the employment of school leavers

All the children in the total Kent sample who were classed as 'poor' readers at the age of eight were transferred to secondary modern schools three years later, and none of them gained a grammar or technical school place at the age of 13-plus, whereas, approximately four out of every five children classed as 'good' readers in their second junior year eventually proceeded to grammar or technical schools.

On the whole, the 'good' readers selected for grammar and technical schools had significantly better test scores for reading and non-verbal ability than those transferred to secondary modern schools. However, there were notable exceptions for which reasons were sought. The selected 'good'

---

[1] See p. 247.

[2] A standardised score on Sentence Reading Test 1 of 85 and below.

[3] Factors contributing to the relative success of late beginners in overcoming their reading difficulties by the end of the primary course and their school days, respectively, are discussed in some detail in Chapters XIII and XIV.

readers had fewer adverse characteristics of any kind but the remaining 'good' readers were equally privileged with regard to their home circumstances and primary school conditions. The difference, therefore, lay in the fact that, on average, the latter had a greater number of unfavourable personal attributes, which naturally lessened their chances of being chosen for secondary education of the grammar or technical type.

Two other considerations may be relevant. First, in allocating children to different types of secondary school, the Kent Education Authority take into account many factors besides those we studied. Second, competition for grammar and technical school places was extra keen for the children involved in our studies because they were born in a 'bulge' year. Perhaps these considerations help to explain why the correlations between heads' predictions and the actual allocation results one and two years later provided to be only 0.77 and 0.65 respectively.

In view of the abnormal situation, inaccuracies in the heads' forecasts for the 'good' readers may not be of educational significance. But, the 100 per cent accuracy of those they made for the 'poor' readers implies that *late beginners in reading are destined for secondary modern schools not only in fact but in the opinion of those responsible for their progress as juniors.* Hence, the importance of the 'early' acquisition of reading skill is emphasised.

Approximately 3 per cent of the 'poor' readers were subsequently sent to special schools for the 'educationally sub-normal'. A further 3 per cent were transferred to approved schools, thereby indicating a link between reading backwardness and juvenile delinquency.

The majority of the original sample of 'poor' readers became manual workers, and the minority who entered skilled or semi-skilled occupations were, on the whole, those who eventually achieved satisfactory reading standards.

This last finding raises the question of whether more could be done to enable children who make a slow start with reading to become effective readers, and so eventually have a wider choice of occupation and a richer adult life. Some of the other findings of the Kent inquiries suggest an affirmative answer.

Appendix F

READING IN INFANT CLASSES[1]
by E. J. GOODACRE

A Survey of the Teaching Practice and Conditions in 100 schools and departments

Aims and findings

The findings reported here are the first results of a three-year programme of research into the problems of teaching beginners to read. The main aim of this present survey is to provide a picture of the infant schools' methods of teaching reading, the schemes, materials and practices used, and how, if at all, the two important factors of school organisation and social area affect this. These broad factors are studied in relation to the final reading attainment of the pupils.

We may now examine the results first in terms of the practice of the infant school by comparison with those of the junior school about which evidence was obtained in the early Kent inquiry. We may then examine the importance of the two variables, school organisation and social area, particularly in the light of how schools might have varied their practice to meet the problems which appear to face them, especially those arising from the social background of their pupils.

The findings in relation to the Kent inquiry

READING METHODS

The Kent inquiry demonstrated the importance attached by junior school teachers to the use of 'mixed' methods in the teaching of reading. The picture in the infant school appears to be similar. The majority of teachers use all the main methods of teaching reading, and tend to differ principally on the order in which they introduce the basic methods and the importance they attach to any aspect at different stages of children's development.

When the type of approach used is distinguished as being either child-centred or curriculum-centred, there appears to be some evidence that during the past five years there may have been a change in infant teachers' opinions and practices. The importance of the basic skills and the value of a controlled and planned classroom environment received more emphasis in the London schools of this survey than the individual freedom of the child and the merits of activity methods which were popular among Kent teachers, and this possibly reflects the pendulum swing of opinion. This is

[1] Cross references in this Appendix are to *Reading in Infant Classes*.

of interest to note, since such a climate of opinion may be more favourable towards other changes in educational method. For instance, the recent interest in the units and stages of learning involved in the development of the total skill is related probably to the introduction and use of teaching machines. The simplification of early reading tasks, such as that provided by the use of materials printed in i.t.a. may have a special appeal to teachers after a period when analytic methods attracted much attention. These latter types of reading methods, with their smaller emphasis upon systematic instruction and their avowed aim to develop reading for meaning rather than mere word recognition, are more difficult to test. Thus, in the early stages at all events concrete results are hard to come by, and the teacher has less satisfactory evidence of successful teaching. It may well be that synthetic methods, because they are dogmatic, tend to lessen teachers' anxieties and provide an emotional satisfaction. As yet there has been no research designed solely to study types of reading methods in relation to the personal satisfaction and security which they provide for the teacher.

Certainly, if teachers are showing less interest in the motivations of learning to read and rather more in the nature and operation of the skill, this was to be expected, since probably sufficient emphasis had been laid upon the importance of the learner's motivation, and what is needed is a re-appraisal of the knowledge which exists about the elements which constitute the total skill. This would involve the definition and simplification of those reading tasks which comprise learning to read, which would increase our knowledge and awareness of the successive stages and developmental nature of the operation. The emphasis would then increasingly be upon the appropriateness of each task to the observed level of motivation.

A change in the climate of opinion is perhaps indicated also in the comparison of Kent and London teachers' answers concerning the major considerations which affected the type of instruction given. The ability and professional skills of teachers, in particular their knowledge and experience of the stages in the teaching of the subject, increase in importance when the curriculum itself is of high significance. Fewer London heads mentioned the needs of individual children as a major consideration, nor did they make much of the size of classes; the relative sizes of the classes in the Kent and London studies were not established in fact. The size of the class assumes less importance, if one's approach is not predominantly child-centred with its emphasis upon individual rather than group or class instruction.

If these differences represent a swing of opinion towards more formal approaches, one might expect there to be a corresponding increase in the use of systematic phonic instruction with five-year-olds, and that the choice of introductory method would be synthetic rather than analytic. Certainly there is evidence from the London teachers that a larger proportion of teachers were giving all pupils systematic phonic instruction earlier. And if we take account of the slight difference in the wording of the question to the London teachers, more were using combinations of methods, including phonics, in their introductory work than in Kent. Despite the view that an early introduction to sounds may affect later fluency and comprehension, and that a minimum mental age of 7 + is necessary for the comprehension of phonic elements, two out of every five infant teachers in London were giving systematic phonic instruction to *all* their pupils, irrespective of either the individual child's mental maturity or home background. A later stage of the research programme will provide information not so much to determine whether these teachers were right or wrong, but whether early systematic reading instruction has different results in terms of the particular social environment of the schools.

READING MATERIALS AND LIBRARY FACILITIES

Five years had elapsed between the carrying out of the Kent inquiry and the London survey. It may be that this lapse of time is alone the reason for the extremely rapid increase in the popularity of a particular reading series, *Janet and John.* This series was reported as being in use in more than half the London schools in comparison with one in five of those in Kent. The scheme had come on the market only three years before the Kent inquiry and an increase in the use of the scheme could have been anticipated from the answers of the teachers at that time, in the same way that there were suggestions in discussions with the teachers during the London inquiry that the McKee reading scheme was gaining ground. Another fact that should be remembered is that the design of the *Janet and John* scheme provides for the choice of a phonic or whole-word approach, so that the scheme has an appeal to a larger group of teachers than one based on a single approach.

However, the immense popularity of a single series is worthy of comment. Only 18 per cent of the London infant schools were using two or more schemes. The reading scheme or series with its set of readers of increasing difficulty appears to be of immense help to teachers and to provide a source of security, especially to infant teachers straight from college. These appeared to find the manual of instruction and the controlled vocabulary of particular help, since some of these young teachers reported that they had had only limited instruction in the actual mechanics of teaching reading in their training colleges; although most had no complaints about the opportunity their lecturers had provided for looking at different reading schemes and materials.

It can be argued also that the use of one particular scheme in so many schools may be of considerable benefit when more and more children change from school to school because their families move. The introductory book of this series is centred on two children, presented as predominantly middle class stereotypes. The appeal of this to children of vastly different social backgrounds is questionable; the writer recalls the disgusted comment of a lower working class five-year-old who summed up John as 'soppy' and refused to show any interest in his exploits.

The popularity of a single scheme and the fact that only nine London schools did not use a basic scheme in the reception class supports the view that teachers' opinions have somewhat changed since the Kent inquiry. Increasingly, emphasis is being placed on the value of the reading scheme itself as a form of curriculum, by publishers in particular. It was therefore not unexpected to find that the infant schools were making considerable use of reading apparatus. But it is important to note that both the published and the teacher-made type were in use, and that only a small proportion of schools was using such apparatus for class purposes only.

Undoubtedly this type of material plays an important part in teaching beginners, providing opportunities for practice and enabling repetitive learning to be more enjoyable. Since reading apparatus was being used so widely in the infant school, the reluctance, reported in the Kent inquiry, of junior teachers to utilise such teaching aids assumes even more importance. Over half the junior schools in the Kent inquiry did not use reading apparatus at all, since they considered that children over seven regarded such material as 'babyish', and therefore tended to derive little benefit from it. Obviously such material must have infant school connotations for junior pupils, but it is difficult to justify the exclusion of aids found of such value to the infant learner for this reason alone—especially when one considers the low reading standards of some children in the first-year junior classes. The present survey shows that the 'infant only' schools had taken every opportunity to establish libraries for their pupils' use and that often an immense amount of thought and imagination had gone into the setting up of these collections. In comparison with Kent these urban schools, especially the 'infant only' ones, were infinitely better placed regarding library facilities. Undoubtedly the efforts by publishers over the last five years to provide reading material suitable for infants have contributed to the generally high standard of library facilities available in infant schools. But it must be added that the view expressed by teachers in the Kent inquiry 'that the material available for lower juniors was too limited' received support from the teachers of the older infants in the London survey. There is still a need at this stage for additional material if publishers could supply it.

ASSESSMENT OF READING ABILITY

It was suggested by the Consultative Committee on the Primary School (Board of Education, 1931, reprinted 1952) that the task of the junior school teacher was predominantly that of developing reading comprehension, since only a few 'backward' children would be in need of systematic instruction in reading mechanics after the age of seven. In fact the Kent inquiry reported that approximately 45 per cent of the children entering the junior school were still in need of the kind of teaching associated with the infant school. In the London survey it was noticeable that infant teachers, especially those in the 'infant only' type of school, experience anxiety in respect to the standards expected of their pupils by the end of their schooling. It is hoped that findings such as those of the Kent inquiry may to some extent alleviate this. Certainly, the unrealistic approach of some educationists towards the problems of teaching infants, permitted assumptions such as that quoted regarding the main function of the junior teacher. The wide range of abilities of children, the varying effect of home background on motivation to read, and the varying length of time spent by pupils in the infant school, must set limitations upon the achievement which can be attained by the majority of pupils by the end of the infant school course. The London infant teachers, estimating the levels of attainment possible by the time of transfer, suggested proportions of good and poor readers similar to those actually found in the Kent inquiry at the beginning of the junior school course. Since the standards attained in Kent by the end of the primary course were above average for the country as a whole, the London teachers were generally setting themselves fairly high standards. The infant teachers were only too well aware of factors which could affect the standards they hoped to attain, and it is one of the aims of the further stages of the research to examine the effect of teachers' aspirations for their pupils on their achieved level of attainment, especially within the different social areas.

The needs of children of below average intelligence, handicapped by unfavourable circumstances, was a major problem of teachers in the junior school, and a number of the Kent teachers considered that the best method of dealing with this was to secure the services of an experienced teacher, who could remain unattached to a class and provide individual help, although in fact this solution was rarely possible at the time of the Kent inquiry. The present survey found these infant schools were, for certain reasons, more favourably placed in regard to having additional assistance, which was used to help pupils making inadequate progress. It was very noticeable that, although both types of infant school were divided as to the applicability of the term 'backward' to infant children, significantly more 'infant only' schools made every effort to make special provision for those pupils in need of additional help, whether they might be described as 'backward', 'slow' or 'late developers'. This appears to be clear evidence of the anxiety felt by the teachers in the separate department schools at the prospect of their pupils' transfer at seven.

Despite the problem of the backward reader, the Kent inquiries found that junior teachers made relatively little use of diagnostic tests. The London infant teachers were asked about their use of standardised reading tests, and almost twice as many schools were found to be using standardised tests as in Kent. This seems more likely to be a reflection of the increasing acceptance of the reliability and value of this form of measurement to the teacher than a difference in practice between the two types of primary education.

TRAINING AND EXPERIENCE OF THE RECEPTION-CLASS TEACHER

An important finding of the Kent investigation was the need for junior teachers, especially those of the transition class, to possess a knowledge of infant methods and experience of teaching reading from the early stages. We were interested to know whether the staffing of the reception class in the infant school presented similar difficulties. The findings seem to suggest that, although there are certain problems, the situation is not comparable. Since few nursery classes exist, it is not surprising that few reception-class teachers have experience of these classes. It is unfortunate that, at the present time, there seems little prospect of any large-scale introduction of nursery classes; new entrants to infant teaching might benefit considerably from working with such classes.

School organisation and social area

The importance of school organisation appears to be closely related to the factor of size, and in Chapter VI it was concluded that the type of organisation mainly affected conditions related to size, such as the use of space, the existence of an infant library, storage facilities, and provision for backward readers which is related to the use of additional staff, as well as the pressure exerted by the transfer at seven. Certainly in this research, organisation appeared to be unrelated to the level of reading attainment, nor did it have any appreciable effect upon the choice of methods or materials.

The Kent inquiry showed that schools of differing social background were faced with very different problems in the teaching of reading, and having estimated the possibility of the effects of school organisation, we shall now turn to the other aim of this research: how do the schools in the different social areas tend to differ in regard to conditions of learning and practice, and the extent to which they adapt their methods and materials as a consequence?

The most important finding of this survey amongst urban infant schools is that, broadly speaking, the social area of the school had little effect upon teaching methods, materials, standards or even school conditions.

'Mixed' methods were those most often reported, irrespective of the social area of the school. Even the whole-word approach often described as suitable for use with duller children, was found to be no more popular in the lower working class area than either of the other two areas, despite the fact that significantly more of the teachers in schools in the former areas believed that their pupils were only of average or below average intelligence. Even when the controversial question of the use of phonics in the reception class was studied, the social area of the school made no appreciable difference in regard to this practice. In each social area, a similar proportion of teachers believed the practice to be effective.

It has already been mentioned that one reading scheme was particularly popular in all areas, irrespective of the pupils' social background and the environmental experiences which they might bring to the reading situation.

Although teachers tended to differ in the type of approach they adopted to the teaching of reading, being either predominantly child- or curriculum-centred in the approach they used, neither type of approach was found to be more favoured by the teachers in one area rather than another.

Asked about the major considerations affecting their choice of instructions, a quarter of the head teachers claimed that the particular social background of the pupils they taught was an important aspect, while a third considered the needs of individual children were the determining factor. In view of these opinions, it would not have been unexpected to find an association between the use of particular methods and certain areas, at least in regard to the choice of commencing method, if not a single basic one. Similarly, one might have expected to find more schools using more than one basic scheme and a greater variety in the choice of scheme. However, it appears that in most cases the needs of individual children and groups of children, of varying degrees of motivation to acquire the skill, are considered by these teachers to be met by the provision of a variety of supplementary reading material and the use of different types of reading apparatus, rather than by the adaptation of either scheme or approach to the problems and difficulties presented by particular environmental conditions.

The lower working class areas are those in which social conditions are such as to be least likely to encourage children to want or need to learn to read. It may be that almost exclusive reliance upon the provision of variety and quantity of reading materials is insufficient to arouse the interest of these children in learning to read, if neither method, reading scheme nor approach are adapted to their background experience and the values engendered by it. This is one of the questions which a subsequent report will consider in detail: whether significantly good or poor levels of reading attainment within particular social areas are associated with differences in method, scheme or approach, and whether it is possible to produce conclusive evidence as to the effectiveness of different methods and practice in the teaching of reading in areas of high or low motivation to acquire the skill.

FACTORS IN THE LEARNING SITUATION

The relationship of reading methods and children's social background has received scant attention hitherto in research into the teaching of reading. The exponents of the synthetic and analytic methods have put forward their claims for success, but the effectiveness of particular types of methods with children of different backgrounds of experience has scarcely been explored. In learning to read there are four very important factors:

1 the time at which systematic instruction is introduced

2 the form this instruction takes

3   the previous experience of the child, including his motivation and his grasp of languages

4   the experience, confidence and background of the teacher.

The stage at which systematic instruction can be introduced can be lowered if the reading task is simplified. The research to date seems to show that early systematic phonic instruction can produce favourable results, but since synthetic methods tend to depend largely on associative types of learning, this initial advantage may not be maintained, especially towards the end of the junior schooling where reading becomes a means of acquiring and using information—a communicative process and not merely word recognition.

In comparison, analytic methods, although possibly slower in obtaining results, produce reading for meaning and a more fundamental grasp of the skill. Also, analytic methods demand considerable opportunities and experiences in order to formulate the basic reading concepts underlying this type of learning pattern. Such opportunities and experience may have been provided by the child's social background. Where this is not so, the teacher may have to supply them and the rate of progress of these disadvantaged pupils is slower as a consequence.

LANGUAGE PATTERNS AND READING METHODS

The social areas differ in regard to the factor of motivation, but of equal importance is the form of language used in the social environment. Papers by Bernstein[1] have suggested that the working class pupils are users of a 'public' language, and experience difficulty in making generalisations and in concept formation, far more so than middle class pupils, whose language pattern is such as to enable them to extend their experience and knowledge by the elaboration of experience and the building up of new concepts. If this is so, it is possible that teachers in lower and working class area schools are setting themselves an extremely difficult task in teaching reading by analytic methods, since they are attempting to change their pupils' language pattern, and not merely to arouse a feeble motivation. Such teachers may ultimately succeed, but the rate at which the skill develops may be slow in comparison with users of synthetic methods, and never equal to that established by teachers, whose pupils have both the necessary motivation and the desirable experiences absorbed long before they reach the classroom. In comparison, teachers who use synthetic methods with working class pupils are using methods which fit in with the existing language pattern. Drill and repetition play an important part, and within the common language system, reiteration of words and phrases is a characteristic of the 'public' language. However, difficulties probably first arise with the introduction of the exceptions to the rules, and neither the language system nor the type of reading

[1] Bernstein, B. (1961), *Educational Research*, Vol. III, No. 3, pp. 163–76.

instruction produce the necessary flexibility of mind to grasp and use these exceptions. Reading for meaning can supply the ability to read the exception, the general sense supplying clues, but since synthetic methods tend to encourage a facility in word recognition rather than comprehension, this is the stage at which the initial advantage may be lost, unless the home and social background has supplied the motivation to carry the child past this learning plateau.

TEACHERS AND THEIR READING METHODS AND EXPECTATIONS

So far the discussion has been concerned primarily with the basic teaching methods in relation to differences in the background experience of the beginner. But one must not lose sight of the teacher. Her values, attitudes and expectations are of equal importance, and are probably intimately related to her own social class origin. For instance, it is quite possible that the teacher of working class origin may be more emotionally secure when using synthetic rather than analytic reading methods, but this does not presume that such methods will automatically produce success, if both teacher and pupils are of working class origin. It may well be that the working class teacher's expectations of working class pupils are lower than those of a middle class teacher, as the former is over critical and underestimates the potential ability of her pupils in order to emphasise her own social mobility and acquired social status, as shown by her gaining entrance to the teaching profession.

As yet there is little evidence regarding the effect of teachers' social class origin on their attitudes and estimation of their pupils' abilities, potential and achieved. But it is possible that such a factor is operating in relation to the tested and estimated reading attainment of the pupils in the London survey. The explanation for the similar reading achievement of the working and middle class area schools, in comparison with the significantly lower achievement of the lower working class children, is that the working class teachers in the lower working class area schools, by reason of their concern for their status, underestimate these pupils' ability. The teachers of middle class origin in the same area, may also do so because they are unfamiliar with such children and their level of achievement. In contrast teachers in the middle class area, irrespective of social class origin, tend to overestimate the ability of their pupils and depress the level of achievement, possibly through setting too high standards, which produce too great a level of anxiety in the pupils or dissipate their interest.

Teachers in working class areas probably have the most realistic view of the situation, tending neither to over- or under-estimate, and as a consequence their pupils' attainment equals that of the middle class pupils of whom possibly an unrealistic standard is demanded. For instance, the estimated proportions of 'poor' or 'backward' readers were similar throughout the three social areas, despite the fact that the lower working class teachers considered they had more children of average and below average intelligence. The trend, although not significant, was for more middle class area schools to make provision for such readers, whether they agreed with the term or not, than the schools in the lower working class area. The implication is that the teachers expect a higher standard from all children of 'better' homes, whereas a proportion of backward readers is considered to be inevitable in the lower social class areas. This attitude was implicit in the two characteristic types of statement which the writer heard from teachers while visiting the schools in the different areas during the field work. Often, in referring to the work of individual pupils, a teacher would comment: 'She should be able to do better, she comes from a good home', or conversely, 'What can you expect? He comes from a poor home'. This question of what teachers really mean by the use of the terms 'good' and 'poor' home background is treated at some length in the second report of the research, and has already been the subject of an article in *Educational Research*.[1]

[1] Goodacre, E. J. (1961), *Educational Research*, vol. 6, no. 1, pp. 56–61.

Appendix G

TEACHERS AND THEIR PUPILS' HOME BACKGROUND

by E. J. GOODACRE

What importance do infant teachers attach to pupils' home background in the teaching of reading?

Generally the teachers considered that the pupils' home background was an important factor in learning to read; they described those aspects of the home which they believed could actively assist that process, and the abilities pupils used in learning to read which they most readily associated with differences in home conditions. They most valued the provision of suitable reading material in pupils' homes on which pupils could practise their newly acquired skill, and the type of atmosphere in which it was taken for granted by parents and child that reading was a desirable skill to be acquired. Differences in home background were most readily connected with a child's desire to learn to read and his rate of learning.

How do teachers categorise their pupils in relation to home background?

The teachers in this study appeared to be familiar with the term 'good' and 'poor' homes as a means of categorising pupils. When asked to describe them in their own words, they used more motivational and cultural characteristics in describing the 'good' home. The 'good' home tended to be described as one which facilitated the teacher's task of instruction by preparing the child for participation in the formal learning situation and also for acceptance of the teacher's role in it. If a child showed no eagerness to learn to read, teachers believed that the difficulty of imparting the techniques of the skill was increased, because not only did they have to provide the appropriate systematic instruction (difficult enough if teacher and pupil used different types of language systems, dialect, etc.) but they had also to demonstrate to pupils that reading was a desirable and necessary skill.

When teachers rated the different characteristics of a 'good' home, the school's social area assumed importance. For instance, there was little difference between the ratings of teachers in middle and upper working class areas, but particular motivational and cultural items assumed importance as distinguishing characteristics between the two working class groups. These items were the ability of the parents to answer their children's questions, to provide stimulating experiences in the home and to help with school work; parents' own levels of education and intelligence, and the presence of 'good' conversation and manners in the home. Comparing the extreme social area groups, the items regarded as most important in providing a stable home background were a religious faith, parental help with school work, stable emotional home life, and a mother who did not go out to work.

Each teacher's ratings for the various items were added up to give a total score for this question, and if high scores can be interpreted as indicative of an interest in the contribution of the 'good' home, it seems likely that such an interest is related to the individual teacher's age and general personality type. The findings suggest that it is more likely to be the older and more authoritarian type of teacher, with unfavourable attitudes to pupils and their homes, who is most likely to categorize pupils in terms of 'good' or 'poor' homes.

What is the extent of teachers' personal contacts with pupils and their homes, and what clues do they use as a basis for their impressions of pupils' home conditions?

It was found that amongst these urban infant teachers, contacts with parents seldom extended beyond meetings on school premises. Few school heads had established parent–teacher organisations, and few teachers ever visited pupils' homes. Two out of three parents[1] were said to visit the school, usually for reasons connected with the child's physical well-being, and since these questions were asked of teachers of young children, parental interest at this stage was largely an expression of maternal concern.

Pupils' records of attendance and lateness were not indicative of social class differences in attitudes towards the value of education, but pupils' reasons for being away or their excuses for lateness provided teachers, to some extent, with information about the pupils' home circumstances. There was, however, some evidence to suggest that certain types of schools might find particular reasons more 'acceptable' than others.

Teachers seemed to have little difficulty in finding evidence of a child's economic circumstances. Conversations, class 'news', or actual observations of personal belongings, etc., brought to school were considered to be indications of a family's pattern of conspicuous consumption. The type and quality of a child's clothing, even in today's welfare state, still seems to be a major 'clue' for most teachers. Obvious signs such as the bare feet of the 1930s have disappeared, but indications such as the suitability of clothing from the point of view of climate and weather conditions, and the care and quality of

[1] Since one in three parents are not seen by the teachers at school (even from the beginning of the child's schooling), one wonders to what extent lack of face-to-face relationships influences the teachers' assessments of parental interest—it may well be that the unknown, unmet parent soon comes to be regarded as the parent who 'takes little interest'. Douglas (1964) assessed parental encouragement by using the class teachers' comments at the end of the first and fourth years in the primary school and their records of the number of times parents visited the school to discuss their children's progress. It was found that on the basis of this assessment of parental interest, when parents took little interest, their children lost ground in tests and gained rather fewer places in the selection examinations than would have been expected from their measured ability.

underclothing provide a basis for comparison to the eye of the practised observer.

The teachers suggested a variety of ways in which the actions of parents could be construed as constituting parental interest in the child's reading progress. However, analysis of their answers indicated areas of difference which could well be the basis of misunderstandings between teachers and parents. There were, for instance, the different responses to the practical suggestion that parents should provide pupils with a copy of the reader in the school reading scheme, so that the child could practise at home. Firstly, provision of the reader and parents 'hearing' their children read at home was more often suggested as a sign of parental interest by the heads than by the class teachers. Secondly, the head's views as to whether the parent was expected to borrow or to buy the book appeared to be related to his own social class origin. A head of working class origin would be likely to consider a request from a parent to borrow a school reader as a sign of interest, but the same request to a head of middle class origin might be considered as a 'trivial' reason for a visit to the school.[1]

There was evidence to suggest that the type of school organisation has a bearing on the role expected of parents. For instance, more heads of the smaller, combined department school expected parents to take an active interest in the work of the school to the extent of visiting the school to ask about the methods in use, whereas more class teachers in the 'infant only' schools emphasized the parents' supportive role, expected them to encourage and sustain their children in their efforts but not, at this early stage in their children's education, to want to help with school work.

If paternal occupation is used as a criterion for assessing pupils' home background, how reliable are teachers as 'judges'?

The findings were that teachers' estimates were least reliable in the lowest social areas, probably because they were unfamiliar with the degrees of responsibility or training involved in manual occupations, and were less likely to be informed about the educational requirements or intellectual concomitants and responsibilities of the newer professions and the more recently developed occupations in technology. Also, these teachers appeared to have certain predetermined notions about the type of occupations associated with particular regions, and these assumptions had considerable influence—even to the extent of being sometimes more effective than the actual recorded occupations of pupils' fathers. The evidence was not conclusive, but it seemed likely that where records of paternal occupations were

[1] Department of Education and Science (1967): 'National Survey of Parental Attitudes and Circumstances Related to School and Pupil Characteristics', Appendix 3, *Children and their Primary Schools* Plowden Report reported that just over a third of the parents had *bought* copies, to have at home, of some of the textbooks their children were using at school. Considerably higher proportions of parents from the non-manual than manual worker families had bought textbooks.

not kept, teachers' inferences about the incidence of particular occupations in certain regions were less in evidence. However, in these circumstances the head's own social class background appeared to assume more importance—he tended to see the social composition of his school more in terms of his own social class origin.

What inferences do teachers make about pupils whose parents follow different types of occupation?

The teachers' lack of knowledge regarding the gradients of status in the manual classes was reflected in the tendency for teachers in lower working class areas to see their classes as homogeneous groups, and pupils as predominantly children of fathers with manual occupations. Their tendency to stress the power and responsibility of occupations which, in the past, were related to educational mobility and hence intellectual capacity, also led them to think of pupils from the lower working class areas not only as *socially* homogeneous groups, but also as being *intellectually* homogeneous; more teachers in the lower working class areas tended to accept that they had no pupils of above average intellectual ability. Further, it appeared from the teachers' comments that their own language system and academically biased education might make it extremely difficult for many of them to recognise unfamiliar forms of intellectual functioning.

To what extent do such inferences affect teachers' ratings of individual pupils?

In reply to the request to complete estimates, records and predictions of individual pupils' abilities, attributes, reading attainment and progress, it was found that the teachers in the extreme social areas were less reluctant to supply information about pupils' home conditions than the teachers in the upper working class areas. This suggested that the teachers in the extreme social areas tended to have well structured stereotypes of the type of pupil and home they could expect. It seemed likely that these expectations were related to their ideas concerning the relationship of occupational level, social conditions and intellectual ability.

Nevertheless, when the teachers were asked to rate pupils' personal attributes, school organisation rather than social area appeared to be the effective factor. The teachers in the 'infant only' schools tended to describe pupils in more positive terms and generally seemed to favour slightly different personality characteristics from those favoured by teachers in the combined department schools.

Again, it was noticeable that the teachers in the upper working class areas had greater difficulty in completing the assessments of environmental conditions affecting progress in reading. Teachers in 'infant only' schools also seemed more reluctant to assess pupils in relation to the quality of their homes and the amount of parental interest, possibly because the teachers in these schools generally seemed to expect less overt signs of parental interest than did those working in the smaller combined department schools. The 'infant only' teachers, therefore, had less concrete evidence on which to base their judgements.

The fact that more lower working class area pupils were rated as being fond of school and, in regard to intellectual ability, were not estimated significantly differently from pupils in other areas (although on the basis of the teacher's general estimates of pupils' intellectual ability, these pupils had been noted as markedly inferior) suggested that the teachers of these pupils may have lowered their standards of assessment; that is, normalized a lower level of ability in relation to their inferences about pupils from these social areas.

Evidence from the teachers' reading readiness estimates of pupils, suggested that the teachers in the upper working class areas, in comparison with those in the lower working class areas, tended to provide more opportunities for assessing pupils' perceptual development and were less likely to wait for pupils' 'readiness'. Their pupils' initial enthusiasm appeared to be steadily maintained and by their second year of schooling, they were well established in the basic pre-reading skills and receiving systematic reading instruction (letter sounds and names) and so were able to attempt unknown words for themselves and to proceed at their own pace. By the second year the lower working class pupils were undoubtedly showing enthusiasm for acquiring the skill, and possibly within a year the difference between the two groups would have been less marked. However, by the second year the approach of transfer to the junior stage of schooling appeared to affect the judgements of the teachers of the lower group, so that they were beginning to use more uniform criteria, e.g. estimates of pupils' progress and chances of success. We do not know to what extent teachers in junior schools in different areas make inferences about the different social classes and adopt diverging standards, but it seems clear that the teachers of the top infant classes react as if they believe that junior teachers will not diverge in their standards, but will rather apply uniform 'junior school standards'.[1]

Do teachers of infants have certain distinctive social and psychological characteristics, distinguishing them from teachers of older children in the educational system, which would be of importance in considering teachers' attitudes to pupils and their homes?

This study provided further evidence of the previously reported high level of professional satisfaction shown by infant teachers. Previous research

---

[1] The continuing influence of the 1931 Report of the Consultative Committee on the primary school, reprinted as recently as 1962, may have encouraged the use of uniform criteria of assessment by teachers in the junior school, since it gave the impression that the main task of the junior school teacher was to develop pupils' reading comprehension. It suggested that few children, except for a few backward ones, would require systematic instruction after the age of seven, and therefore the implication was that top infants would achieve a specific standard irrespective of length of infant schooling or social background.

indicated that, as a group, infant teachers had outstandingly good personal relationships *in school*. The present study suggested that the class teachers found their greatest satisfaction in their relationships with the children rather than with adults (colleagues or parents), whilst the major dissatisfactions were the low status accorded to infant teachers by the community[1] and the lack of opportunities for intellectual development.

These infant teachers saw themselves as cheerful, conscientious, sensible and adaptable. They believed their principle deficiencies were lack of ambition, originality, confidence and foresight. Their social background was mainly that of the intermediate and skilled occupational levels, and they tended to be predominantly 'first generation' professionals. It was not surprising, therefore, to find that they did not read widely in a vocational sense; but perhaps the most important implication of their social background lies in the fact that as a group within the education system they are likely to be verbally less fluent and articulate, less capable of putting ideas into words and arguing convincingly, which may be important considerations when they need to act as spokesmen for their pupils' educational needs. There was evidence to suggest that it was the heads who were more likely to be aware that such social and psychological characteristics acted as limitations on the scope of their role.

How far are differences in teachers' attitudes to pupils' home background related to psychological rather than sociological factors?

Whilst the infant teachers appeared generally to attach considerable importance to environmental factors, the way in which they reacted to these professional or group generalisations and the extent to which they used them—imposing preconceived and stereotyped categories upon their experiences with pupils and parents—were more likely to be related to their own basic personality. It was the more authoritarian type of teacher who tended to have an unfavourable attitude towards pupils' home backgrounds,[2] particularly in relation to pupils' parents. They were also more likely to feel pessimistic about the school's ability to change pupils' values.

Generally, heads had more favourable attitudes to pupils than had the class teachers, and the attitudes of women heads were more favourable than those of men heads. Teachers who preferred teaching pupils individually

[1] Bacchus (1967) reported that the male teachers in secondary schools with unfavourable views of their pupils tended to be 'more dissatisfied with what they got out of the job in terms of status, salary, opportunities for promotion, etc.' It should be noted that, in the present study with *infant* teachers, association between teachers' attitudes to pupils and homes and their satisfaction with their status in the community did not reach a statistically significant relationship. Generally, these infant teachers seemed to be relatively uninterested in opportunities for promotion. Only in regard to the *heads* was it found that those dissatisfied with their status appeared to be less optimistic about the school's power to change pupils' values (5 per cent level of significance).

[2] These findings, that infant teachers' attitudes to pupils' home background are significantly associated with the personality dimension of authoritarianism, agree with those of Bacchus (1967) in relation to male teachers in the secondary modern school.

rather than in groups, tended to be more favourably disposed towards their pupils and their types of background.

> *Do the personality and attitudes of the head have any direct bearing*
> *on the level of pupils' reading attainments?*

A head's personality did not appear to be related to his school's standards or to the staff records of pupils' progress or reading achievement; but there may perhaps be an indirect relationship, through the medium of the head's attitudes to pupils and their homes, which could affect the staff's morale and consequently their expectations of pupils' future achievements. It seemed likely that head's attitudes to pupils and their home background assumed most importance in relation to schools in the lower working class areas. The head's personality and attitudes may well be a crucial factor in determining the extent to which his staff are able to 'break through the barrier of IQ depression'[1] which tends to operate so strongly in these areas.

> *To what extent are these findings affected by (1) the type of organisation*
> *of the school in which the teacher works: (2) the teacher's position in*
> *the school: (3) the teacher's own social class origin?*

1. Some of the differences reported in relation to school organisation were undoubtedly related to the distinguishing organisational characteristics of school size and pupil range. The 'infant only' schools tend to have more pupils on roll, and their teachers have only a short period in which to become acquainted with pupils, so it is not surprising to find that the teachers in these schools experienced more difficulties in completing assessments about pupils' home conditions. However, there may be a further reason. The infant school philosophy of education may be more pervasive in the single department school, and since one of its basic tenets is the importance of the needs of the individual child, this may mean that less emphasis is being placed upon group relationships—pupils, parents, teachers. Certainly there was evidence that the teachers in the 'infant only' schools were less concerned about overt signs of parental interest, of parents being interested in the school's methods and activities. They may, of course, be more prepared to approach parents and to provide them with information. They seemed to take up a more positive approach towards both pupils and parents. They were probably less interested in achieving parental approval of their approach and methods than in ensuring that parents appreciated and encouraged their children's efforts, thus strengthening pupils' motivation to learn.

[1] Professor Kenneth B. Clark used this phrase in *Education in Depressed Areas* (1963) when describing the crucial role of the school in determining the level of scholastic achievement. He argues that standards and quality of education need not be lowered by the limitations set by home conditions; far more significant were the *general attitudes of teachers toward their pupils and the manner in which these were communicated.* Too many teachers, Clark suggested, maintain 'the pervasive and archaic belief that children from culturally deprived backgrounds are by virtue of their deprivation or *lower status position* inherently ineducable'. He proposes that schools 'break through the barrier of IQ depression', since many ideas about the absolute nature of intelligence are more relevant to assumptions about class than about education.

The findings of the present study suggest that the combined department school may more nearly resemble the traditional school system developed in the past in which the role of socialisation tends to be of primary importance, whereas the 'infant only' schools seem to develop an autonomous role, thereby cutting across local traditional reactions and possibly facilitating social change. How much these basic differences can be related to the organisational factors of school size and age range of pupils, and how much to the generally ignored fact that 'infant only' schools are staffed solely by women under a woman head, would seem to require further research. It can be stated, however, that there were no significant differences between the attitudes of the teachers working in the two types of schools. Again, further research would be necessary to evaluate the importance of the finding in relation to heads, which indicated that they had more favourable attitudes towards pupils than their staff, and that women heads had more favourable attitudes than men.

2. Where differences existed in relation to the teacher's position, they appeared to be mainly the result of differences in the degree of contact with parents and pupils respectively. For instance, more heads described the 'good' home in emotional and moral terms, since they were often more aware than the class teacher of the parents' personal problems and were therefore in a better position to realize the importance of an emotionally stable home for both personality development and scholastic progress of pupils. More heads mentioned parents' attendance at Open days as a sign of parental interest, since, for them, this offered clear evidence of an additional visit made out of interest and not simply because of admission requirements. Too much weight should not be given to this point, but the reception-class teachers' answers gave the impression that many of them felt that parents only came to school to see them about lost property!

As has been previously noted, the existence of footwear and a pupil's general physical appearance were formerly considered to be the most reliable 'clues' to the economic circumstances of the home, whereas today the quality and condition of pupils' clothing, particularly underclothing, may assume more importance. The latter is more likely to be seen by the class teacher when supervising pupils' changing for physical training. Heads, however, appear to be more likely to rely upon their observations of parents for their 'clues'. In these circumstances the attitudes of the heads towards parents may have a more profound effect than those of their staff. One thinks, for instance, of the head who makes rules and tries rigidly to control the conditions of parents' visiting the school—an action which, in itself, may be a factor which contributes to the formation of parental and neighbourhood opinion. Since parental esteem is the head's main 'feedback' for awareness of his authority and prestige in the area, it is his actions in relation to parents in particular which will directly affect his status and satisfaction with his role. That this can be a vicious circle is probably exemplified by the case of the authoritarian head whose characteristic attitudes tend to antagonise parents, thereby bringing about the very social isolation which this type of personality fears.

3. In comparison with the other three variables, the factor of social class origin appeared to have much less effect. It seemed that generally these teachers had adopted the middle class values associated with their profession. When differences occurred, they related to attitudes concerning the use of money. Although teachers with a working class background appeared to have adopted the cultural values of the social class to which they aspired, they retained their original attitudes towards money. Probably their upbringing was characterised by financial difficulties, and entry into a higher social class involved for most a fight against economic odds.[1]

Differences in attitude towards the use of money may explain some differences in practice between teachers. One example brought to light in this study concerns the provision of the school reader for practice at home: teachers of working class origin probably assume that parents would borrow a copy if they wanted one, whereas the middle class teacher would expect the copy to be bought. There are probably other instances of differences and misunderstandings between school and home, which in fact involve differences in 'values' in the monetary sense rather than in the sense of moral principles.

REFERENCES

Bacchus, M. K. (1967) 'Some factors influencing the views of secondary modern school teachers on their pupils' interests and abilities' *Educational Research* vol. 8, No. 3, 147–50

Clark, K. B. (1965). 'Educational stimulation of racially disadvantaged children' in Passow, A. H. (ed.) *Education in Depressed Areas*, New York Bureau of Publications; Teachers College, Columbia University

Department of Education and Science: Central Advisory Council for Education (England) (1967) 'The 1964 National Survey: survey among parents of primary school children by Roma Morton-William, The Government Social Survey', Appendix 3 in *Children and their Primary Schools*, HMSO

Douglas, J. W. B. (1964) *The Home and the School* MacGibbon & Kee

Klein, J. (1967). 'The parents of school children' in Croft, M. *et al.* (eds.) *Linking Home and School* Longman

---

[1] Josephine Klein (1967) has outlined some of the differences which distinguish the traditional 'roughs' in the working class from the 'respectable' working class family. Presumably most teachers with a working class origin would tend to come from the latter type of home. In this connection, Klein makes an interesting point when she describes how the 'respectable' family takes pains to achieve standards of domestic behaviour and social interaction which will distinguish them from the 'roughs' amongst whom they live. However, the children in these families are brought up with the knowledge that the 'roughs' are 'different' from them only in style of life, but not in economic circumstances, and that a period of illness or unemployment or some other misfortune may be sufficient to push a whole family below the poverty line.

Appendix H

A SUMMARY OF i.t.a. AND THE TEACHING OF LITERACY

by JOHN SCEATS

In this book John Sceats makes the following points, based on his own observations and on his conversation with teachers who have used i.t.a.; they deserve to be considered carefully by those who already use i.t.a. or who may decide to do so.

A. *The problem of ensuring that the children are reading with understanding*

This can be a particular problem for those children who 'catch on' very quickly to the new code. Once learnt they can literally read almost anything —as one teacher said: 'This class could make a good showing at reading *The Times*.' Sceats comments:

> The temptation for teachers using i.t.a. with bright children was that the facility and fluency of children's reading might well blind them to the child's lack of understanding of the concepts and words used.

The headmaster of this particular school thought it was necessary to *de*celerate the reading process and treat it more casually, at least in the early stages. He thought that pioneer teachers of i.t.a. were often over-enthusiastic, even obsessional, about reading, and children's progress was therefore speeded up unnecessarily. In another school, however, the teacher (of second-year juniors) was impressed not only by their ability to attack and pronounce words that they had never heard before, but also by how well they phrased and expressed what they read, thus showing their understanding.

B. *The dangers of a 'caste' system*

It was put to Sceats in one school that where i.t.a. readers had become a small minority in a class the other children identified them clearly as a backward group.

A related difficulty is the question of how much classroom material to put in i.t.a. and how much in t.o., once some but not all children in a class have entered—or passed—the transfer stage.

C. *Writing fluency*

In many schools, Sceats found that the value of i.t.a. in improving children's writing was felt to be at least as great an advantage as its help in reading. Bright children were writing fluently in their second term at school ($5\frac{1}{2}$) and the majority were doing so by their fourth term ($6\frac{1}{2}$). In one school Sceats was told that written work which *had* been stilted and halting had become fluent and fresh, but in another, although children were no longer frightened of writing, they were 'without any ideas of what to write about. News written on a Monday morning is stereotyped and dull: they simply have nothing interesting to report.' i.t.a., in other words, is not a magic tool which the child can use to make his thoughts imaginative and interesting—but given that other stimuli are also present, i.t.a. can be very helpful in releasing the child's thoughts into written language.

D. *Spelling in t.o.*

Sceats noted that the time for 'spelling transfer' seems to vary considerably; in some schools pressure to conform to correct t.o. spelling begins in the infant classes while another teacher was happy to accept i.t.a. characters in a second-year junior class.

It is certainly not clear yet, from the available research, when is the optimum time for any attempt to persuade the child to write consistently and correctly in t.o. The whole question of the preferability of early or late transfer is confused. Downing appears to waver between a preference for a relaxed unpressured approach which does not hurry the child into t.o., and the more recent hypothesis since the Second Experiment that the more familiar the child becomes with reading and writing in i.t.a. the greater the degree of interference when he comes to switch to t.o.

E. *Some problem areas in the use of i.t.a. for teaching literacy*

Sceats picks out the following areas for renewed attention and investigations:

1 How much and what kind of pre-reading experience should be arranged?

2 What method or methods of teaching reading is it best to adopt?

3 Are reading and writing to proceed simultaneously or is one (which one?) to be seen as primary?

4 How is oral work to be planned?

5 Is i.t.a. to be used for *all* children in the school or only some? If only for some, what principles will guide their selection?

6 Is the transfer to reading t.o. to be arrived at as soon as possible or at leisure?

7 What criteria will be adopted for this transfer?

8 What principles of selection will be applied to the choice of books?

Books of 'good quality' have been stipulated, but what is meant by 'good quality'?

9 Which writing system will be used at which times for classroom communication?

10 How are children to be taught the mechanics of writing? With what method, and with what materials?

11 Are the children to write freely in the early stages without correction? If so, for what aims?

12 What will be the procedure for the transfer of children's writing to t.o.?

13 If 'creative writing' is to be aimed at, what conditions are necessary to achieve it?

14 What procedures will be adopted for the teaching of spelling after transfer?

15 Should the aim be to improve measurable standards of performance in reading (over a certain standard) or to achieve the same standards with more ease?

16 How can we use literacy for the improvement of general education?

Appendix I

i.t.a. AN INDEPENDENT EVALUATION

The report of a study carried out for the Schools Council, 1969

by F. W. WARBURTON and VERA SOUTHGATE

A. The extent to which i.t.a. was being used at the time of the survey (1966)

The results quoted by Warburton and Southgate are based on completed questionnaires received from 158 out of 163 Local Education Authorities.

1 Of the 158 LEAs returning completed forms, 140 were using i.t.a. in one or more infant schools or departments.

2 In 20 of these authorities only *one* school was using i.t.a. with infants and in a total of 57 authorities it was being used in four or less infant schools.

3 In contrast, in some LEAs i.t.a. was being used in large numbers of schools—in the case of one county borough 100 per cent of the infant schools were making use of the device.

4 The total number of schools in England and Wales in which i.t.a. was being used with infant pupils in the summer of 1966 was 1554; a figure which represents 9.2 per cent of the total number of infant schools in the 158 LEAs from which completed questionnaires were received.

5 The returns showed that i.t.a. was by no means evenly spread throughout the country. There appeared to be a tendency for schools in the south of England to have adopted i.t.a. less frequently than those in the north although there were exceptions to this pattern.

6 One further geographical trend which was most noticeable was the small proportion of Welsh schools using i.t.a. in comparison with English schools.

7 At the end of 1966 it was clear that only a negligible number of schools (32) had returned to the use of t.o. with infants after using i.t.a. chiefly for administrative reasons.

8 In these areas where i.t.a. was being used in infant schools, a total of 459 junior or secondary modern schools in 1966 were also using i.t.a. for

remedial purposes, compared to a total of 1554 infant schools using the device as a first approach to the written language.

9 Seventy-eight of the 140 authorities using i.t.a. in infant schools were also using it for handicapped and maladjusted children in ESN schools, remedial centres and classes for adult illiterates.

10 None of the 18 LEAs which did not use i.t.a. in infant schools made use of it in other circumstances.

B. *Southgate's summary of the verbal evidence*

GENERAL COMMENTS

1 Verbal evidence on the use of i.t.a. with infants was obtained from interviews with nearly 400 people.

2 The majority of the verbal evidence reflected favourable reports; only a small minority expressed doubts. The most noticeable trend was that the people nearest to or most knowledgeable about actual teaching and learning in infant classes were most favourably impressed while those who saw dangers and had misgivings were generally those who had neither used i.t.a. themselves nor closely observed it in use.

3 By 1966 local officials had observed i.t.a. being used with infants in schools which exhibited every possible variety and combination of such factors as socio-economic level, range of intelligence, size, organisation, attitudes to reading and formality and informality of working procedures.

OBSERVED RESULTS OF USING i.t.a.

Reading:

1 The majority of teachers who had used i.t.a. as a method of beginning reading with infants found that children made better progress than could have been expected with t.o. The children learned to read earlier, more easily and more happily. They understood what they were reading and developed habits of independent reading which led to an extension of their interests in many subjects.

2 The observations of HM Inspectors supported those of teachers regarding children's reading progress, their improved attitude to reading and their comprehension of what they read.

3 The majority of those local advisers with wide experience of observing i.t.a. in infant classes were in agreement with teachers and HM Inspectors regarding children's reading progress.

4 A minority of local advisers thought that the introduction of i.t.a. had made little difference to infant reading standards. While certain of these

advisers had only slight experience of i.t.a., others had observed its use quite closely.

5 The parents of infants who had been taught to read by i.t.a. were generally pleased with their progress.

6 The effect on children's reading standards of having learned to read initially with i.t.a. was not nearly as pronounced by the age of about eight as in the early infant classes. Opinions were fairly equally divided as to whether or not those infants who had learned to read early and quickly with i.t.a. retained this advantage in junior classes.

7 Certain teachers of junior classes, containing children taught to read originally both by i.t.a. and by t.o., found their reading performances at eight and nine to be indistinguishable. Other teachers, although stating that the level of reading ability was similar for the groups of children taught by both methods, had nevertheless noted that children who had originally learned to read with i.t.a. read independently, more often, for longer periods and with greater interest and understanding than children taught to read entirely with t.o.

8 Some headteachers with class teachers of junior schools, HM Inspectors and local education authority advisers commented that the use of i.t.a. had resulted in fewer non-readers and slow readers entering junior classes. Others had noted no reduction in the numbers of such children.

9 Not one teacher who had used i.t.a. with infants, or who had been in charge of such children when they entered junior schools or classes, remarked on any injurious effect on children's reading progress which he or she had observed. The same was true of HM Inspectors, local inspectors and other frequent and knowledgeable visitors to i.t.a. schools.

10 Without exception, every teacher who had seen children transfer from i.t.a. to t.o. in reading was of the opinion that this transition caused no difficulty. HM Inspectors, local inspectors and other visitors to schools who had closely observed this stage were in full agreement with the teachers.

11 Teachers themselves, as well as knowledgeable visitors to schools, commented that the use of i.t.a. had resulted in less dependence on basic reading schemes in infant classes.

12 Doubts were expressed by all concerned as to whether the quantity and quality of books available was yet[1] adequate to cater for children's expanding reading ability and interests.

[1] This refers to the summer of 1966. Many more books printed in i.t.a. were available by 1968.

13　Teachers who were in charge of classes in which children were transferring from i.t.a. to t.o. found themselves faced with difficult tasks.

Writing:

1　An overwhelming majority of infant teachers who had used i.t.a. expressed their pleasure in the increase in the quantity and quality of children's free writing; many of them rating this as the chief advantage of i.t.a.

2　It was particularly emphasised that this free writing arose spontaneously, at an earlier stage than when t.o. was used, and that children were able to pursue this form of expression almost independently of the teacher.

3　The majority of HM Inspectors and local inspectors supported the views of teachers regarding the free writing of infants.

4　The minority of infant schools in which no improvement in children's free writing was observed, consisted mainly of very good schools which had always excelled in this respect with t.o.

5　The opinions of teachers of junior classes were divided concerning the free writing of children who had learned to read initially with i.t.a.; about half of them noted an improvement, while the remainder saw no difference or made no comments.

Spelling:

1　The overwhelming opinion of infant teachers and all knowledgeable visitors to schools was that the use of i.t.a. as a writing system had enormously simplified the task of spelling for children. It was this factor which was mainly responsible for the increase in children's free writing.

2　It was generally concluded that children's attempts at spelling in i.t.a. were much more often correct than they would have been in t.o.; even young children soon gained confidence in their own ability to spell any word and so become relatively independent of the teacher.

3　Certain parents rated it as a disadvantage that, when their children were writing at home, they were unable to help them with i.t.a. spelling.

4　Infant teachers did not consider that the transfer from i.t.a. to t.o. spelling caused children any difficulty, but a few teachers in junior schools took the opposite view.

5　There was general agreement among infant teachers, as well as among advisers and inspectors, that the transfer in spelling should take place later than the transfer in reading and that mixed t.o. and i.t.a. spellings should be accepted for a considerable time. Many infant teachers found some direct instruction in t.o. spelling rules to be helpful to children at the transition stage.

6   No infant teachers expressed the view that children who had been taught by i.t.a., once they had made the transfer to t.o. spelling, were less able spellers than children who had used t.o. from the beginning.

7   Most teachers of junior classes had little to say concerning children's spelling ability. Of those who did comment, some spoke of an improvement in children's spelling ability while others had doubts about the transfer. The views of HM Inspectors and local advisers also varied regarding the effects of i.t.a. on the spelling ability of junior children.

8   The one main fact which did emerge from the small amount of available evidence on the spelling ability of junior children was that there had been no clearly observed deterioration in the spelling of children who had learned to read and write with i.t.a. and later transferred to t.o., although such a result had originally been rather widely feared.

Effect on other aspects of school life:

1   Infant teachers who had used i.t.a. were generally impressed by its beneficial effects on subjects other than the language arts. It was noted that the shorter time required to master the skills of reading and writing enabled more time to be spent on other aspects of the curriculum. Children's early skill in reading and writing helped them with other subjects, for example mathematics, and facilitated an increase in the use of individual heuristic methods of learning. Most HM Inspectors and local advisers also counted this as one of the advantages of i.t.a.

2   On the whole, junior teachers had much less to say about the effect of i.t.a. on other subjects than had infant teachers, although certain head-teachers mentioned this point.

3   The majority of infant teachers who had used i.t.a. commented on improvements in children's attitudes and personal behaviour; interest, liveliness, confidence, independence and responsibility being mentioned in this context.

4   Many junior teachers, although not such a large majority as among infant teachers, commented favourably on the general attitudes of children taught by i.t.a.

5   More than half of HM Inspectors had noted an improvement in children's attitudes and behaviour; most of the remainder saw little change. The views of local inspectors on this point were similarly divided.

Results related to children's intelligence:

1   Most of the comments regarding the results of using i.t.a. with children of different levels of intelligence came from infant teachers rather than from visitors to schools. More than half of the teachers who had used

CHRIST'S COLLEGE
LIBRARY

i.t.a. were convinced that children of all levels of interest made better progress in reading and writing than they would have done with t.o.

2 A small minority of infant teachers thought that as the brightest children were likely to learn to read quite easily with t.o., there was probably no need for them to use i.t.a. In contrast, certain teachers considered i.t.a. to be particularly valuable for the brightest children by 'stretching' them, in that its use permitted them to forge ahead on their own in so many subjects.

3 A minority of infant teachers spoke of their disappointment that i.t.a. had not helped the dullest children as much as they had hoped. A few local advisers also expressed their doubts on this point, in contrast to other local inspectors and HM Inspectors who remarked on significant improvements in the reading and writing progress of less able children.

Results in junior classes:
1 Although opinions were divided regarding the long-term effects of using i.t.a. to be observed in the reading, writing and spelling of eight- and nine-year-olds, two clear trends of belief emerged from the evidence:
   (a) Junior children had not suffered by learning to read and write initially with i.t.a.
   (b) The exceptional rate of progress noted by most infant teachers was decreasing rapidly and had often reached a normal rate by the time children were in first- and second-year junior classes.

2 Certain reading experts, teachers and other skilled observers had formed the opinion that teachers of upper infant and junior classes had not yet learned to capitalise on the early reading skill gained by children who had used i.t.a. It was considered that teachers of junior children needed not only to increase their expectations of what children could do but also to realise the need for giving children guidance and instruction in the more advanced reading skills, as part of a continuous developmental programme.

OBSERVATIONS REGARDING STAFF
1 Headteachers and local advisers were in complete agreement that all teachers did not achieve the same results with i.t.a. even when the children in their classes were considered to be of equal achievement level. In other words, exactly as in any other teaching situation, the results obtained by the most able and experienced teachers were always better than the results of less able and inexperienced teachers.

2 There was also an extensive measure of agreement between headteachers and local officials that, with teachers of all levels of ability and experience, children's progress was better with i.t.a. than with t.o. The exception to

this statement was represented by the views of certain local inspectors who concluded that children's progress in reading and writing was equally as good with the 'best' teachers using t.o. as with the 'best' teachers using i.t.a.

3 Support for the idea that the introduction of i.t.a. had led to a general improvement in the level of reading tuition came from teachers themselves, headteachers, inspectors and most other visitors to schools. It was concluded that the publicity about i.t.a., and the fact that many teachers had read reports on the subject and attended lectures and workshops, had contributed to a renewed interest in both i.t.a. and t.o. schools, resulting in many staffroom discussions on varied aspects of reading. Greater thought had thus been given to the actual learning and teaching process, leading to a noticeable improvement in the standard of reading tuition.

4 Many local inspectors and certain headteachers were particularly favourably impressed by their observations of less able and inexperienced teachers using i.t.a. with infants. They noted that, as the comparative regularity of the alphabet simplified the initial process of learning to read and write, inexperienced and below average teachers were able to teach these skills more competently, with beneficial effects on the children in their classes.

5 One of the problems originally feared by headteachers concerned frequent staff changes, resulting in an influx of teachers who were neither trained to use i.t.a. nor experienced in its use. In practice, however, the majority of headteachers and local inspectors had been pleasantly surprised by the ease and speed with which new members of staff, including young teachers straight from college and married women returning to teaching, had familiarised themselves with the alphabet—a view corroborated by the teachers concerned.

6 A proportion of headteachers and advisers, as well as members of The i.t.a. Foundation, believed that teachers' competence in the use of i.t.a. could be increased by tuition in the form of lectures, correspondence courses and workshops.

7 Certain headteachers were of the opinion that the use of i.t.a. had contributed towards a friendlier attitude between members of staff.

OBSERVATIONS REGARDING EXPERIMENTS

The reading unit's first experiment:

1 Knowledgeable visitors to schools were mostly of the opinion that, in the Reading Research Unit's first experiment, the schools which had volunteered to use i.t.a. were usually in the charge of good headteachers who took a lively interest in new ideas in education. In most of these

schools there was a belief in an early rather than a delayed stage for beginning to read.

2   The main reasons given by the headteachers themselves for adopting experimental methods in their schools were, in this order: an interest in new developments in reading, dissatisfaction with the difficulties caused to children by the irregularities of the traditional alphabet, and concern about the reading standards in the school.

3   There was general agreement among headteachers of experimental schools that the most experienced or most able teachers in the school had been placed in charge of the original i.t.a. class, a view which was endorsed by local inspectors and other visitors to schools.

4   The majority of the teachers in the first experimental classes spoke of the original stimulus of knowing they were part of an important experiment, and their increasing enthusiasm as they observed children making good progress with i.t.a. Local advisers, HM Inspectors and other visitors to these schools also remarked on this exceptional wave of enthusiasm.

5   Teachers, advisers and inspectors all mentioned the shortage of books printed in i.t.a. during the first few years of the experiment.

6   Many teachers of experimental classes commented that, in spite of the lack of books, the results in their first year were better than the results in succeeding years. Headteachers, advisers and inspectors had noticed the same trend. These exceptionally good results in the first year were attributed to the quality of the teachers in charge of experimental classes, the pioneering spirit which resulted from being the first to experiment with this new alphabet, and the stimulation arising from early success. (Despite the less striking results in succeeding years, the majority of the first experimental class teachers were still favourably impressed by i.t.a. and hoped to continue to use it in preference to t.o.)

7   Teachers in the experimental classes stressed that they had tried to continue to use their former methods of teaching, as requested. Yet in many cases they had found that the sounding of words and grasping of phonic rules had arisen quite naturally in children at an earlier stage than with t.o. Nevertheless, neither the teachers themselves, nor local and national inspectors saw this trend as a movement towards more formalised phonic work—a trend which would have been disapproved of by many of them.

8   Many educationists, including lecturers, writers, inspectors and advisers and numerous teachers, had taken strong exception to the publicity surrounding the Reading Research Unit's first experiment, to the fre-

quent visitors to certain of the experimental schools and to what they considered to be the premature publication of results.

9 The large amount of testing and recording which took place in both experimental and control classes was deplored by the majority of teachers concerned. It was considered by them to be a strain on young children and far too time-consuming both from the point of view of the children and the teachers who had to undertake it. On the other hand, a minority of headteachers reported that they found the task of carrying out the testing interesting.

10 A proportion of advisers in those local authorities which took part in the first experiment also criticised the amount of testing which had to be carried out. Even more seriously, the quality of the testing and the reliability of the results were questioned by a few of these officials; their views, in certain instances, being supported by independent test results.

11 As the nine control schools visited in the Reading Research Unit's first experiment form only a small proportion of the total number of control schools, and as no special rules of guidance for the selection of these schools were employed, it should be noted that general conclusions regarding control schools cannot be drawn from the following observations.

12 The main reason given by the headteachers of the nine control schools for taking part in the first experiment was interest in new developments in reading. They were eager to be involved in such an experiment and many would have preferred to be experimental rather than control schools, but they had been prevented from doing so by the doubts of their staff. In fact, by 1966, seven of these nine control schools had begun to use i.t.a.

13 Of the nine control schools visited, two had been provided with new *Janet and John* reading books, while the remaining seven had continued to use *Janet and John* books already in the school.

14 The majority of the control schools had had few visitors and only occasional meetings and lectures had been arranged for them. No teacher or headteacher indicated that any of the lectures had been helpful and many voiced the reverse opinion.

15 Local authority advisers, as well as HM Inspectors, were divided in their views as to whether control schools had been well or badly served in the way of meetings and lectures.

16 Not one of the control schools visited appeared to have regarded the experiment as a contest between different schools using different media

for beginning reading. The staffs stated that they had consciously tried to give no more emphasis to reading than formerly and to continue to use their normal methods. The majority of local inspectors concerned endorsed these statements. Further corroboration came from the results of standardised reading tests which were given annually at 7+, in some instances, and which showed little variation after the schools became control schools.

The reading research unit's second experiment

1   As only two of the schools taking part in the Reading Research Unit's second experiment were visited, it cannot be assumed that the views expressed were representative of all the experimental schools.

2   Although the teachers concerned had been interested to take part in the experiment, they had found the experimental conditions neither easy to work under nor personally satisfying. The separation of the day's timetable into two parts, in the charge of two separate teachers, represented an artificial division, at variance with normal infant-class routine in which all the subjects of the curriculum overflow into, merge with, and reinforce each other.

THE ADVANTAGES AND DISADVANTAGES OF i.t.a.

It should be emphasised that the majority of the verbal evidence collected in this evaluation weighted the advantages of using i.t.a. for beginning reading and writing with infants much more heavily than the disadvantages; the latter being frequently expressed as doubts or dangers rather than disadvantages.

When asked about the advantages and disadvantages of i.t.a. more than half the infant teachers who had used it approved of it so thoroughly that they could see no disadvantages and, accordingly, were only able to list advantages. Other teachers who basically approved of i.t.a. were nevertheless aware of certain dangers. The same was true of HM Inspectors, local officials, other educationists and parents, who noted a few disadvantages, even when their conclusions were in favour of i.t.a.

Many of the misgivings originally felt by certain people, when the use of i.t.a. was first proposed, had proved in practice to be unfounded. Nevertheless, some of these doubts continue to be expressed by people who are lacking in personal experience of working with, or observing, children using i.t.a.

The main advantages and disadvantages put forward by all the different categories of people interviewed are summarised in the following lists. Those doubts or dangers which were mentioned by people who had seen little of i.t.a. in practice, and which experience had disproved, have not been included.

The main advantages of i.t.a.:

1 The use of i.t.a. has made the early stages of learning to read easier and more enjoyable for children. As a consequence they learn to read earlier and in a shorter space of time.

2 This early reading is not merely sounding words but is usually reading with understanding.

3 Children soon find they can make successful attempts to read unknown words themselves, without help from teachers. As a result, young children choose to read individually more often than when t.o. is used, read for longer periods of time and read many more books.

4 The materials read by infants soon extended beyond those of a basic reading scheme into a wide variety of story books, information books and reference books, as well as comics, newspapers, magazines, pamphlets and so on.

5 i.t.a. has brought about a reduction in the number of non-readers and struggling readers in infant classes and has consequently reduced the frustration and lack of confidence formerly experienced by children who found difficulty in reading with t.o.

6 The beneficial effect of the introduction of i.t.a. on children's free writing was listed as one of its main advantages quite as frequently as its effect on reading.

7 The comparative regularity of the sound/symbol relationship has resulted in children's early discovery that they can make good attempts at spelling any word for themselves. The result has been a marked increase in the quantity and quality of children's free written work.

8 Children who have learned to read and write easily and happily with i.t.a. tend to develop confidence and independence and to show initiative and responsibility in other aspects of school life at a quite early age.

9 The early mastery of the skills of reading and writing, together with the independent and confident attitudes developed by children, has led naturally to an increase in individual study and exploration which is in line with current heuristic methods of learning.

10 The use of i.t.a. has benefited work other than reading and writing in infant classes in two different ways. Firstly children's earlier skill in reading and writing has been instrumental in extending their understanding of other subjects, for example mathematics and science. Secondly, the fact that children master the basic skills of reading and writing with greater ease and speed has enabled the teacher to devote more time to the needs of individual children and to aspects of the curriculum other than the language arts.

11 Teachers themselves obtain greater pleasure and satisfaction in children's progress in reading and writing. They spoke with feeling of the end of the 'long uphill grind' of children learning to read with t.o., and the abolition of long queues of children waiting to ask for help in spelling words.

12 Teachers also rated it as an advantage that the introduction of i.t.a. has stirred up a great interest in reading among themselves; attendances at lectures and conferences, as well as staffroom discussions, have contributed to an increase in teachers' own understanding of children's learning, with a consequent increase in their teaching proficiency. This view was supported by headteachers, local advisers and other visitors to schools, who also noted particularly an improvement in the proficiency of less able and less experienced teachers when they use i.t.a. rather than t.o.

13 Teachers and others counted it an advantage of i.t.a. that its introduction has resulted in an increasing interest by parents in their children's reading, often exemplified by closer co-operation between parents and teachers.

The main disadvantages of i.t.a.:

1 Certain people, including teachers, parents, local inspectors and educationists, who were not only familiar with i.t.a. being used with infants but also favourably disposed towards it, continued to have misgivings about the effect on the children of using i.t.a. in the classroom while encountering t.o. in every other situation in their total environment.

2 There were instances of parents reporting the frustrations experienced by children, who were not yet ready to transfer from i.t.a. to t.o., when they attempted to read t.o. print at home in books, comics, newspapers and other printed materials.

3 Certain parents find it a disadvantage to be unable to give the help requested by their children who are reading or writing in i.t.a. at home.

4 Many parents, teachers and other educators are very conscious of the problem which arises when a family moves and a child who is not a fluent reader in i.t.a. has to attend a school using only t.o.

5 Local inspectors, as well as teachers themselves, are aware of the danger of infant teachers endeavouring to hasten children's transition in reading from i.t.a. to t.o. This problem is most likely to arise when slower infants are about to be promoted to those junior schools known or thought to be not very favourably disposed towards i.t.a.

6 Owing to publishers' doubts regarding the possible extension of the use of i.t.a. the number and variety of books and other reading materials available in i.t.a. for beginning readers is still small compared with

early reading materials printed in t.o. Furthermore, experience with i.t.a. has not yet been extensive enough to result in the most appropriate reading materials for the early stages being devised.

7 Once children have mastered the initial stages of reading, HM Inspectors, local advisers, teachers and others do not consider that the quantity and quality of books available for infants cater adequately for their expanding reading ability. This lack is felt not only in i.t.a. books but also in suitable t.o. books for young readers who have made the transition from i.t.a.

C. *Conclusions drawn from verbal evidence*

At the commencement of her own conclusions drawn from the verbal evidence, Southgate does not shirk the possibility of coming to a definite decision about i.t.a. rather than sitting on the fence:

> The basic question in the mind of a headteacher who has never used i.t.a. with infants runs somewhat along the following lines: 'If we were to change the medium of reading instruction in this school from t.o. to i.t.a. would the children be given a better start to reading, would they be happier and would certain children be prevented from failing? On the other hand if we continue to use t.o. in preference to i.t.a. should we be depriving children of certain benefits which they might otherwise gain?' These represent direct and practical questions to which an evaluation of this nature ought to attempt to give definite and honest answers unless the evidence proves to be either so inconclusive or so conflicting as to preclude straightforward answers. This as we have seen is not the case with the present evidence.
>
> Accordingly, before adding several riders, the straightforward answer to the headteacher's straightforward question is: 'Yes'; as far as the verbal evidence is concerned, if the headteacher of a school now using t.o. decides to use i.t.a. with infants as the medium for the initial stages of learning to read, there is a strong likelihood that in a large majority of cases, such a change will be to the advantage of most children.

CONVINCING EVIDENCE

As convincing evidence Southgate points to the fact that teachers from every kind of infant school including teachers with many years of experience in using t.o. 'have concluded that when i.t.a. is used with infants better progress is made than previously was the case.' The observed results include easier and earlier reading skill acquired without frustrations for the child; an increase in the time children choose to spend on reading, in the number of books they read and on their understanding of the contents of the books; an increase in the quantity and quality of children's free writing; an improvement in children's attitudes and behaviour and beneficial effects on other school subjects and the general life of the school.

ORIGINAL DOUBTS WHICH PROVED UNFOUNDED

According to the verbal evidence, experience with i.t.a. has shown that some of the original fears, of which the following three are the most important, are unfounded:

1. *The transition in reading*: In the whole of the verbal evidence collected in the course of this enquiry, no teacher or anyone else who had closely observed children at the stage of transfer reported children experiencing difficulties.

2. *The transition in spelling*: The evidence collected in this evaluation indicated that the early use of i.t.a. had not adversely affected later spelling in t.o.

3. *Changing staff*: Headteachers were anxious about how those probationary teachers and married women returning to the teaching profession, who were entirely inexperienced in using i.t.a. would manage. In the event, it has proved little of a problem, the teachers concerned soon feeling quite at home with i.t.a.

REMAINING DISADVANTAGES

About half of all those teachers experienced in working with i.t.a. and basically approving of it, nevertheless noted certain disadvantages, although these were considered to be less important than the advantages. The four main disadvantages which follow are arranged in the order of their importance as judged by Southgate from the verbal evidence:

1. *Continuity of i.t.a. instruction*: The greatest danger to a child who begins to learn to read with i.t.a. lies in the possibility that the learning process may be interrupted at a stage before he is ready to transfer to t.o.—either because he moves to an area in which i.t.a. is not being used—or if he is promoted to a junior school which is not anxious to continue i.t.a. instruction although the child may not be fully ready for total transition to t.o.

2. *The transition and the teacher*: Another disadvantage mentioned frequently in the verbal evidence was the heavy demands placed on the teacher in a class where *both* i.t.a. and t.o. are being used. Southgate points out that whether or not vertical grouping is used most teachers face this situation in an i.t.a. school 'because children transfer from i.t.a. to t.o. at such widely different ages'.

3. *t.o. outside school*: There is also the difficulty of the child being faced with one form of words in school and another outside it.
(a)   A few of the teachers already using i.t.a. expressed this fear.

(b) Parents' verbal evidence gave a certain amount of confirmation of such a fear.

(c) Most of the verbal evidence given by teachers who had used i.t.a., as well as Southgate's own observations, lead to the conclusion that this represents less of a danger than the preceding two disadvantages. Southgate adds: 'It could well be that it is simpler for many children to reconcile themselves for a short period to i.t.a. in school and t.o. outside school, than to adapt themselves in the initial stages to all the various rules governing the pronunciation and spelling of words in t.o.' She concludes that the real truth about this particular danger 'is that we have very little evidence available. Research into this question is certainly needed. What does seem fairly certain is that it cannot constitute a a very serious problem; if it did so the reading progress of those children whose early medium of reading instruction was i.t.a. would not be so great as the verbal evidence so clearly shows it to be.'

4. *Reading materials*: By the academic year 1966–67 certain teachers, local advisers and HM Inspectors still considered the supply of reading materials to be inadequate in quality and in variety and consequently counted this as one of the disadvantages of i.t.a. Southgate herself regards this as the least of the disdavantages, however, on the grounds that 'it can be said that many children have already learned to read easily and speedily with i.t.a. despite the shortage of books'.

EARLY READING

All the verbal evidence, as well as published reports, emphasises that children begin to read and write earlier with i.t.a. than with t.o. Southgate comments that in spite of apprehension on this score by some educationists, 'Early reading *per se* is not to be decried unless the child is being forced to attempt something beyond his capabilities. There is no evidence whatsoever of this happening with i.t.a., in fact the reverse is true, in that the impetus towards early reading comes from the child and not from the teacher. Most children come to school eager to learn to read and write and with this particular simplified spelling system, they soon find themselves able to do so.

Southgate continues: 'It is concluded that this trend towards earlier reading and writing which springs from the child himself, carries with it considerable advantages ... Among them should be counted the child's pride and satisfaction when he masters the skills of reading and writing; the value to him of acquiring an additional means of communication; and the development of his confidence, initiative and independence which results in an extension of his interests. Moreover the early reading and writing of the large majority of children leave the teachcr more time to devote to slower children and those with other special needs.'

DIFFERENT CLIMATE IN SCHOOLS

When t.o. is the method of initial reading instruction its irregularity makes it inevitable that children are dependent upon the teacher for perhaps the first year or two, sometimes considerably longer. The child needs to be taught to recognise new words and then to practise them in a variety of ways before he is ready to progress to the next page or story in a reading scheme, the timing of each stage of progress usually depending on the teacher's decision. When the child begins to make attempts at reading and writing on his own he is handicapped by the necessity to consult the teacher frequently regarding the pronunciation or spelling of words. Within this sort of working framework in which the teacher always initiates the next step in the learning process, and the child frequently needs to consult her, it is inevitable that the teacher should, to some extent, represent an authoritarian figure. On the other hand, when i.t.a. is employed, the diminution of the necessity for the teacher to teach and the child to consult leads the child to regard the teacher as much less of an authoritarian figure and himself as more of an equal. Thus the relationship between teacher and child and the classroom regime nearly always becomes more democratic and more informal.

Secondly, the independence gained by the child using this simplified spelling system frequently results in the development of confidence, initiative and so on in the child. These two forces working together have increased the noticeable movement in infant schools towards heuristic methods of learning, embodying individual interests and exploration within informal working relationships.

TEACHERS OF READING

Southgate points out that in view of the inadequacy still of the 'learning-to-read' courses in many colleges of education, in addition to the number of married women returning to teaching who may never have taught in infant schools before, 'the teacher who is experienced and knowledgeable may well be the exception rather than the rule'. In view of this the fact that 'learning to read with i.t.a. requires less skilled teaching than learning to read with t.o.' can be regarded as a positive advantage from the teacher's point of view as well as from the child's.

THE ADVANTAGES OF i.t.a. DO NOT LAST

Comments made by teachers in junior classes and by knowledgeable visitors to schools, as well as reports of research findings, all indicate that by the approximate age of eight, the early advantages in reading and writing gained by children who have used i.t.a. are diminishing or have almost disappeared. Southgate's visits to junior classes generally confirmed this view, although certain junior teachers spoke of other advantages in the form of personal attributes which they had observed in the i.t.a. children.

Southgate suggests that this 'levelling out' is not surprising in view of the fact that 'the acquisition of reading skills in schools is not looked upon as representing a continuous task for all teachers with all pupils, from infants to school leavers . . .' She adds that 'it is a rare event to find a comprehensive reading programme planned for systematic improvement in word analysis skills, vocabulary extension, comprehension skills, varying rates of reading and so on, or specific training in the utilisation of the various skills which comprise the total subject of reading'. At the same time, Southgate attributes the loss in many junior schools of the 'original free flowing writing' characteristically found in many i.t.a. infant schools to 'an undue emphasis on punctuation, paragraphing and the formal planning of essays, in a manner likely to obliterate the spontaneity of children's free written expression'.

Southgate also points out that such a levelling out round about the age of eight, 'does not discredit the use of i.t.a. for the initial stages of reading and writing. The aim was to simplify the initial task of learning—thus if learning to read has been easier and more pleasant for them, if fewer children have experienced frustrations and failures and if many have known the enjoyment and value of reading a year or so earlier than they would have done, it can be fairly claimed that the use of i.t.a. was justified.'

SLOW-LEARNING CHILDREN

Contrary to Downing's assessment (1967) on the results of specified reading tests that i.t.a. was not very helpful for slow readers, on the strength of the verbal evidence and of her own observations, Southgate maintains that the simplified system is of use for the following reasons:

1 Many teachers and advisers spoke of how the introduction of i.t.a. had resulted in a reduction in the number of non-readers and poor readers. Numerous examples have been quoted of schools in poor economic areas, using i.t.a. with children of below average ability, in which whole age groups of children were being promoted to junior classes with practically no non-readers among them.

2 Teachers who were disappointed when slow readers did not make easy or spectacular progress with i.t.a. were forgetting that it was only one of many facets of learning to read. They may also have made the attempt to introduce the child directly to the written language too early—whatever the spelling system they used.

3 Possible reason for the poor performance of slow readers on reading tests are as follows:
   (a) with slow-learning children, whatever the medium of instruction, measurable progress in *reading* should not be expected in the first year.
   (b) Reading readiness tests are not generally used in this country and thus the progress made in this preparatory stage is judged intuitively by the teacher.

(c) The reading tests currently used are extremely blunt instruments for the task.

(d) To test children in a different method from the one in which they are engaged in learning to read is not a practice to be generally commended. The exposure of the slowest children to this trial is to be strongly deprecated as it may undermine the children's confidence in their own ability to read and furthermore is unlikely to give meaningful results regarding their actual reading standards.

(e) If one accepts that the slowest children will take much longer than bright children to learn to read, it might be agreed that for such children to be able to read easy books in i.t.a. in about three years, even if at that point they have not transferred to t.o., would be acceptable progress. Southgate suggests that the most meaningful comparisons between groups of slow-learning children using t.o. and i.t.a. would be the results of tests administered, in the method being currently used, at the end of the infant school, supplemented by later tests in t.o. after the i.t.a. children had transferred to t.o.

(f) In the verbal evidence, teachers noted additional improvements with regard to slow learners 'far removed from test scores'; these included more interest in reading, a greater eagerness to attempt to read and write and an increase in the pleasure and satisfaction of so doing, with a concomitant decrease in the frustrations and occasional despair which some slow-learning children experience when using t.o.

(g) Even though they did so mechanically, slow-learners using i.t.a. were able to read aloud to the teacher and thus prevented from feeling different from the other children, or a complete failure as a reader.

i.t.a. NOT NECESSARILY THE FINAL ANSWER

Although Southgate's independent evaluation of i.t.a. is on the whole extremely favourable, she is concerned to avoid any encouragement of the assumption that 'i.t.a. is the total and final answer to the perennial question of the best way of initiating children into the skills of reading and writing'. She comments:

What has been achieved in the six years between 1961 and 1967 is remarkable ... That so many schools have been willing to experiment, that so many children should have learned to read and write so easily, that so many original fears should have proved groundless, that so much discussion about reading should have taken place among teachers and that the public at large should also have evinced such interest, has represented a phenomenon unique in the history of primary education in this country.

Nevertheless 'to conclude from the results that the use of i.t.a. is the final answer to initial reading instruction would mean that the ultimate benefits which might spring from this adventurous undertaking could be partially or almost wholly wasted. The experiments with i.t.a. have demonstrated other points than the obvious one that a simpler code is easier to learn than a complex one, of which the following three may be most important:

1 We have been brought face to face with the realisation of how little we all know about how children really do learn to read.

2 When someone who is not a reading expert can produce an idea which has proved so advantageous, one must consider what might be done if experts from different fields—for example, teachers, linguists, reading experts, educational psychologists, educational researchers, neurologists and so on—combined to consider the teaching of reading.

3 It has been demonstrated that given sufficient stimulus and support, British teachers, parents and educators, who are traditionally rather conservative, can be caught up in and become deeply involved in an interesting experiment with mutual gain for everyone.'

These points, according to Southgate, lead to one major conclusion: The use of i.t.a. over six years has shown that an alteration in only one of the factors which affect reading progress can effectively simplify the task of learning to read. The time is now clearly ripe for pursuing these investigations into simplifying reading and writing for beginners by comparing all possible means of simplifying the task, including comparisons of different media, materials, methods and procedures.

TESTS AND TESTING

An assessment of the evidence collected in Part Two of this report has led the writer to form the following conclusions regarding the testing of infants and lower juniors in reading experiments.

1 Testing programmes, even when these are undertaken by external testers, and the keeping of records, represent a serious additional burden to primary school teachers, most of whom are already fully occupied in catering for the needs of large classes of children of mixed abilities and attainments. Consequently, testing, record keeping and so on should be reduced to a minimum.

2 All testing should be undertaken by external testers who are not only adequately trained but also used to dealing with young children. If the testing is not properly conducted by reliable, independent testers, the whole edifice of statistical calculations which often forms the bulk of research reports, and likewise the conclusions based on this evidence,

can prove valueless or downright misleading. It follows that any research report based on test results should include full details of the backgrounds and training of the testers who were employed.

3　In experiments relating to the use of i.t.a., it would appear unnecessary in future to continue to test every child after the age of transfer to junior classes. All the evidence indicates that most children have not suffered by using i.t.a. as an initial alphabet. The continued testing of children who have long ago transferred to t.o. more nearly represents an assessment of what later teachers have taught, or failed to teach, than an appraisal of the approach used in the children's first year or so of schooling.

4　To make a regular practice of administering reading tests in t.o. to children who have not yet transferred from i.t.a. is unkind, unnecessary and misleading. It would be well worth considering the possibilities of testing children at certain functional stages in their reading progress, rather than at stated intervals of time. For example, every child might be tested in i.t.a. immediately before he made the official transfer to t.o. books, and then in t.o. at stated intervals for a specified period afterwards. Thus the only children to be tested in junior classes would be those who had transferred to t.o. immediately prior to, or after admission to, these classes.

In those circumstances, the comparison of results between t.o. and i.t.a. children would need to be arranged on some other basis than that of whole classes. One possible method would be, at specified intervals, to test the proportion of i.t.a. children in a class who had transferred and compare their results, on t.o. tests, with an identical proportion of the best children in the t.o. class. Alternatively, individual children might be matched and compared at intervals.

5　The majority of reading tests standardised and employed in this country represent inadequate assessments of the skills they attempt to measure: this is particularly true of tests for the youngest children. The evidence collected in this part of the present research project reveals the following flaws in test materials purporting to assess reading attainments in the first three years of children's schooling:

(a) No one reading test, standardised in Britain, appears to be comparing, in the early stages, the attainments of children who have begun to learn to read by different approaches. For instance, certain tests in common use favour children who have begun to read by phonic methods. To apply such tests to children whose phonic training will not take place until a later stage is clearly a meaningless exercise, in that processes which are taught later can only be fairly assessed later. In contrast, certain other tests favour children whose early reading experience is based on a look-and-say method; yet the opportunities of such children to score on these tests are unequal in that the early sight words they have learned by using different schemes or approaches may, or may not, be included in the early items of the test. Moreover, such children, because of the way in which they have started to learn, are not usually equipped to attempt to read words other than those already constituting part of their reading repertoire.

Chall's (1967) work in the USA also has a bearing on this point. Reporting on the 1962–65 Carnegie Study, in which numerous research results relating to beginning reading were evaluated, she concluded that 'different methods . . . tended to produce a different course of growth. They showed strengths on the different components of reading and spelling at different times. Thus, depending on what was tested and when it was tested, one approach tended to come out better than the other.'

In future, in reading research relating to infants, it would be advisable, even before deciding on the form of test to be used, to give prior consideration to the question of the earliest stage at which children taught in different ways can fairly be compared on the results of the same test. The writer would suggest that two or three years after entering school would be more likely to represent a realistic estimate than two or three terms.

(b) The inadequacy of current tests of the earliest stages of learning to read, for instance those administered in the first year, was clearly illustrated by the number of children using both t.o. and i.t.a. who failed to score on the Reading Research Unit's early tests, and by the evidence relating to slow-learning children. Test results consistently indicated a much larger proportion of children to have failed to make a start at reading than teachers and inspectors knew to be the case. Teachers working with these children were able to recognise certain stages in their progress which standardised tests were unable to measure.

The conclusion is drawn that assessments of reading attainments in the earliest stages should probably be more in the nature of diagnostic tests, attempting to map, in exact detail, those areas in which some learning has taken place, as well as disclosing those areas of reading skills into which the child has not been initiated. Tests such as those in current use, consisting of brief samples of items standardised in respect of average children at various ages, are of very little value when applied to young children who, although they have taken the first important steps in the process of learning to read, have done so by learning quite different words in different ways.

(c) The third flaw concerns the child who has acquired fluency in reading i.t.a. or t.o. He has learned to concentrate on the ideas being developed in the prose and to make rapid appraisals of the probable and actual meanings of new words, in relation to the whole context of the story or passage. To present such a child with a list of unconnected words is to ask him to perform an entirely different task from the one he has learned to enjoy. The results may show statistically significant differences between children, but these certainly cannot be taken to represent operational differences. Furthermore, even when so-called 'comprehension tests' of reading ability are employed, they rarely represent adequate assessments of what is meant by 'reading with understanding' in its broadest sense.

It is concluded that, in future research projects designed to compare different ways of beginning reading, attempts should be made to devise methods of assessment which more closely reflect the functional reading of children, at every stage, than do tests in current use.

D. *Conclusions drawn from the research evidence*

In his summary of the conclusions to be drawn from his own evaluation of the research findings which were available up to 1967, Professor Warburton supports the conclusions drawn by Southgate from the verbal evidence:

> The general conclusion drawn from these various researches is that i.t.a. is a superior medium to t.o. in teaching young children to read, and that this advantage may be lost after transition.

In the researches summarised in the present report only Swales (1966) finds that i.t.a. does not have the overall advantage. If there were no real trend running through all the researches we would expect the results to be less one-sided, sometimes favouring i.t.a. and sometimes t.o. On this ground our final recommendation is in favour of the use of i.t.a. (albeit with many qualifications).

Appendix J

USING WORDS IN COLOUR

1. *A summary of observations of children's responses to WIC in two English schools*

(made by Joan Dean, Chief Inspector for Surrey County Council)

In the Second International Reading Symposium, Dean (1966) reports on the use of WIC in two schools. School A, a six-class-entry infant school, had previously used the *Beacon* phonic scheme and continued to do so with all classes but one when WIC was first introduced. In the year following the introduction of WIC, the *Janet and John* scheme was used for the first time with a new entry. A comparison of the average reading age (set against the average chronological age) for classes using all three schemes (*Beacon*, WIC and *Janet and John*) reveals clearly 'that all classes except one, the WIC class, are reading at a level below their chronological age. The difference varies from −0.10 with the oldest group to −0.85 with the youngest. The *Words in Colour* group have a difference between average chronological age and average reading age of +1.61.' It should be added that the measurement as to how adequately or not the children were 'reading' was Schonell's Word Recognition Test; in other words, what was being measured was chiefly the child's ability to decode rather than to understand but clearly in this school *Words in Colour* had proved to be an effective way of teaching decoding skills.

'In another junior and infant school', Dean reports, 'the scheme is in use much as Gattegno suggests and is used as the main reading scheme for all beginners and for remedial groups of older children who originally learnt by other methods. The school is a lively one and it provides a really good reading environment with plenty of books and many interests for the children. The speed at which they learn to read and write is impressive and nearly all children read at levels above their chronological age.' (Dean also points out that 'it is difficult to know how much to credit this to the scheme since this sort of progress is not unusual in this kind of area'.) *The ability to discriminate sounds and symbols and to play with words and to puzzle out new ones is very strong* and these seem to be the special gains from this scheme.'

2. *A summary of a longitudinal study of two beginning reader programs; Words in Colour and Traditional Basal Readers*

(Doctoral study by William Dodds at Case Western Reserve University, Cleveland, Ohio, under Dr Mary C. Austin)

Statistical tests showed WIC to be a more effective 'language arts' program. Highly significant differences were found by Dodds in *word recognition skills* and in *spelling* at the end of first grade. These differences tapered off somewhat during second grade, but continued to be statistically significant. Mean comprehension scores for the WIC pupils were in every case higher than for pupils in the traditional programme, although statistically significant differences *did not* appear in terms of comprehension skills with the primary children.

One of the most encouraging results of the kindergarten–primary study was the *range* of achievement of the WIC pupils at the end of the first and again the second year. The *bottom* of the range was considerably higher each time for the WIC pupils. *The simultaneous learning to read, to write and to spell* was clearly evident. Dodd's conclusions were that: 'The visual imagery and attention holding assets of WIC at the initial stages of decoding, together with its constancy of columnar organisation, helped to produce the significantly superior scores of elementary age pupils.'

Appendix K

COLOUR STORY READING
A SUMMARY OF THE RESEARCH REPORT

In September 1967 Kenneth Jones published his research report on Colour Story Reading, 'An investigation into the value of phonetic colour in early reading', financed by the DES and carried out in association with the Reading Research Unit of the University of London Institute of Education. It is published by Nelson, and I give here a brief summary of its contents. The main experiment covered 19 schools, each school acting as its own control. The control group consisted of more than 400 children who entered the 19 schools in September 1964, and who were tested in reading and spelling at the end of their first year and at the end of their second year in school. The experimental group comprised a similar number of children entering these 19 schools one year later (September 1965) who were also tested in reading and spelling at the end of their first and second years in school. None of the children was tested in colour—all the tests were in normal black print.

MATERIALS

The teachers taking part in the experiment were provided with a manual explaining Colour Story Reading, *The Nineteen Stories*, the three small reading books, three sets of cards printed with pictures, letters and words in CSR dealing with the characters in the stories and the wall chart. During the second year tape recordings of *The Nineteen Stories* were made available to the schools in the experiment.

CONDITIONS FOR TEACHERS

There were 2 basic conditions for a class to be considered experimental:

1   The wall chart had to be on permanent display; the coloured reading books had to be readily available and coloured pencil and crayons on hand to permit the children to write in colour if they wished to do so.

2   The teacher had to read *The Nineteen Stories* to the children and to spend not less than *half an hour a week* on presenting the scheme in the classroom (this included the time taken for reading the stories); the time spent on CSR activities was not to be in addition to the usual allotment of reading time.

During the second year there were no conditions at all about the minimum use of the scheme. The reasons for continuing the experiment for a second year were to see if gains were maintained and to what extent teachers could use the colour symbols code as a frame of reference for helping children with their black print reading and spelling problems. Five of the nineteen schools did not use the scheme at all during the second year.

TEACHERS' ATTITUDES

Teachers' attitudes to the scheme were assessed on a 5 point scale in a questionnaire sent out during the second term of the first year. The teachers in the experimental group were asked to assess retrospectively their attitude to CSR before they started to use it and to make a second assessment on the same 5 point scale of their present attitude. The five points were: very sceptical, fairly sceptical, neutral, fairly keen and very keen. The results showed a substantial shift from 'sceptical' to 'keen' which would seem to indicate that the enthusiasm arose as a result of experiences in the classroom.

TEACHERS' METHODS

Teachers in the experimental group were recommended not to 'teach' reading but to present the materials in such a way that the children were able to use 'discovery' methods. General findings both from the investigator's own observations and from replies to the two questionnaires in the second and sixth terms of the experiment indicate that the teachers in the experimental group used direct phonic teaching to a *lesser* degree than they had in previous years.

TEACHERS' COMMENTS

From the teachers' comments it was clear that the children had enjoyed the stories and frequently asked to hear them voluntarily and that even the slowest children (the scheme was used with retarded as well as normal readers) had been able to remember many of the letters and their sounds from the clues provided by the stories. There was no case of a child experiencing difficulty owing to colour blindness in the experimental group. The use of colour for writing by the average children appeared to be less successful as it slowed them down; the retarded children, on the other hand, enjoyed using colour, although as they improved they gave up coloured pencils except when they wanted to spell a word they were doubtful about.

The headmaster of the ESN school made the further point that where previously difficulty had arisen with his children in the sounding of words through what appeared to be an inability to distinguish between short vowel sounds and other sounds, the use of CSR helped the children to overcome this apparent learning difficulty and in addition helped to eradicate the difficulty many children had of sounding letters without the ability to form them into words.

The question of *transfer of learning* from the coloured medium to black print was rarely mentioned. Jones suggests that this was probably because the amount of coloured reading material was so small that the children were never entirely 'on' colour. Also, the two media were identical in the shape of the letters and the spelling of the words.

Many teachers, in reply to the questionnaire, stressed an increased awareness themselves of the spoken sounds which the symbols of traditional orthography represent.

As far as regional accents were concerned, the only difficulties encountered in two of the northern schools were with impediments of speech and sometimes lazy pronunciation of vowels. The children remarked on the different 'u' sound for umbrella but they all agreed that it was the man on the tape who was pronouncing it strangely!

RESULTS

Within schools the two main variables appeared to be (a) the ability of the teacher (where the teacher of the control group did not follow through and take the experimental group) and (b) CSR itself, including the extent to which it was used in the classroom

SCORES IN THE MAIN EXPERIMENT

The tests used were the Schonell Graded Word Reading Test and the Schonell Spelling Test 'A', when a comparison was made at the end of the second year of the mean scores for Reading and Spelling between (a) schools which had used CSR as their main reading scheme, (b) schools which had used it as a subsidiary teaching device, and (c) schools in the control group which had not used it at all. The main score for (a) was 13 months ahead of (c) on the Reading and 11 months ahead on the Spelling Test, and the mean score for (b) was 2 months ahead of (c) on both tests.

CONCLUSIONS

Jones concludes that these results do not support the view that CSR would be of little value to the brighter children who 'would learn to read without difficulty anyway', nor do they support the expectations which might have been formed by the results of the first and second i.t.a. experiments, that there would be little or no measurable difference between the scores of the control and the experimental groups *in the lowest achievement categories*.

The results *do* appear to suggest that:

1 Children find it easier to learn to read and spell *in black print* when their early reading material is coded in colour and the sounds are conceptualised in story form.

2 The less the teacher relies on black print in the early stages the greater the achievement in black print in the later stages.

3 Children over the whole range of measurable intelligence are helped by Colour Story Reading to decode in the traditional orthography of the English language.

Appendix L

D. K. STOTT'S PROGRAMMED READING KIT

A detailed summary of the 30 pieces of apparatus of which the kit is comprised

I. TOUCH CARDS

These aim to make children *aware of letters and sounds* and to teach and practise *the associations between them*. The cards have a picture and a letter on one face and the letter by itself on the other. They are introduced in groups, e.g. the first series of Touch Cards only introduce the letters *m,s,n,g,t,r,c,w,l*. The making of the sound-letter associations is broken up into three stages:

Stage 1: Each of the children is given an *m* and an *s* card, with the pictures of *monkey* and *star*. They are told that the teacher will say one of these words and the game is to touch whichever picture they think it is to be. They hold a finger poised ready to drop it on a picture. The teacher pronounces *monkey* or *star*, stressing and prolonging the first letter. (cf. *Structural Reading*: the pre-reading programme.) The children are encouraged to touch as soon as they can tell by hearing the *m* or *s* sound which picture is going to be named. These two words are repeated in random order until it is apparent that the children are chiefly listening for the beginning sound and touch the picture even before the rest of the word is said.

Stage 2: The same procedure is repeated but the children are told to touch the letter beneath the picture.

Stage 3: Each child turns his pair of cards face downwards so that only the letters on the back are visible. They are then told to shuffle the cards round a few times so that they cannot remember which picture is on which card. The teacher once again says *monkey* or *star* and the children touch the letter; they then turn over their cards to see if they are right before placing the cards face downwards again and reshuffling.

The asking game

The children sit opposite each other in pairs. Each puts 3, 4 or 5 cards in a holder in such a way that he can see the pictures but the player opposite can only see the letters. One asks 'Where is the rabbit?', etc. The other takes the card where he thinks the rabbit is. If he is right he keeps it and places it in the holder alongside his own or on the table beside him. As soon as it is observed that the children choose the correct card for the first nine letters

242

reliably they should be introduced to the corresponding series of the Morris cards and then to the written exercises practising the same nine easy sounds—the '27s' and the Find-the-letter-strips.

2. MORRIS CARDS[1]

These are used 'to practise the letter–sound associations until they are firmly established; the children should finally be able to pick the right card instantaneously and with certainty'.

A Morris card is a single piece of card folded in two so that it will stand up, with four pictures and the words which they represent printed on the inside and the initial letter which is common to all four words printed on each fold on the outside.

Before the children play the Morris Cards game the teacher asks the children to identify the pictures to ensure that they are all using the same labelling word for each. The children play in pairs facing each other; each has 4 cards which are stood up like dominoes so that the child can see his own pictures but only the letters on the back of his partner's cards. The children ask in turn 'where is the . . .?' If the player asked takes the correct card *first* time he keeps it and adds it to his own.

'Children should be allowed to continue with this game until they pick the right card with alacrity, thus indicating that the letter–sound associations have become habits which need no pondering.'

3. '27s' CARDS

'Practice and testing of the letter-sound associations is an individual exercise.'

These cards have 27 pictures printed on them and the 9 letters which have now been practised on the two previous sets of cards in the top left hand corner. The rows of pictures are numbered 1–17.

The child writes out the row numbers 1–17 beneath one another on a separate sheet of paper, leaving room for letters to be put beside them. He then begins at the first picture and chooses the correct beginning letter from those given at the top left hand corner of the sheet. The teacher should do the first row with the children and should explain that each letter may be needed more than once in each row. The object of this arrangement is to impress still further upon the child that many words may begin with the same sound.

4. '9' CARDS (for further practice of the letter–sound associations)

A set of 6 cards form a pictorial lotto-type game. Each child has a card and nine counters. The teacher says to the group, 'Find a picture with a sound like *cat*'.[2] It should be explained[!] that there is another word *beginning* with a 'c' like cat. Each child finds the picture (present on *every* card but in

[1] Named after Ronald Morris who first evolved very similar cards (cf. his book *The Quality of Learning*, 1951, Methuen).
[2] This seems to be very badly phrased—only the word *cat* has a sound like *cat* . . .

varying positions) and places a counter over it. The satisfaction lies in filling the cards which the game allows all the children to do. The teacher is easily able to observe a child who is getting muddled because all the pictures will not be covered or some will have 2 counters.

5. FIND-THE-LETTER-STRIPS

These provide another written exercise in the beginning letters for use when all the sounds have been learnt. The strips of card are divided horizontally into two with five pictures spaced along the top half and above each picture the labelling word minus the first letter, e.g. -up (cup), -un (gun), etc. On the bottom half of the card the five initial letters are printed in a mixed order and the child has to write the appropriate letter at the front of each unfinished word.

6. CAPITAL AND LOWER CASE LETTERS

'To teach capital letters.'

A pair of children have a set of 6 or 7 interlocking capital and lower case letters. One child places the capitals in a row, the other fits the lower case letters. The *interlocking* is identical: the child is encouraged to match by the letters and not by the shape of the card. The letters are arranged so that there is approximately the same proportion of letters identical in their capital and lower case forms in each series; this makes the pairing of the dissimilar ones easier. After the children have got used to the exercise and are fairly proficient each can have a series and play a game of who can match up first.

7. 'ACTIVITIES'

'Practising capital letters and transferring knowledge of the sounds to them.'

The cards are in duplicate sets of different colours. The class or group is divided into two halves, each half having a set of the cards bearing the name of an activity. The children place their cards on the edge of their desks ready to lift quickly if theirs is called. The first to raise the card called by the teacher wins a point for his half.

8. BAT AND DUCK CARDS

'A revision exercise for those children who, despite all previous practice, still confuse *b* and *d*.'

The two master cards bear the pictures of the duck and the bat and ball. These are drawn to give visual tags to the direction of the letters. The remaining cards numbered 1–17 bear pictures and words with the beginning letters (either *b* or *d*) missing. The child completes each word by placing a *b* or *d* card against it, and then writes down the word. When in doubt he uses the master cards as a reminder of which way round he wants the letter.

9. HALF-MOON CARDS

It comes naturally to many children by this time to read simple phonic words. Others *do not get the idea at all*, and—what can be as bad—confidence-lacking children taught by the traditional phonic method may cling to a stereotyped 'building' of each word without making any attempt to advance to the reading of the word *on sight*. According to Stott this is a frequent but little observed sticking point.

The Half-Moon Cards are the central teaching aid for this stage. Their basic purpose is to help the child convert his knowledge of simple letters into phonic-sight habits *of two and three sounds*. He is thus provided with a stock of known syllables which enables him to tackle words by their natural parts rather than by breaking them up into single sounds. Stott records in a paper printed in the first *International Reading Symposium* (1964) how 'we reached our first major sticking point with our laboratory group when it came to "fusing" (or blending). We observed them struggling, full of tension; but no amount of cajoling "build it up" produced the fusion. Then we tried a shot in the dark—supposing we symbolised the fusion *visually?* We made up a set of the Half-Moon Cards with a kind of tongue joint holding the vowel and consonant together. They worked straight away.'

'If a child knows the sounds *c* and *a* we find that when they are placed together in the interlocking half-moon he "just knows" "*ca*". What actually seems to happen is that the fusing of sounds takes place unconsciously. Just as we avoided teaching the single sounds in isolation so we now avoid the traditional phonic method of building c-a-t. The teacher should encourage the child to read "cat" in a way which emphasises and prolongs the "ca", pronouncing the "t" very lightly' (cf. *Structural Reading*).

Stott adds further, 'Simple though this apparatus is, it is surprisingly attractive to children. The locking together of the shapes seems to give a primitive aesthetic satisfaction; it also symbolises the fusing of sounds. In addition the child seems to be encouraged by having to solve only one circumscribed problem at a time. By contrast, a page or even a sentence of reading matter brings within the child's vision a chain of problems which at this stage may be frightening.

'How many of the consonants and vowels are laid out to begin with will depend upon the mental development of the children. As soon as the idea of making words has been grasped the children can play with the Half-Moons by themselves with the help of printed word lists. One child reads out a word, another makes it, and the reader checks, awarding a counter if it is correct.'

10. TWO-LETTER CARDS

    (i) 'To establish the main two-letter word parts as phonic-sight habits.'
   (ii) 'To give the child a lead into the *middle* of the word thus overcoming any tendency to limit attention to the beginning letters.'

Each player has five folded stand-up cards with four pictures on the inside and the first two letters of each word represented by the pictures on the outside. The game is played in pairs again: the choosing child points to the card which he thinks contains the picture asked for and if correct is awarded a counter. Each of the five cards contains words with an initial letter in common so that the child has to sound the word out for himself, and then choose correctly from the second letter/sound as well as the first.

11. PORT-HOLES

'This gives further practice in establishing the phonic-sight habits of 2-letter word parts.'

The cards have 4 lines of 4 pictures on one side with the labelling word printed beneath each picture and a 'port-hole' directly beneath each word. On the reverse side the first two letters of each word are printed above the appropriate hole.

Each of a pair of children has a card of 'port-holes' which he holds up so that he can see his own pictures while the other child can only see the word parts (2 letters) on the reverse side. They ask each other where the pictures are and the answering child pushes his pencil through a port-hole. If he is right he receives a counter from his partner.

12. '25s' CARDS

These cards are similar to the '27s' cards and are designed to help the child distinguish vowel sounds in the middle of simple phonic words and the reading of such words with the help of pictures.

13. WHICH-OF-TWO CARDS

'To accustom the child to give due attention to the *end* letters of words and syllables and to give practice in reading simple phonic words.'

Stand-up cards are used with the *end* letter of each labelling word printed on the outside of the cards.

14. BRICK WALL

'To give abundant practice in the making and reading of simple phonic words; the familiarising of the common consonant combinations (*st, br,* etc.) and to introduce the idea of a dictionary.'

The 'starting frame' with the first two letters of five words printed on it and indentations for bricks to be slotted in, is placed on the left side of a table. About four feet of space is needed if all the 'bricks' are used. The bricks on which the last letter or letters of one word are printed and the first two letters of the next are dealt out to the players (2 to 4) who stack them with the letters upwards. Each in turn tries to place the topmost brick of his pile on one of the open ends of the 'wall' to make a word. If he cannot so do he may place the top 'brick' underneath his pack and try with the next one.

As the children become adept at the game the 'dictionary' card can be introduced. This acts as a check to which words are permissible. Sometimes

Stott notes that a child likes to build the wall alone, consulting the 'dictionary' as he places each brick.

15. NOUN CARDS I

These cards introduce the reading of more difficult phonic words with a very few irregular ones. The nouns used are those which will be met in the Sentence Cards I. The most meaningful words in the latter are thus read in advance. The cards are similar to Morris cards with the picture plus word on the inside and the whole word on the outside.

16. SENTENCE CARDS I

These cards are designed to encourage 'the fluent reading without tension of sentences mainly composed of simple phonic words and the perfecting of sight habits of a number of common words'.

The cards are similar to the Morris Cards and the children take it in turns to win a card touched by their opposite number if they can read it correctly. When these sentences seem to be known almost by heart the children should do the Sense and Nonsense I as a written exercise.

17. SENSE AND NONSENSE I

The purpose behind these cards is practice in reading for meaning, in coping with familiar words in a slightly altered context and the closer observation of words which is given *by writing*.

The sentences on the Sentence Cards I have been split into two and the endings paired with nonsense wordings which have a certain humorous appeal. The child chooses the proper endings and writes the rejoined sentence in his book (cf. *Structural Reading*, Mix-Ups and Fix-Ups).

18. CINEMA SEATS I

Whole words including adjectives, adverbs, and prepositions are placed on lotto-type cards in 'cinema rows' of four. The words of each row should be called separately to allow the child to limit his scanning to four words only, thus helping the slow reader. When a child has filled a row the teacher may ask him as a check to read back the words.

19. MAKE-A-STORY GAME

The purpose of this game is to familiarise the child with the most common irregular words such as what, which, there, are, come, together with practice in the sight reading of simple but slightly longer regular words. The simplest of the suffixes, *-er*, *-ing*, *-ed*, also *kn* and *y* as a vowel are introduced here.[1]

The scenes on the fronts of the cards indicate the story-sets, there being seven cards in each. The order of the cards in each set is given by the numbers

[1] The only other conventions used are those occurring in the most common 200 words based on the word-count of children's reading *Key Words to Literacy* by J. McNally and W. Murray (*Schoolmaster*, 1968).

in figures at the top of each picture, and in words on the story side. Each child is allowed to play with a set individually, arranging them in order and trying to read the story. A group of children may be allowed to work together informally in this way. They should also be encouraged to read the irregular words on the picture-sides.

20. TRICKY BITS

These charts are to let the children see that there are certain additional sounds which are written with two or more letters. (The analysis of these sounds was based on that made by W. S. Gill and Kathleen Gill (1952) in *The Phonic Side of Reading*.) The child reads the words beside the pictures and his attention is drawn to the new sounds. He is helped to read the 6 or so sample words. He then copies them into his book and underlines the letters representing the sound in question. The 8 charts may also be used for group reading and pinned up round the walls of the classroom for reference and spontaneous reading by the children to each other.

21. NOUN CARDS II
22. SENTENCE CARDS II
23. SENSE-AND-NONSENSE II
24. CINEMA SEATS II

In these cards the child meets specimens in sentences of the words which follow the newly learnt orthographic conventions, and becomes familiar with them outside the context in which they were first met. Each series of Sentence Cards is the equivalent of a simple Reader but with the advantage that a sentence is read several times in the course of the game. The sentences are designed to include as many as possible of the most frequent words used in children's reading.

25. 'LAZY E' CARDS

'These cards are designed for the learning and practice of the "Lazy E"— the unsounded E which modifies and lengthens the preceding vowel.'

The idea should be demonstrated by simple comparisons of words with and without the Lazy E. The child then writes out the completed words in his book using the pairs of pictures as a key to the appropriate sound for each word.

26. NOUN CARDS III
27. SENTENCE CARDS III
28. SENSE-AND-NONSENSE III
29. CINEMA SEATS III

In these cards the child meets the Lazy E in simple sentences together with further examples of the orthographic conventions. Both are further practised independently of their context in the sentences. Cinema Seats III also familiarises the child with numbers one to twelve in words.

30. LONG WORD JIGSAWS—'SYLLABLE CARDS'

These cards are designed to give the child the confidence to tackle long words and to show how the phonic sight habits already acquired can be used in reading them. Words of 3 and 4 syllables (*re-mem-ber, en-ter-tain-ment*) are cut into uniquely angled shapes: ⟩⟩ ⟨⟨ etc. The words are sorted by different border patterns common to one word only. As well as assembling the words the children should write them out and read them to the teacher.

Appendix M

STRUCTURAL READING

An outline of the scheme developed

by CATHERINE STERN and TONI GOULD

Structural Reading is a combination of a teaching method and a teaching scheme, with appropriately devised materials to accompany the whole programme. I have included this detailed outline as an appendix because at present there is no similarly highly structured scheme on the English market, and it provides an excellent example of such a 'reading program'.

WHY STRUCTURAL?

The scheme was formulated by two American educationists, Catherine Stern and Toni Gould, and it is described fully in their book *Children Discover Reading*, first published in the States in 1963. They gave the name Structural Reading to their scheme because at every stage the emphasis is placed firmly on the child learning by insight—in preference to learning by rote: 'the latter method of learning involves drill and memorisation, the former always involves an awareness of the structure of what is to be learnt.'

A. *Choice of reading method*

disadvs.

The two authors reject the use of the analytic *look and say* method of teaching reading for the following reasons:

1 Because it teaches by mechanical drill.

2 Because it involves 'rote' memorisation with no real insight into what is being memorised.

3 Because the *shape* of a word gives no indication of the meaning of the word.

4 Because the whole, even according to Gestalt psychology, is not meaningful without a knowledge of the parts.

5 Because with this method the child is given no clue as to the similarities of certain word patterns which will enable him to extend his written vocabulary for himself.

Stern and Gould agree that 'the proponents of the *phonics* (or *synthetic*) method are right to condemn the *sight* (or *analytic*) method because it teaches by mechanical drill', but they criticise the paired association drill for letters and sounds which teachers using a *synthetic* method often introduce to their classes prior to any 'blending' practice: 'The usual procedure is to draw the child's attention to the form of a printed letter[1] and tell him the sound it records. Unfortunately the association of a strange letter with a meaningless sound merely glues together two unfamiliar items; the child can only learn them by rote.'

Because in their view 'teaching by phonics and teaching by sight forces the child to learn to read by the use of rote memorisation', Stern and Gould propose an approach based on 'the study of the whole *spoken* word which is already full of meaning to the beginning reader'. They explicitly reject the use of any nonsense words or syllables, on the grounds that 'it is a dangerous practice to give the child the feeling that reading is just the unthinking rendition of the sounds the letters indicate'. Interest must be focused on the sounds of the *spoken* word which can be divided for the child into *ready-made blends* rather than uniform letter units.

B. *The stages involved in the Structural Reading Scheme*

The Structural Reading programme is clearly defined *on a step-by-step basis*: 'The basic tenet of the course of Structural Reading is that every step in the process be intelligible and both thinking and reasoning are developed from the start.' Briefly the steps to which, one at a time, the child is introduced, are as follows:

1   In the 'pre-reading' programme the child is encouraged through various games (cf. Gattegno) to listen to the sounds that spoken words make—especially the initial sound.

2   When the child can distinguish between these initial sounds easily and confidently he is taught how sounds are put down on paper by letters. (Stern and Gould give no indication as to whether the entire range of possible sound/letter combinations are covered at this stage.) He is encouraged to write the letters for himself at this point. 'Nothing fixes the form of a letter in the mind better than the kinesthetic experience of writing it repeatedly.'

3   *Picture.* 'Experience Charts' are used to encourage discussion and thus 'to expand the children's spoken vocabulary'. Written Experience Charts are deferred until the child can read simple words. Throughout the Structural Reading course pictures are used (cf. Gattegno who deliberately *avoids* pictures) 'to induce children to *name* the object that they see and thus to pronounce the word before they see it in print'.

[1] According to Joyce Morris (*Educational Research*, vol. I) it is now increasingly common for advocates of a synthetic method to use a *syllabic* rather than a *letter* approach to word building.

4   *Monosyllabic words.* The children move from the 'pre-reading' programme to a study of *monosyllabic* words in which each sound is represented by one letter to which it corresponds. *Colour* is used to emphasise
the structure of each word (blue for consonants, red for vowels, gold
for 'magic *e*', green for prefixes and suffixes, and broken grey lines for
silent letters) and the words are broken up into *word parts*: 'the children
are handed as it were, ready-made blends.' These word parts, according
to Stern and Gould, follow the order of natural speech so that although
in the first stage the children are encouraged to listen for initial letter
sounds, now they are encouraged to listen for, and to recognise in print,
initial blends: *ma-n, ca-t, fa-n*, etc.

5   *Word groups.* These *monosyllabic* words are then grouped so that the
child can see for himself the similarity between groups of word patterns.
He is not faced from the start with a bewildering confusion of letter–
sound combinations. The words *ma-n, ha-t, ca-t, ra-i*, and *pa-n* all
appear on the same page along with provision for the children to write
the words *after they have read them aloud*: 'From the start, each child
must learn to write from his own dictation.'

6   'The next step is building words with dominoes: there is a domino for
each of the main parts *ma, ha, ca, ra, pa* and for each ending. The children
listen to the teacher pronouncing one of the words and then construct
it with their dominoes.' Stern and Gould claim that 'Building the
word *man* with dominoes to self-dictation is excellent preparation for
learning how to write *man*. It is a way of teaching the *thinking* part of
writing while eliminating the strain of forming the needed letters' (cf.
Stott's Programmed Word Reading Kit).

7   *Single words rather than sentences.* Stern and Gould insist that 'Before a
child can begin to read sentences we must be sure that he can read each
word of a sentence independently and accurately.' They refer to 'the
lamentable practice of teaching children to read sentences while they
can as yet only guess what the words say', and defend their focus of
attention upon single words on the grounds that it 'is in complete
harmony with the development of each child. To the young child a
word always brings to mind a complex of ideas.'

8   *A sight vocabulary.* From their observations of children using the Structural Reading scheme, Stern and Gould note that: 'For quite a time
many children will read a printed word as *map* in two pieces *ma p*, but
will then immediately repeat it as a whole word with the right intonation.[1] In this way a *sight* vocabulary is built upon the child's *insight*

---

[1] It is difficult to see how any intonation can be 'right' if the word is pronounced *outside* the
context of a sentence.

into the structure of a word, and not presented as in the analytic approach as a *fait accompli*.

9   *Word meanings.* While they are still at the stage of decoding single words, children are required not only to read the word out loud but to follow this with an explanation of its meaning. In this rather naive way the authors believe that 'barking at print' is avoided, and 'reading for meaning' instilled in the beginner.

10   *From words to sentences.* Again the emphasis in teaching the child to read sentences is placed upon the *meaning* which the sentence is expressing: 'The usual phonics teacher . . . seems to assume that the only requirement for the fluent reading of a sentence is the ability to read separate words. This is not so. Often a child who has been taught in this way correctly reads aloud one word, then the next and the next but the expression on his face shows clearly that he has no insight into the meaning of the sentence. He has learned to read words, not sentences. Accordingly, Stern and Gould suggest, for instance, that 'the teacher must teach the child to read sentences as he speaks them—with a varied intonation. It is not enough simply to read each word, however fluently; the voice must bring out what the mind finds important'.[1]

Sentences are introduced as soon as the first group of *a* words have been mastered; 'by restricting ourselves to sentences containing only short *a* words the child, knowing the words, can concentrate on getting the meaning of the sentence'.

e.g. Sam has a cat.
      Sam has a mat. etc.

The shortcoming, of course, as with all tightly graded vocabularies, is that the sentences make sense without being very meaningful. The authors of the scheme admit this but maintain: 'In the Structural Reading method this deficiency is counteracted in incorporating the simple sentences in an amusing context. In the workbooks the meagre sentences are used as significant parts of interesting tasks which the children enjoy.'

11   *Stimulating the children's imaginations.* In the Structural Reading scheme the 'powers of the child's imagination' are 'stimulated' by encouragement from the teacher to invent stories from simple facts. They are encouraged, for instance, to expand the very simple sentences composed for them to read into a narrative.

e.g. Sam has a cat.
      The cat had ham.
      Sam hit the cat . . . because the cat ate all the ham.
      The cat is sad . . . The cat is sad because Sam hit him, etc.

[1] Cf. Mackay and Thompson's approach where the child is encouraged to *produce* sentences rather than to *read* them.

How far the children are actually drawn into such a story imaginatively is questionable. There is inevitably something artificial about a situation with which the child has no genuine links: the sentences are not about real people doing real things at all.

12 'At a *later* stage children write their own sentences and illustrate them.[1] The teacher writes on index cards the words the children cannot yet spell and explains their structure. At this time many children like to start their own dictionaries, filing newly discovered words for later use.'

13 *Reading stories.* 'From concentrating on sentences the child progresses to read simple stories and to grasp their content as a whole. Here again, instruction should start on the *spoken* level.' Stern and Gould suggest that, 'The teacher should frequently tell simple stories to the class, interupting herself and asking the children to figure out what might happen next,' because 'this gives the children *insight into the structure of the story*'. In the work books, for instance, the first 'stories' consist of five short sentences, each sentence carrying the narrative one step forward. When larger 'stories' are used the teacher is urged 'to check and develop comprehension by asking the children to sum up in their own words the information given'. Slow children are to be 'interrupted' by the teacher after every paragraph which they read, and asked to tell the story so far in their own words. This *may* help the child to form a clear picture of the narrative structure but frequent interruptions may also effectively kill any imaginative response that the story might otherwise have sparked off in the child.

14 *Silent reading and oral reading.* The teacher is given specific directions on how to foster each kind of reading with the children in her class; e.g. for silent reading: 'It is most important that the teacher help all her pupils to develop the ability to disperse with the sounding-out process'; for oral reading: 'The teacher should begin teaching this skill by reading a text first without and then with correct intonation . . .'

15 *Extended reading.* From their pilot studies Stern and Gould claim that '*by the end of the first grade* [i.e. by the end of the first year] a veritable reading explosion occurs. Children suddenly break loose! To their own delight and that of their parents and teachers, the children discover that they can read books!' They continue: 'Our records give ample evidence of the confidence with which children enlarge their reading vocabulary by themselves once a secure foundation is laid.'

C. *The systematic expansion of the reading and writing vocabulary*

1 Stern and Gould claim (as would other advocates of *synthetic* methods)

[1] This provision of words for the child is similar to Mackay and Thompson's scheme where children are encouraged to form their own sentences *from the start*.

that encouraging a child to listen to the sound of a word in order to record it on paper increases the child's ability to extend his written vocabulary for himself, whereas, if any *analytic* method is used, the dual task of memorising the word's *shape* in order to recognise it, and memorising a sequence of named letters in order to spell it, only increases the complexity of both decoding (reading) and encoding (writing and therefore spelling).

2   Colour is used to indicate various word patterns (red for vowels, blue for consonants, gold for 'magic *e*', green for prefixes and suffixes and broken grey lines for silent letters), though with far less precision than in either *Words in Colour* or *Colour Story Reading*.

3   The child moves in a series of clearly defined steps from monosyllabic words which contain each of the five short vowel sounds, to monosyllabic words where the short vowel sound is ended or preceded by a consonant blend (la-*mp*, *fla*-g, ri-*ng*), to monosyllabic words which contain the long vowel sounds and a final *e*, introduced not as five groups but as one group under the 'magic *e*' rule. Words which follow these patterns are all that the child is expected to learn in the first year. They are all lexical words: nouns, adjectives, main verbs. Pronouns, conjunctions and prepositions occur infrequently in the examples quoted and attention is certainly not drawn to them.

4   In the second year (age 7–8 in the United States) vocabulary continues to be presented in structurally related groups, with the child's attention directed consistently with each new word group to *the sound of the spoken word first*: 'By now self-dictation has become a customary procedure available to the children at every level of difficulty.' Groups of words in which an identical sound is represented differently in the orthography (*meet*, *meat*) are not taught together to avoid confusion as far as possible. Words which contain silent letters that have no 'sound' function (unlike 'magic *e*' which affects the sound of another vowel) are introduced after the children are familiar with a wide range of 'regularly spelt' words. The authors describe these words (*lamb*, *knot*) as containing silent letters 'which have no *visible* function'.[1]

5   *Spelling tests.* Stern and Gould believe that spelling tests should be 'tests in which the teacher says a word and the child writes the word from self-dictation'. They raise a strong objection to 'spelling tests where the children have to decide whether a certain printed word is spelled correctly or wrongly'.

6   *The child's 'Three Vocabularies'.* Stern and Gould conclude their account of

---

[1] This is not true; (see Mackay and Thompson). The function is not an *audible* one but the 'k' in knot distinguishes the word *visually* and grammatically from 'not', just as 'bee' is similarly distinguished at sight from 'be' and 'two' from 'too', etc.

how Structural Reading extends the child's ability to read and to write by noting that 'the three vocabularies that the child has at his command each have a different scope. His *speaking* vocabulary is the most comprehensive, his *reading* vocabulary is next and his *writing* vocabulary is least.' They claim that 'the greatest difference between our method and others is the expansion of the writing vocabulary', but if Structural Reading with its careful step-by-step introduction to the patterns of English orthography is compared to either i.t.a. or Colour Story Reading, where some device to simplify and regularise the writing system is used, the child's ability to encode the sounds he makes into recognisable *patterns* would seem to be greatly enlarged in scope by either of these devices more quickly than by the Structural Reading programme.

D. *The introduction of spelling rules and grammatical concepts*

1   'Children must grasp that what they say spontaneously does not apply to this word or that only, but that there are rules that hold true generally. Attention is first drawn to the fact that in the *spoken* language special changes regularly occur that must similarly be observed in writing, e.g. how plural nouns are indicated.'

2   Considerable emphasis is placed by the authors on the importance of *allowing the child to discover these rules for himself*: 'To teach the rule first before it is understood, means that it can only be learned by memorization; such recitation does not ensure "insight" into the structural characteristics underlying the rule.'

3   The first rule that children grasp intuitively in Structural Reading is the 'magic *e*' rule. The golden colour in which this *e* is always printed 'reminds the children that the *e* at the end of words like *lake*, *cube* and *slide* has a magic quality: it keeps silent but makes the preceding vowel say its alphabet name'. This kind of word pattern is introduced in the 1st Grade; so is the pattern for plural words where only the addition of an *s* is required. Words ending in *es*, *ss*, *sh*, *ch*, *z* and *x* are deferred until the following year, though undoubtedly if they are allowed to do any free reading or writing the children will come across examples before the second year of the programme.

4   'One of the most important concepts children learn in Second Grade is the inflection of root words.' Here again 'children must be guided by their own natural use of word forms; the pronunciation of a spoken word indicates what the printed and written word must *say*'. Again, as with the introduction of any new focus of attention in Structural Reading 'functional drawings on the teaching page lead the children to the discovery of the general rule'. Prefixes and suffixes, for instance, are printed in green so that they are easily differentiated from the root word to which they are affixed.

5 Once the child has learnt how to pick out the root word from prefixes or suffixes the ground is prepared for understanding syllabic patterns. (These will differ in many cases from the spoken word parts into which the child has been accustomed to split words in self-dictation, e.g. *men-ding* correctly divided into syllables becomes *mend-ing*, *prin-ter* becomes *print-er* and so on.) Stern and Gould illustrate clearly how a prior grasp of prefix and suffix patterns enables the child to move easily and with insight to the process of correct syllable division. Similarly the syllabic division which depends upon the length of the vowel sound (e.g. *lem-on*, *de-mon*), is quickly understood by children who can already distinguish with confidence between long and short vowels.

6 *Word functions.* Stern and Gould do not advise that children should be taught any technical grammatical terms in the first two grades (years), but their work books are so structured that children do learn that 'each word in a sentence has a definite function'; for example: 'On page 3 of Book D children are asked to choose the proper adjective to fit a given noun and to reject two that would not fit; they learn in this exercise that an adjective is a word that describes or modifies a noun.' And: 'On page 74 of Book E they find that adding -*ly* to an adjective makes it into an adverb. From studying the *effect* of these words children are prepared to understand that this set of words describes or modifies verbs.'

Lastly, in the 'Mix-Ups and Fix-Ups' game, Stern and Gould observe that the children enjoy hunting for a word that would make sense in the context and look quickly over the work text page 'looking for the part of speech in each sentence which they need for the Fix-Ups.' In each case they learn to examine only the subjects or only the predicates or only the objects of the given sentences. 'Thus this favourite task in the work texts prepares children for the understanding of a complex study that is so often difficult—the diagramming of a sentence.' The authors conclude their account of how grammatical concepts are first introduced to the child by noting that: 'One of the greatest advantages of *Structural Reading* is that subject matter that is often considered dull and distasteful by older children is made interesting and amusing to children in Grades One and Two and makes the later introduction of grammar challenging and welcome.'

The structural reading program: preliminary test results

'During the 1963–64 school year, the S.R. program was tried out in 24 classrooms including several pilot projects scattered across the country.[1] All

[1] The 'exuberant interest in reading' which teachers using other new schemes and devices have reported (i.t.a. Colour Story Reading) was characteristic of children in Structural Reading Groups also. It is also not unusual for 'the experimental teachers' to be unanimous in their certainty that these children had made 'exceptional progress'—or at any rate to be enthusiastic about the degree of interest and involvement which the children using the new scheme (or device) had portrayed.

the teachers reported that the children enjoyed learning to read with this method and that they were reading at a high level of interest ... The experimental classes taught by the S.R. method received significantly higher scores on standardized tests than comparable groups do.' (No details are given by Stern and Gould as to which tests were used or what schemes the 'comparable groups' were using.)

Details of results
When Stern and Gould's book was published (1964) preliminary test results were only available for two pilot classes of the Structural Reading programme. Both sets of results showed the S.R. Group to have performed outstandingly on the standardised tests that were used (the Gates Word Recognition Test and the Sentence Reading Test). One experimental group, for instance 'which scored 15 points below the comparison class in IQ and which rated next to the bottom in the school, advanced through the S.R. program both in Word Recognition and Sentence Reading to a level matching that of the highest rated class which was taught by one of the leading basal reading programmes supplemented by phonics'.

Stern and Gould also record that Structural Reading has proved effective in remedial class situations. 'In one class of severely retarded second graders in the New York City School system, the whole group tested at the Readiness level in the Autumn achieved grades two scores higher by the end of the first year of the S.R. program.' The authors claim in fact that: 'Not one pupil taught with this method (which they have been using since 1944) has failed to learn to read.'

Comments on 'structural reading'

The advantages of the scheme:

1　Children are encouraged to learn by *insight* and not by rote memorisation at every stage of the scheme.

2　Hence the careful attention to structure, of words, sentences and simple continuous prose, which makes insight possible.

3　The child is consistently reminded in this scheme of the fundamental connection of written language with spoken language.

4　The authors stress the importance of 'extracting meaning' from the written text at every stage (although in the initial stages they interpret meaning somewhat narrowly). Their scheme goes beyond decoding the substance of the language. The child is encouraged to become aware of basic concepts of grammar and syntax and at the stage when he is reading continuous prose there is some attempt to develop 'comprehension skills'.

5　Through the use of word games, pictures and colour the authors have made every effort to devise a scheme which is enjoyable for the child as well as instructive.

The limitations of the scheme:

1 The emphasis throughout the first year workbooks is chiefly on *decoding skills* hence an inevitable preoccupation with the *substance* of the language.

2 Although the child is said in the pre-reading programme to be taught the letter shapes which represent every sound, this introduction to sound/symbol relationships does not appear to be comprehensive, nor does it become comprehensive in the reading scheme itself. I can find no reference, for instance, to the neutral vowel sound *a* and the ways in which it can be represented in the orthography, although it is the most common vowel sound in the English language and the authors stress the importance of listening to sounds in order to *encode* them correctly and *decode* them into natural speech sounds at every stage in their programme.

3 The continual stress on the importance of structure leads to a great deal of 'course imposed' material. The carefully formulated steps which are a major feature of Structural Reading are necessarily teacher controlled. Literacy skills develop in close conjunction with the workbooks which enable the child to discover what the authors have decided it is appropriate for him to discover. Clearly a structured environment has a great many advantages for the learner, but if it is very highly structured or 'programmed' the learner may be prevented from discovering other useful and related features; for instance the step-by-step approach to written vocabulary is certain to prevent the child from recording thoughts and feelings *which are important to him*. A child using *Structural Reading* would have to wait for many months before he could write 'I dreamt about a giant last night' or 'Yesterday I had a birthday party'.

4 The authors do not differentiate between the single word 'caption' produced in writing *by the child* in the initial stages of literacy and the single word presented to the child 'from outside'. In the first case the single word may well represent a much fuller spoken comment of which the child is aware when he writes the word, in the second case the word is *not* embedded in a prior speech formulation and cannot therefore have the same breadth of meaning.

5 In spite of the authors' emphasis on the importance of meaning they suggest strongly that the motivation for learning in the early stages should come from enjoying the act of decoding or encoding simple words successfully. Even if 'successful' decoding and encoding involves a recognition of what the word represents this seems to be a very narrow interpretation of a 'meaningful response'. The child's own experience is involved only in so far as he recognises the objects to which the words *man, hat, fan*, etc., refer. Any wider response is not open to him and *is not encouraged* at this stage.

6 The concern for structure could well act as a brake on the child's imagination at several stages in the course. In the early stages, for instance,
Stern and Gould write 'It is important to encourage the invention of
stories from simple facts to stimulate the powers of the child's imagination.' The kind of invention they envisage here is a linking together of the
simple sentences in the work book to form a story, but although in this
way the child is forming a narrative, it is an exercise; there has been no
genuine impulse on the child's part to 'tell a story', let alone to *write* one.

Later the suggestion is made that when a child is reading aloud the
teacher should stop him (especially if he is a slow child) after every paragraph and ask him to tell the story so far in his own words. This may
ensure that he follows the thread of the narrative correctly but such
enforced recapitulation may kill any feelings of excitement or anticipation
on the part of the reader.

Appendix N

by DAVID MACKAY and BRIAN THOMPSON

Our writing system: English orthography

'Traditional ideas about orthography are as false as the school grammars of the past, and traditional approaches used with children of 5 years of age sometimes wrap up the facts in whimsy. This makes it no easier for children and indeed may well get in the way of the child's understanding. A model of the orthography that is derived from teaching about "letters that hold hands" or "letters at the front door" of a word are not likely to be of much use except to pixies.'

A. *English orthography: what is it?*

1   The substance of language must be either PHONETIC—that is, made of *sound* perceived *aurally*—or ORTHOGRAPHIC—that is, made of *marks* perceived *visually*.

2   The writing system of English is an ALPHABETIC writing system (although no writing system with a history like ours can ever be wholly alphabetic). The basic stock of letters is 26. Each of these has two shapes—a lower case and an upper case—with many variants of these shapes in both printed and hand-written texts.

3   The writing system uses letter space to separate letters and word space to separate words. Sentence, paragraph and verse space are also used.

4   The writing system has punctuation marks for marking certain linguistic boundaries.

5   Italic variation of letter forms is used to draw attention to part of a text and to mark stress.

6   A small set of *logograms* such as the ampersand, numerals, those which indicate currency units, and *contractions* such as Mr Mrs and Dr are used.

7   The apostrophe is used to indicate possessives and contractions.

8   It is worth noting that the English writing system, alone of all European writing systems, uses no *diacritics* (such as the circumflex ^).

B. *English orthography: what it does*

'Many attempts to describe orthography have been made, including some made by linguists in which it is considered full of inconsistencies and exceptions to the rules. These criticisms arise in part from inadequate observation or incomplete descriptions of the structure of the orthography. They stem basically from the deep-rooted belief that in English orthography the letters of the alphabet represent the sounds of the spoken language simply and directly and that *this is all that the orthography does. But* in English orthography (as in French and German) the visual symbols not only give information about the *sounds* of the words, *they also give other kinds of information*. English orthography does this in a number of ways:

1   it distinguishes certain grammatical items from lexical items

2   it distinguishes, by spelling patterns, words from different sources, such as Graeco/Roman, Romance language, etc.

3   it has a system for writing proper names

4   it presents syllables in the same way whether they are stressed or unstressed (and thus provides visual unity)

5   it has a system for distinguishing words that may sound the same in the spoken language

6   it has a system for distinguishing monosyllables from polysyllables.'

Mackay and Thompson comment: 'An adequate account of English orthography must account for all systems such as these. When this has been done and the patterns of the orthography have been described exhaustively, there will be relatively little data that can be labelled "exception to the rules" or "inconsistent".'

C. *English orthography: what it does not do*

1 ƒ One of the points to which Mackay and Thompson call special attention is 'the way in which the writing system excludes certain features of spoken language such as stress and intonation—apart from the extent that we are able, in writing, to indicate intonational features by means of italic forms and by the use of the question mark'. Because there are so few clues as to *how* the written language should be read aloud 'almost all young children when they first begin to read do so as though they were reading a list of words. They do not use the intonation proper to the spoken form of the sentences they are reproducing'. There could be several reasons for this 'list-like' chanting that young children use: concentration on the act of decoding to the detriment of the meaning, the artificial English in which many reading primers are couched anyway,

and so on. But the lack of clues in the orthography to stress and intonation must certainly be a factor.

2 The writing system also disregards the *flow* and *pause* of normal speech, and uses spaces of conventionally varied lengths to separate letters, words, and sentences. The writers of this paper suggest that: 'In the initial stages of becoming literate this presents difficulties. The child whose perceptions are keenly tuned to receiving and producing spoken language in continuous flowing stretches has, for the first time, to deal with the familiar in an unfamiliar guise.'

3 *The failure of orthographic symbols to represent sounds on a one-letter-to-one-sound basis.* Mackay and Thompson spend some time explaining why critics who resent the inconsistencies of English orthography on these grounds perhaps regard it more positively by rejecting 'one-sound-to-one-symbol' as the only criterion for an acceptable writing system. An interesting and useful distinction is drawn, for instance, between letters and symbols. Letters, as letters, have no sounds; it is only when letters function as symbols in word combinations that they can be said to have sounds—and the sound which they symbolise *will depend upon their environment* although they remain identical in shape regardless of their environment (e.g. *cat, chat, cent*). 'From the basic stock of 26 letters a very large number of symbols (nearly 300) are derived.'

Some symbols in our orthography correspond invariably to one sound, e.g. *sh, th, ch.* Other symbols correspond to more than one sound. An important aspect of orthographic patterning is that by which the sound correspondence of one symbol is marked by another symbol (*cap, cot, cup, clap; cent, ace, cite, acid*). *Words in Colour* indicates sound/symbol relationships by adding colour to the twenty-six letter shapes in the orthography, i.t.a. introduces extra shapes, *Colour Story Reading* uses colour and additional shapes. Mackay and Thompson give comprehensive lists of vowel and consonant symbols and two interesting frequency lists of RP vowels and RP consonants.[1]

D. *English orthography: the rules it follows*
In their paper, Mackay and Thompson formulate a number of rules which English orthography observes and which underlie some of the 'spelling patterns' which are frequently present (if we know how to look for them) in our so-called 'chaotic' language. I do not intend to cite all these 'rules' but, for example:

1 When letters *a, e, i, o, u* occur as simple vowel sounds in monosyllables, if these monosyllables are lexical words (nouns, main verbs, adjectives),

[1] RP: 'Received Pronunciation'.

the vowel is almost always followed by a consonant symbol, e.g. *bad,
bed, red*. But if the monosyllable is a grammatical word (preposition,
pronoun, article), there need be no closing consonant: *I, he, she, the, to, do*.

2   Similarly, if there is no consonant at the *beginning* of a lexical monosyllable, the final consonant is always doubled: *ebb, add, egg, odd, inn*. It
is not doubled if the word is a grammatical word: *at, in, on, as*.

Appendix O

'REAL' BOOKS FOR READING IN INFANT CLASSROOMS

One of the chief conclusions that I have reached in the course of this survey of factors which affect the child's response to reading is that a wide range of 'real' books should be used *centrally* at every stage of the child's education, including the very early stages. Many infant teachers use a 'look and say' approach initially which could just as effectively (in my view more effectively) be applied to simple story books as to artificially constructed 'readers'. Children could then be offered a substantial choice of books (plus tapes) to look at and to listen to and in this way their first attempts to grapple with the problem of converting speech sounds into visual symbols would at least be related to stories that interested, pleased, amused or excited them rather than to material about unreal people doing unreal things. In my opinion all the books in these lists have something to offer the child in terms of content as well as form. Since these lists were compiled many more attractively produced books have been published. Some of the titles listed may be out of print now, but should still be available in libraries.

List A—Books with no more than two or three sentences to a page; suitable in my opinion for use with five-year-old infants.

ABELARD–SCHUMAN
Do you move as I do? H. Borten
Do you see what I see? H. Borten
My Brother Bernard Shan Ellenbuck
(Most effective for 'A' children with tape)

ALLEN & UNWIN
The Beautiful Island Meg Rutherford
(A very beautiful black and white fantasy—the text is very brief, the illustrations a work of art)

ANGUS & ROBERTSON
Just Me Marie Hall-ese

E. J. ARNOLD & SON
Umbrella Books (large clear print) by David and Guillemette Cox
Sam at the Picnic　　*Sometimes Sam*　　*The Gymkhana*

BANCROFT
Books for me to Read—Red, Blue, Green and *Yellow* Series
(These vary in quality but there are some attractive ones)

BENN
Benn's *Beginning to Read* Books
Hello Lucy   Donald Bisset
Little Bear's Pony   Donald Bisset, illustrated by Shirley Hughes
Peter Climbs a Tree   Elizabeth Beresford, illustrated by Margery Gill
Looking for a Friend   Elizabeth Beresford

(There are more than 20 titles[1] in this series in the hardback edition and
18 titles printed in i.t.a.)

Benn's Books For Very Young Readers by Kathleen Brooks, illustrated
by Fredun Shapur
Spot and the Paint   *Blackie and the Wool*   *By the Pool*
The Christmas Tree
Single Titles:
The Happy Owls   Celestino Piatti
The Nock Family Circus   N. Haber and Celestino Piatti
Teddy Bears 1 to 10   Susanna Gretz
Roundabout Ride   Robina Beckles Wilson, illustrated by Margery Gill

A. & C. BLACK

Things I Like Series by Peggy Blakeley, illustrated by Philippa Thomas
Colours   *Fast and Slow*   *Shapes*   *Fur and Feather*
Big and Little   *Sounds*   *Hot and Cold*   *Heavy and Light*

BLACKIE
Isabella the Fishing Boat   L. Leher, illustrated by Ursula Kirchberg
After the Sun Goes Down   written and illustrated by Rainey Bennett
The Secret Hiding Place   written and illustrated by Rainey Bennett
Where is Peterkin?   Wilfrid Blecher
The Cloud's Journey   Ehrhardt Heinhold, illustrated by Ursula Kirchberg
(Especially with a tape)
Buy Me a China Doll   Harvé Zemach, illustrated by Margot Zemach
(Best with a tape. A traditional lullaby)
The Bubble Book   Kathleen Norris

BODLEY HEAD
Rosie's Walk   illustrated by Pat Hutchings (no words)
Tom and Sam   illustrated by Pat Hutchings (no words)

[1] Some of these titles are more suitable for list 'B' readers than list 'A'.

Hide and Seek (a picture story)   Renata Meyer (no words)
Vickie (a picture story)   Renata Meyer (no words)
Whistle for Willie   *The Story Day*   *The Little Drummer Boy*
Peter's Chair   *A Letter to Amy*
All by Ezra Jack Keats

Henny Penny   *The Three Little Pigs*
The Three Billy Goats Gruff   *A Frog He Would A-Wooing Go*
All illustrated by William Stobbs
(These would be suitable with a tape because they have a strongly repetitive pattern)

The *Angus* Books (about a little Scottie dog) written and illustrated by Marjorie Flack
Angus and The Cat   *Angus and The Ducks*
Angus and Wag-tail Bess   *Angus Lost*
Angus and Topsy

BROCKHAMPTON

Christmas in the Stable   Astrid Lindgren
The *Jeanne-Marie* Books by Françoise
Springtime for Jeanne-Marie   *Jeanne-Marie Counts Her Sheep*
Jeanne-Marie in Gay Paris   *Jeanne-Marie at the Fair*
The Big Rain
(All printed in very satisfying thick black text)
The Kitten that Came to Play   Elle Kari Hojeberg
(Best with tape)

BURKE

'*Read for Fun*' Words: *Your Children Use* Books
Peter Johnson and his Guitar   Hans Peters, translated by Marianne Turner, illustrated by Iben Clanbe
The Lost and Found Ball   Jerrold Beim / Marianne Turner / Ylvä Kalström
Billy's Birthday Lollipop   Lenhart Hellsing / Marianne Helweg / Stig Lindberg
Robert Goes Driving   Karin Numan / Marianne Helweg / Ylvä Kalström
(All stage 1)

CHAMBERS

Billy, The Littlest One   Miriam Schlein, illustrated by Lucy Hawkinson
Here Comes Night   Miriam Schlein, illustrated by Harvey Weiss
Snow Time   Miriam Schlein, illustrated by Joe Lasker
Big Lion, Little Lion   Miriam Schlein, illustrated by Joe Lasker
Days I Like   Lucy Hankinson
All in One Day   Lucy Ozone

CHATTO & WINDUS
  A Train to Spain   Ray Wade

COLLINS
  Bright and Early Books for *Beginning Beginners*
  The Foot Book   Dr Seuss
  The Eye Book   Theo le Sige
  The Ear Book   R. Perkins
  Inside   Stan and Jan Bernstein
  Outside   Stan and Jan Bernstein
  Upside Down   Stan and Jan Bernstein

  (Collins and Harvill)
  Beginner Books (40 titles)
  First:
  Hop on Pop   *One Fish, Two Fish, Red Fish, Blue Fish*
  Both by Dr Seuss
  Then:
  The Cat in the Hat   *The Cat in the Hat Comes Back*
  Both by Dr Seuss, and at least twenty-five other titles, including
  The Sleep Book   Dr Seuss
  The Beginner Book Dictionary   Bennet Cerf
  I Wish that I had Duck Feet   Theo le Sige
  The Book of Animal Riddles   Bennett Cerf
  If accompanied by a tape:
  The Owl and the Pussy Cat   Edward Lear, illustrated by Dale Maxey
  The Pobble Who Has No Toes and other nonsense verses   Edward Lear,
  illustrated by Dale Maxey

  Collins *Colour Camera* Books (colour photographs)
  First things   *Zoo Book*

  Collins' *Easy-to-Read* Books by Mollie Clarke
  The Blue Velvet Cat   *Little Nuisance*   *The Toy Owl*
  The Useful Cart   *Tom Cat and the Three Mice*   *Hobby Horse*

  Now I can Count   Dean Hay (full-colour photographs)
  I See a Lot of Things   Dean Hay (full-colour photographs)
  What Whiskers Did   designed by Ruth Carroll (no words)

DENT
  One times One   Horst Lemke
  A Lion in the Meadow   Margaret Mehy, illustrated by Jenny Williams

ANDRÉ DEUTSCH
  The *Madeline* Books by Ludwig Bemelmans
  Madeline   *Madeline's Rescue*

Madeline and the Bad Hat   *Madeline and the Gypsies*
Madeline in London
(Especially as the rhyming stories have also been taped)

DINOSAUR PUBLICATIONS (Willingham, Cambridge)
  Althea Books
  George and the Baby   *Jeremy Mouse*
  Peter Pig   *Desmond the Dinosaur*
  Desmond goes to Scotland   *Desmond the Dusty Dinosaur*
  Desmond and the Fire   *Cuthbert and Bimbo*

DENNIS DOBSON
  The Black Pencil Marcello Minale
  The Yellow Flowers Fiona Saint and Ralph Steadman
  The Bald Twit Lion Spike Milligan and Carol Barker
  (Especially with a tape)

EVANS
  Run, Run, Chase the Sun Robin and Inge Hyman, illustrated by Yutaka
  Sugita
  (Lovely glowing pictures)

FABER
  The Pied Piper of Hamelin Robert Browning
  *Bedtime for Frances Russell Hoban
  Bread and Jam for Frances Russell Hoban
  *A Baby Sister for Frances Russell Hoban

GOLLANCZ
  Lucy and Tom's Day written and illustrated by Shirley Hughes
  Willy is My Brother Peggy Parish, illustrated by Shirley Hughes

HAMISH HAMILTON
  The Little Wooden Farmer Alice Dalgliesh, illustrated by Anita Lobel
  The Elephant and the Bad Baby Elfrida Vipont, illustrated by Raymond
      Briggs
  (It would be possible for reception class children to enjoy both these
  books if a tape were available with the book)

HAMLYN
  The *So High* Books
  I am a Bunny   *Animals*   *I am a Bear*   *Words*
  I am a Mouse   *Up and Down*   *I am a Fox*

* Also available in Faber paper covered editions.

Hamlyn—*contd.*
The *Little Tiger* Books
Little Tiger Colours Everything   *Listen, Little Tiger*
Little Tiger Takes a Trip

HARRAP
All the *Père Castor* Books

HEINEMANN
The Great Big Enormous Turnip Alexei Tolstoy, illustrated by Helen
Oxenburg
Look at the Fair Margery Sharp, illustrated by Rosalind Fry
Benjy's Blanket Myra Berry Brown

LONGMAN
Longmans Young Books
Tim and Terry J. R. Joseph and Desmond Knight
Judy and Jasmin
Twirly Elaine Moss, illustrated by Haro
The Wait and See Book Elaine Moss, illustrated by Sally Ford
Where is John? Lilly Mosheim, illustrated by Sally Ford
Peter's China Pig   *Peter and his Tricycle Flash*
Garden Picnic for Elizabeth and Peter   *Elizabeth's Cat Tiny*
Elizabeth and her Doll Susan   *A Secret Birthday Present for Elizabeth*
All by Lilly Mosheim, illustrated by Andrew Walker
Toby Moves House   *A Seaside Holiday for Jane and Toby*
Toby Stays with Jane   *Jane and Toby Start School*
All by Ann Thwaite
Harold and the Purple Crayon   written and illustrated by Crockett Johnson
Boots   Wheels   Water   Wind   Tea   Sunday
All by Jenny Joseph

MACDONALD
Joanjo J. Balet
The *Mr Bear* Books written by Chizuko Kuratomi, illustrated by Kozo
Kakimoto
Mr Bear goes to Sea   *Mr Bear in the Air*   *Remember Mr Bear*

MACMILLAN
The *Nippers* Series by Leila Berg (1st grade blue)
(A fair amount of print, but the text is reiterative—best probably used
with a tape)

METHUEN
Bruna Books by Dick Bruna

The Little Bird	*Tilly and Tessa*	*The Fish*
The Egg	*Circus*	*The King*
The Sailor	*The School*	*The Apple*
Pussy Nelly Miffy	*Miffy at the Seaside*	*Miffy in the Snow*
Miffy at the Zoo		

3 × 3 Three by Three James Kriss, illustrated by Eva Johanna Rubin
(In verse. Most effective with a tape.)

Wet Albert Michael and Joanne Cole
Bod Books by Michael and Joanne Cole
Bod's Apple   *Bod's Present*   *Bod's Dream*
Bod to the Cherry Tree

Jenny and Simon Series by Oliver Jones

The *Helen Piers Animal Books* (with colour photographs)

Mouse Looks for a House	*How Did it Happen*
Mouse Looks for a Friend	*Hullabaloo for Owl*
Fox and Hen	*Goose Laid an Egg*
What can Monkey do next?	*Five Little Pigs*
The Kitten who Couldn't get Down	

MOWBRAY

Glow-Worm Books all designed by Gordon Stowell

This is God's World—Listen	*I Open my Eyes*
Praise Him	*All Things Bright and Beautiful*
Smells I Like	

MULLER

Muller *Easy Readers* (some more suitable for list 'B' than for list 'A'
readers) 24 titles altogether, including
The Clumsy Cowboy   Jean Bethell
Will You Come to My Party?   Sara Asheron
The Monkey in the Rocket   Jean Bethell
The Boy who Fooled the Giant   Tamara Kitt
Adventures of Silly Billy   Tamara Kitt
The Day Joe Went to the Supermarket   Dorothy Levenson

NELSON

The *Red Bus* Series
(This is a series of rhyming stories written by 'Miss Read', and five-year-
olds would certainly enjoy them, especially with a tape)

The Red Bus	*Plum Pie*	*No Hat*
The New Bed	*Chuck*	*The Little Black Hen*
The Little Peg Doll		

OXFORD UNIVERSITY PRESS

The *Papa Small* Books by Lois Lenski

Papa Small	*The Little Farm*	*The Little Sail Boat*
Cowboy Small	*The Little Aeroplane*	*The Little Fire Engine*

The *Davy* Books by Lois Lenski

Davy's Day   *Davy and His Dog*   *A Dog came to School*

Mother Goose (nursery rhymes)   *Wild Animals*   *Fishes*   *Birds*
All illustrated by Brian Wildsmith

Fables by La Fontaine illustrated by Brian Wildsmith
The Hare and the Tortoise   *The Lion and the Rat*
The North Wind   *The Miller, the Boy and the Donkey*

Books written and illustrated by Charles Keeping
Alfie and the Ferryboat   *Charlie, Charlotte and the Golden Canary*
Shawn and the Carthorse   *Joseph's Yard*

PENGUIN—Picture Puffins
Anatole   Eve Titus / Paul Galdone
Fee Fi Fo Fum   Raymond Briggs
The Frog in the Well   Alvin Tressell / Roger Duvoisin
Harry the Dirty Dog   Gene Zion / Margaret Bloy Graham
No Losses for Harry   Gene Zion / Margaret Bloy Graham
The Story about Ping   Marjorie Flack / Kurt Wiese
The Story of the Three Little Pigs   William Stobbs
(Best with a tape)
Time Mouse   Judy Brook
The Twelve Days of Christmas   Robert Broomfield
Two Can Toucan   David McKee
Whistle for Willie   Ezra Jack Keats

Young Puffins
My Aunt's Alphabet   Charlotte Hough
The Story of Ferdinand   Munro Leaf

SCHOFIELD & SIMS

The *Through the Rainbow* Series by E. S. Bradburne, illustrated by Joanna Carter
(Plus colour photographs in same books)

SCHOLASTIC PUBLICATIONS

Easiest-to-Read Books
(Sixty-eight titles, all attractively printed and illustrated, all suitable for reception-class children to look at, listen to and begin to read)

Particularly recommended
Stop, Stop   by Edith Thatcher Hurd, illustrated by Clement Hurd
One, Two, Three, Going to Sea   written and illustrated by Alain
Clifford Gets a Job   written and illustrated by Norman Bridwell
Clifford Takes a Trip   written and illustrated by Norman Bridwell
Who Took the Farmer's Hat?   Joan L. Nodget, illustrated by Fritz
Siebel
The Gingerbread Man   illustrated by Ed Arne
(With tape if possible)

EDMUND WARD
The *Ant and Bee* Books by Angela Banner, illustrated by Bryan Ward

Ant and Bee	*More Ant and Bee*
More and More Ant and Bee	*Ant and Bee and the ABC*
Ant and Bee and Kind Dog	*One Two Three with Ant and Bee*
Around the Word with Ant and Bee	*Ant and Bee and the Rainbow*
Happy Birthday with Ant and Bee	

The '*Starting-to-Read*' *Noggin* Books by Oliver Postgate and Peter Firmin

Noggin the King	*Noggin and the Whale*
Noggin and the Dragon	*Nogbad Comes Back*

WARNE
Springboard Readers (most attractive 'chalk drawing' illustrations)
Twelve titles including
In the Plane   *To the Zoo*   *Tom is Sick*

Getting Ready to Read
Ten introductory readers including
Sally Wants a Horse   *The Broken Toys*   *A Holiday with Grandma*

Teddy Bear Coalman Series

Teddy Bear Coalman	*Little Blue Clock*
Three Kittens in a Boat	*Umpty Elephant: Window Cleaner*
Percy Pig: House Painter	

Johnny Crowe's Garden   illustrated by L. Leslie Brooke

WHEATON
The *Spot* Books
A Book for Spring   *A Book for Summer*   *A Book for Autumn*
A Book for Winter
All by Mollie Clark

WORLD'S WORK
Early I Can Read Books
Albert the Albatross   written and illustrated by Syd Hoff

World's Work—*contd.*

Come and Have Fun   Edith Thatcher Hurd illustrated by Clement Hurd
Who Will be My Friends?   written and illustrated by Syd Hoff
Cat and Dog   Else Holmelund Minarik, illustrated by Fritz Siebel

I Can Read Books
Some of these could be used in an infant reception class: any of them are
suitable for six-year-old children. There are 82 books in this series
all simply written and attractively illustrated including the *Little Bear*[1]
books by Else Holmelund Minarik, illustrated by Maurice Sendak;
early 'science' books like *Seeds and More Seeds* by Millicent Selsam,
illustrated by Tomi Ungerer; *Sammy the Seal* and *Julius* both written
and illustrated by Syd Hoff and many other stories with a strong appeal
for five-plus-year-olds)

The *Mother Goose Library*   all illustrated by Peter Spier
London Bridge is Falling Down   *To Market to Market*
The Fox Went Out One Chilly Night
(These would be especially suitable with a tape)

The Very Little Girl   Phyllis Krasilovsky, illustrated by Ninon
Falling Down   Gene Zion, illustrated by Margaret Bloy Graham
Giant John   Arnold Lobel
Part-time Dog   illustrated by Seymor Fleishman
Wake up Farm   illustrated by Roger Duvoisin
One Step Two   Charlotte Zolotov, illustrated by Roger Duvoisin
Big Sister and Little Sister   Charlotte Zolotov, illustrated by Marina
Alexander

'REAL' BOOKS FOR CHILDREN IN THE 6–7 AGE GROUP (*List B*)

ABELARD SCHUMAN
The Blue Marble   H. G. Lenzen, illustrated by Marie-Luise Pricken
The Little Boy and the Big Fish   written and illustrated by Max Vetthuijs
The Four Seasons   Gertrud von Walther, translated by Patricia Crompton, illustrated by Uta Glauber
The Rhine Pirates   written and illustrated by Hans P. Schaad
The Cats Go to Market   Joan Cass, illustrated by W. Stobbs
The Canal Trip   Joan Cass
Ivor's Outing   O. Postgate

ALDUS BOOKS
Daniel's New Home   Karen Gunthorp, illustrated by Attilio Cassinelli

[1] Two little bear books are also printed in i.t.a.

ANGUS & ROBERTSON

My Own Little Cat   M. Gerland-Ekeroth, photography by Gosta Nordin
Sir Charles and the Lyrebird   Joyce Nicholson (with photographs and strong black print), photography by Brian McArdle

Kerri and Honey (two koalas)   *Granky the Baby Australian Camel*
Andy's Kangaroo   *Ringtail the Possum*
(All by Joyce Nicholson)

E. J. ARNOLD

Robert Andrew Books by Leonard Clark, illustrated by James S. Scargill
Robert Andrew Tells a Story   *Robert Andrew and Tiffy*
Robert Andrew by the Sea   *Robert Andrew and Skippy*
Robert Andrew and the Indian Chief   *Robert Andrew in the Country*
Robert Andrew and the Holy Family

BENWIG BOOKS

Grimm's Fairy Tales
Cinderella   *Snow White*   *The Musicians of Bremen*
Red Riding Hood   *Hansel and Gretel*   *Sleeping Beauty*

A. & C. BLACK

Things I Like by Peggy Blakeley, illustrated by Philippa Thomas
Colours   *Fast and Slow*   *Shapes*   *Fur and Feather*
Big and Little *Sounds*   *Hot and Cold*   *Heavy and Light*

Let's Read and Find out Science Books
Air is all around you   Franklyn M. Branley
Big Tracks, Little Tracks   Franklyn M. Branley
The Bottom of the Sea   Augusta Goldin
The Clean Brook   Margaret Bartlett
A Drop of Blood   Paul Showers
Ducks Don't Get Wet   Augusta Goldin
Find Out by Touching   Paul Showers
Floating and Sinking   Franklyn M. Branley
Follow Your Nose   Paul Showers
Flash, Crash, Rumble and Roll   Franklyn M. Branley
How a Seed Grows   Helena J. Jordan
How You Talk   Paul Showers
Icebergs   Roma Gans
The Listening Walk   Paul Showers
The Moon Seems to Change   Franklyn M. Branley
My Five Senses   Aliki
My Hands   Aliki
Rockets and Satellites   Franklyn M. Branley

A. & C. Black—*contd.*

> *Spider Silk*   Augusta Goldin
> *Straight Hair, Curly Hair*   Augusta Goldin
> *The Sun: Our Nearest Star*   Franklyn M. Branley
> *A Tree is a Plant*   Glyde Robert Buller
> *Watch Honey Bees with Me*   Judy Hawes
> *What Makes a Shadow?*   Clyde Robert Buller
> *What the Moon is Like*   Franklyn M. Branley
> *Where the Brook Begins*   Margaret Bartlett
> *The Wonder of Stones*   Roma Gans
> *Your Skin and Mind*   Paul Shower

BLACKIE

> *Uncle Toby's Picnic*   Hans G. Lenzen, illustrated by Sigrid Hanck
> The *Topsy and Tim* Books by Gareth and Jean Adamson

> *Topsy and Tim's Monday Book*   *Tuesday Book*
> *Wednesday Book*   *Thursday Book*
> *Friday Book*   *Saturday Book*
> *Sunday Book*   *Topsy and Tim Go Fishing*
> *Topsy and Tim's Holiday*   *Topsy and Tim Go to School*
> *Topsy and Tim's Foggy Day*   *Topsy and Tim at the Seaside*
> *Topsy and Tim at the Football Match*

> *Buy Me a China Doll*   Harvé Zemach, illustrated by Margot Zemach
> *Nail Soup*   Harvé Zemach, illustrated by Margot Zemach
> *Pip and the Six Cooks*   Joan Beales
> *I Wish, I Wish*   Lisl Weil
> *The Musicians of Bremen* (retold)   Eva Figes, illustrated by Horst Lemke
> *Too Much Nose*   Harvé and Margot Zemach
> *The Flying Jacket* and other stories   Betty Wilsher

BLACKWELL

> *Zig Zag and His Friends* (retold in English)   Joyce Hole, illustrated by
> Thora Lund

BODLEY HEAD

> The *Petunia* Books by Roger Duvoisin (5 titles about a goose)
> The *Veronica* Books by Roger Duvoisin (6 titles about a hippopotamus)
> *Lazy Jack*   Joseph Jacobs / Barry Wilkinson
> *The Extraordinary Tug of War* (retold)   Letter Schatz, illustrated by John
> Burningham
> *Mr Rabbit and the Lovely Present*   Charlotte Zolotow, illustrated by
> Maurice Sendak
> *Where the Wild Things Are*   written and illustrated by Maurice Sendak
> *The Tale of a Turnip*   A. Howett

Mrs Mopples Washing Line   A. Howett

The Three Billy Goats Gruff   *The Three Little Pigs*
The Story of the Three Bears   *A Frog he would a Wooing Go*
The Golden Goose   *Jack and the Beanstalk*
All illustrated by William Stobbs
The Five Chinese Brothers   C. L. Bishop
The Story of Ping   M. Flack
Mr Fairweather and his Family   M. Kormitzer
Captain Pugwash   J. Ryan
The Diverting Adventures of Tom Thumb   Joseph Jacobs, illustrated by Barry Wilkinson
The Speckled Hen   Harvé Zemach
The House that Jack Built   illustrated by Paul Galdone
The Old Woman and Her Pig   Paul Galdone
Old Mother Hubbard and Her Dog   Paul Galdone
The Little White Hen   Anita Howett, illustrated by William Stobbs
Anatole by Eve Titus, illustrated by Paul Galdone
Anatole over Paris   *Anatole and the Cat*   *Anatole and the Robot*
Anatole and the Poodle   *Anatole and the Piano*
All Around You (a first Science Book)   Jeanne Bendick

BROCKHAMPTON

The *Buzzy Bear* Books by Dorothy Marino
Buzzy Bear goes South   *Buzzy Bear's Busy Day*
Buzzy Bear goes Camping   *Buzzy Bear and the Rainbow*

The House of Four Seasons   Roger Duvoisin
Simon in the Land of Chalk Drawings   Edward McLachlan
Sandman in the Lighthouse   Rudi Stahl
Andy Pandy Books (29 titles)
The Two Giants   Michael Forman
Gumdrop and the Farmer's Friend   Val Biro
Gum drop, the Adventures of a Vintage Car   Val Biro
Gumdrop on the Rally   written and illustrated by Val Biro
Christmas in the Stable   Astrid Lindgren
Six Foolish Fisherman   B. Eikin

BURKE

'*Read for Fun*' *Words your Children Use* Books (Stage 2) classroom edition
The Little Woman Who Forgot Everything   Janet Beattie
Little O's Naughty Day   Edith Unnerstad
Matthew and Eva in the Toyshop   Ann Mari Falk
Matthew Comes to Town   Ann Mari Falk
The New House   Hans Peterson

Burke—*contd.*

   Brenda Helps Grandmother   Astrid Lindgren
   The Old Man and the Bird   Hans Peterson
   Matthew Blows Soap Bubbles   Ann Mari Falk
   Patrick's Aeroplane   Ulf Lofgren
   The Ambulance   Ann Mari Falk
   The New Road   Hans Peterson
   Simon Small Moves In   Astrid Lindgren
   Lena and Lisa Have Measles   Grete James Hertz
   The Town That Forgot It Was Christmas   Alf Prøysen
   Grandpa's Straw Hat   Grete James Hertz
   Mr Hazelnut   B. G. Hallquist

JONATHAN CAPE

   Jack and Nancy   written and illustrated by Quentin Blake

   Cannon Ball Simp
   Borka
   Trubloff, The Mouse that Played the Balalaika
   Humbert, Mr Firkin and the Mayor of London
   Harquin
   Seasons   John Burningham
   All written and illustrated by John Burningham

   The *Fenella* Books
   Fenella in Greece   *Fenella in the South of France*
   Fenella in Spain   *Fenella in Ireland*

   Patrick   written and illustrated by Quentin Blake

W. & R. CHAMBERS

   The Little Black Hen   Lene Hille-Brandts, illustrated by Sigrid Heuck
   Guess What! (rhyming riddles)   Lene Hille-Brandts, illustrated by Doris Dumley
   Happy Harry and the Scarescrow   Anne Geelhaar, illustrated by Ingeberg Meyer-Rey
   Noah's Ark   Ivy Eastwick, illustrated by John Mackay
   Toby's Friends   Laura Bannon
   The Very Special Animal   Rudolf Newmann
   Animals at Home
   The Penguin   *The Mouse*   *The Whale*   *The Bee*   *The Beaver*
   The Stork
   (Especially useful with a tape)

   The *I Want To Be* . . . Series by Carla Greeve
   Thirty-one titles including
   I Want to be a Cowboy   *I Want to be a Dentist*

I Want to be a Policeman   *I Want to be a Space Pilot*
I Want to be a Nurse   *I Want to be a Teacher*
I Want to be an Airplane Hostess

GEOFFREY CHAPMAN
Tabarin Tales
The Gardener's Daughter (a tale from Gascony retold)   A. F. Scott, illustrated by Rene Moren
The Savage King of the Seven Seas (a tale from Turkey retold)   A. F. Scott, illustrated by Jacques Le Scanff
Clot and the Sound of the Sea
The Vixen, the Bear and the Blacksmith
The Devil's Hat
The Jealous Lionness

CHATTO, BOYD & OLIVER
The *Open Gate* Library

Explorers	*Dinosaurs*	*Outer Space*
Museums	*Time*	*Flight*
Electricity	*Magic People*	*Ocean Wonders*
Travel by Land	*Travel by Water*	*More Magic People*

The *Lyle* Books by Bernard Waber
Lyle, Lyle, Crocodile   *Welcome Lyle*
Lyle and the Birthday Party

Henry the Explorer   Mark Taylor, illustrated by Graham Booth (Oliver & Boyd)
Exactly Alike   Evaline Ness (Oliver & Boyd)
Mrs Popplecorn   N. Werner

CHATTO & WINDUS
Elizabeth   H. A. Rey

The Story of Little Black Sambo   *The Story of Little Black Quibba*
The Story of Little Black Bobtail   *The Story of Little Black Mingo*
The Story of Little Black Quasha   *The Story of Little White Squibba*
All by Helen Bannerman

Zozo takes a Job   H. A. Rey
Zozo goes to hospital   H. A. Rey

The *Flap* Books by H. A. Rey
See the Circus   *Feed the Animals*   *Anybody at Home?*
Where's My Baby?   *How do You Get There?*

COLLINS
Grandmother Lucy and Her Hats   Joyce Woods and Frank Francis

Collins—*contd.*

The Bee Man of Orn   Frank Stockton, illustrated by Maurice Sendak
The Owl and the Pussy Cat   Edward Lear, illustrated by Dale Maxey
The Pobble Who Has No Toes and other nonsense verses   Edward Lear, illustrated by Dale Mavey

Easy Reading Series of *Wonder Colour* Books
Jo-Jo's Day Out   *Let's Have a Circus*   *Little Crazy Car*
Georgie's My Dragon   *A Home for Henry*   *Susan's Secret Garden*

Preep   M. Schulmann
Preep in Paris   M. Schulmann

The *Richard Scarry 'Mystery'* Books e.g. *The Supermarket Mystery*

What Do People Do All Day?   Richard Scarry
Busy Busy World   Richard Scarry
Great Big Schoolhouse   Richard Scarry
Epaminondas (retold)   Eve Merriam, illustrated by Trina Schart Hyman
The Wedding Procession of the Rag Doll and the Broom Handle   Carl Sandburg and Harriet Pincus
Who Was In It?   Carl Sandburg and Harriet Pincus
The Tiger Who Came to Tea   Judith Kerr

Information Books (also a Wonder Colour Series)
Book of Aircraft   *Space Book*   *Book of Farming*
The Book of Cowboys   *The Book of Indians*   *The Book of Pirates*

The Trouble with Timothy   Dale Maxey

Fidgit   written and illustrated by Dale Maxey
May I Bring a Friend?   Beatrice Schenk de Regniers and Beni Montresor

ANDRÉ DEUTSCH
The Banger   Eva Figes / Joanna Stubbs
Farmer Barnes Buys a Pig   John Cunliffe, illustrated by Carol Barker
Farmer Barnes and Bluebell   John Cunliffe, illustrated by Carol Barker
Farmer Barnes at the County Show   J. A. Cunliffe, illustrated by Jill McDonald
The *Madeline* Books by Ludwig Bemelmans (cf. list 'A')

Kermit the Hermit
Huge Harold
Hubert's Hair-raising Adventure
Smokey   *Ella*   *Farewell to Shady Glade*
The Pinkish Purplish Bluish Egg
All written and illustrated by Bill Peet

DINOSAUR PUBLICATIONS
Althea Books

Ocky Octopus and the Shell   Ocky and the One-man Band
Ocky Octopus and the Races   Christmas with Ocky Octopus

DENNIS DOBSON

Creatures Great and Small Michael Flanders/Marcello Minale
(Best with a tape)
Mr Benn—Red Knight David McKee
Tobias Pilgrim Builds a Stow Ship Malcolm Carder
Tobias Pilgrim and the Toks Malcolm Carder
Just One Apple written and illustrated by Janosch (beautiful glowing illustrations)
Noise in the Night Anne Alexander, illustrated by Abner Grabott
The House Next Door John Chalon
Elmer David McKee
Fly Away Peter Frank Dickens, illustrated by Ralph Steadman
Ali Baba and the 40 Thieves (retold) Emannete Luzzati
The Bald Twit Lion Spike Milligan/Carol Barker
The Boy and the Lion written and illustrated by Carol Barker
The Lady of Shallott Alfred Lord Tennyson, illustrated by Bernadette Watts
(With a tape if possible)

EVANS

Humphrey Goes to Town Marianne Richter
The Happiest Elephant in the World Minami Nishiuchi, illustrated by Seichi Horiuchi, adapted by Robin and Ingë Hyman

Keith and Sally Books illustrated and designed by Alain Gree adapted by Anne Marie Ryba
Keith and Sally in the Woods   *Keith and Sally Look at Ships*
Keith and Sally at the Seaside   *Keith and Sally Out and About*
Keith and Sally Go Abroad   *Keith and Sally on the Farm*
Keith and Sally by the River   *Keith and Sally Look for Oil*
Keith and Sally Look at Television

Barnabas Ball at the Circus
Runaway James and the Night Owl

FABER[1]

Snippy and Snappy Wanda Gag
Millions of Cats Wanda Gag
How St Francis tamed the Wolf   *Old Winkle and the Seagulls*
The Sorcerer's Apprentice   *The Magic Suit*
Good King Wenceslas   *St George and the Fiery Dragon*

[1] All asterisked titles available in Faber paper back editions.

282Learning to read

Faber—contd.

Punch and Judy Carry On   The Big River
Wuffle Goes to Town   Charlie on the Run
All by Elizabeth and Gerald Rose

*Mike Mulligan and his Steam Shovel   written and illustrated by Virginia Lee Burton

*The Little House   Katy and the Big Snow
Calico the Wonder Horse   Choo Choo
All by Virginia Lee Burton

The House that Grew   L. M. Boston
The Story of William Tell   Aliki
*In the Forest   Marie Hall Ets
The Bigger Giant   Nancy Green
*Bedtime for Frances   Russell Hoban
*A Baby Sister for Frances   Russell Hoban
Bread and Jam for Frances   Russell Hoban
Jim Tiger   Charlotte Hough
Morton's Pony   Charlotte Hough
The Animal Game   Charlotte Hough
King Arthur's Sword   Errol Le Cain
*The Story of Peter and The Wolf   Prokofiev
*The Gingerbread Man (retold)   Barbara Ireson, illustrated by Gerald Rose
The Three Little Mermaids   Denise and Alain Trez

Goodnight Veronica   *Circus in the Jungle
*The Butterfly Chase   The Magic Paintbox
The Little Knight's Dragon
All by Denise and Alain Trez

The Dog Who Couldn't Swim   Jill Tomlinson, illustrated by Gillian Shanks
Suli and the Kitchen Cats   Jill Tomlinson / Gillian Shanks
Salt   Harve Zemach, illustrated by Margot Zemach

GINN

'Rescue Stories' by James Webster (for sale direct to schools)
Martin the Mouse   Shorty the Hero
Shorty and Tom Rabbit   Shorty and the Bank Robbers
Sally the Seagull   Brown Beauty

GOWER PRESS

A Mare's Nest   John Paul Sayer (humorous verse)

HAMISH HAMILTON
The Perfect Present Michael Forman
The Old Bullfrog Berenice Freschet, illustrated by Roger Duvoisin
The Elephant and the Bad Baby Elfrida Vipont illustrated by Raymond Briggs
The Great Sleigh Robbery Michael Foreman
The Giant of Grabbist written and illustrated by John Lawrence
The Legend of the Willow Plate Alvin Tresselt and Nancy Cleaver, illustrated by Joseph Low
The Trojan Horse James Reeves, illustrated by Krystna Turska

HAMLYN
(Hamlyn books are not always readily available; good stories are some-times—frustratingly—not reprinted but if they *are* still in print the following are well worth a look)
The Ha-ha Bird written and illustrated by Penelope Janie
Emma and the Captain's Cat (a Golden Pleasure Book)
Weatherwise and I can See You (a Golden Pleasure Book)
Peter and the Wolf Sergei Prokofiev, illustrated by Jiri Trinka
Happytime Series (Golden Pleasure Books)
Jack's Adventure Edith Thatcher Hurd
Puss in Boots (retold by Kathryn Jackson)
The Little Red Hen   *Old Macdonald Had a Farm*
The Happy Little Whale

Pondus the Penguin (a Golden Pleasure Book)   written and photographed by Ivar Myrhøj

HARRAP
Mr Crankle's Taxi written and illustrated by Jane Paton
Pickle and Pepper and the Sea Monster written and illustrated by Robert Barrat
Shen-ti's Dragon Kay King, illustrated by Penelope Jackson
Pink-Abu and the Rockett written and illustrated by Robert Barrat
The Magic Boots written and illustrated by Penelope Jackson

HART–DAVIS
First Folk Tales (retold) Mollie Clarke
The Remarkable Rat—from India
Silly Simon—from England
Momotaro—from Japan
Little Mother Lime-tree—from Russia
Rabbit and Fox—from Canada
The Three Feathers—from Germany

HEINEMANN
   The Quangle Wangle's Hat　Edward Lear, illustrated by Helen Oxenbury

HUTCHINSON
   Hutchinson Junior Books
   Ronald and the Wizard Calico　Emmanuele Luzzati
   The Story of the Green Bus　J. Chalon
   The Flying Steam Roller　J. Chalon

LONGMANS (cf. also Longman Young Books)
   Reading by Rhythm
   My Blue Book—four stories to read
   My Red Book—four stories to read
   My Green Book—four stories to read
   My Yellow Book—four stories to read
   My Orange Book—four stories to read
   All by Jenny Taylor and Terry Inglesby

LONGMAN YOUNG BOOKS
   The Sea Monkey (a picture story from Malaysia)　Geraldine Kay, illustrated by Gay Galsworthy
   Nuki and the Sea Serpent (a Maori story)　Ruth Park, illustrated by Zelma Balkely
   The Tomten (adapted)　Astrid Lindgren, illustrated by Harold Wiberg
   The Fox and the Tomten (adapted)　Astrid Lindgren
   The Adventure of Tommy　written and illustrated by H. G. Wells
   The Great Automobile Club　Michael O'Leary, illustrated by John Haslam
   A Penny to see the Pier　Michael O'Leary, illustrated by John Haslam
   Mrs Cockle's Cat　Philippa Pearce
   Away in a Manger　M. Nussbaumer
   The Snow Queen by Hans Andersen (adapted)　Naomi Lewis, illustrated by Tom Bogdanovic
   Paul, the Hero of the Fire　Edward Ardizzone
   Little Hedgehog　Gina Ruck-Pauquet, illustrated by M. Richter

   Value Books
   Three Little Cats　Anna Standon, illustrated by Edwards Standon, also
   Little Duck Lost　　*A Flower for Ambrose*

   Adolphus the TV Horse　Lois Castellain
   Ben Goes to the City　Antony Maitland
   The Little Girl and the Tiny Doll　Aingeld Ardizzone
   Phewtus the Squirrel　V. H. Drummond
   Richard Goes Sailing　Janet Duchesne
   Jack and the Beanstalk　William Stobbs

How Edward Saved St George   Delia Huddy
Snow White and Rose Red   Barbara Cooney
Sarah and Simon and No Red Paint   Edward Ardizzone

MACDONALD

Monsieur Bussy—The Celebrated Hamster   Pascal-Claude Lafontaine, illustrated by Annick Delhumeau
The Magic Fish   Maria Francesca Gagliardi, illustrated by Stepan Zavrel
Ferdi and Ferdinand   Gunter Spang, illustrated by Beata Rose

METHUEN

Bruna Books by Dick Bruna
Red Riding Hood   Snow White   Cinderella   Hop-o'-my-thumb

The Giant Alexander
The Giant Alexander and the Circus
The Giant Alexander in America
The Giant Alexander and Hannibal the Elephant
All by F. Hermann and illustrated by George Him

Little Spook   Inge and Lasse Sandberg
The Three Robbers   Tomi Ungerer
Crictor   Tomi Ungerer
Little Owl   Reiner Zimmik and Homne Axman

The *Babar* Books by Jean de Brunhoff
The Story of Babar the Little Elephant   Babar at Home
Babar's Travels   Babar the King
Babar and Father Christmas   Babar's Friend Zephir

Little Babar Books by Jean and Laurent de Brunhoff
Babar's Childhood   Babar and the Old Lady
Babar's Coronation   Babar's Balloon Trip
Babar's Kingdom   Long Live King Babar
Babar's Children   Babar and the Crocodile
Babar Goes Ski-ing   Babar at the Circus
Also the *Adventures of Babar on Television*   Laurent de Brunhoff
Babar goes visiting   Babar learns to drive   Babar Keeps Fit!

Harry's Bee   Peter Campbell
Serafina the Giraffe   Laurent de Brunhoff
Serafina's Lucky Find   Laurent de Brunhoff
Captain Serafina   Laurent de Brunhoff
Three Men Went to Work   Leila Berg and Dorothy Clark
Bill the Bus Conductor   Miki the Mechanic   Bert the Builder

Look Around Books by Alain Grée
I Know about Colours   I Know about Counting

Methuen—*contd.*

I Know about Flowers   *I Know about Travel*
I Know about Our World   *I Know about Cars*
Find the Yellow Chicken   *Find the Goldfish*
Flat Stanley   Jeff Brown, illustrated by Tomi Ungerer
Little Hippo   Christine Chagnoux
Frances Face-Maker   William Cole, illustrated by Tomi Ungerer

MULLER

Muller's Junior Reading (not outstandingly lively, but better than reading primers)
Will You Carry Me?   E. W. Chandler / M. Seltzer
The Perky Little Engine   *Johnny and the Monarch*
Lucky and the Giant   *The Man Who Walked Round the World*
Ekorn the Squirrel   *Next Door to Laura Linda*
Who Was Tricked?

NELSON

See How They Grow Series (with photographs)
Galahad the Guinea Pig   *Dinah the Dove*
Percy the Parrot   *Poppet the Pup*
Hannibal the Hamster   *Let's grow a Hyacinth*
Patrick the Piglet   *Kahi the Lamb*
Twitter the Tit   *Teresa the Tortoise*
Snuffle the Hedgehog   *Velvet the Kitten*

The *Candy* Books by Gwyneth Mamlock
Candy and Ginger   *Candy and the Pony*
Candy and Peppermint   *Candy and the Rocking Horse*
Candy at the Tower   *Candy and the Golden Eagle*
The Sun Shone on the Elephant   Gwyneth Mamlock

Favourite Books in 'easy-to-read type' including
Aladdin   *Ali Baba*   *Dick Whittington*   *The Snow Queen*
Robin Hood
Reading with Winnie-the-Pooh (adapted) Rosemary Garland, from original stories by A. A. Milne, Walt Disney illustrations
Pooh's Book   *Piglet's Book*   *Tigger's Book*
Eeyore's Book   *Rabbit's Book*   *Christopher Robin's Book*

OLIVER & BOYD

The Picnic   Edith Unnerstad, illustrated by Ylvä Kalström
Mrs Popplecorn   N. Werner

OXFORD UNIVERSITY PRESS

The Sea Horse Frans van Anrooy, illustrated by Jaap Tol
The Sleeping Beauty (story by Brothers Grimm) illustrated by Felix Hoffmann, translated by Peter Collier
The Three Poor Tailors Victor G. Ambrus
The Brave Soldier Janos Victor G. Ambrus
Little Red Riding Hood (retold) Bernardette Watts
The Wolf and the Seven Little Kids (stories by Brothers Grimm) illustrated by Felix Hoffman
The Two Windmills Maryke Reesink
Gennarino Nichola Simbari
Freddy the Fell Engine Peter Walsh, illustrated by Papas

The *Tim* Books by Edward Ardizzone:

Little Tim and the Brave Sea Captain   *Tim All Alone*
Tim and Ginger   *Tim and Charlotte*
Tim and Lucy Go to Sea   *Tim's Friend Towser*
Tim in Danger   *Tim to the Rescue*
Tim to the Lighthouse
Also
Nicholas and the Fast-Moving Diesel   *Johnny the Clockmaker*
Peter the Wanderer

The *Wildsmith* Fables La Fontaine
The Lion and the Rat   *The North Wind and the Sun*
The Hare and the Tortoise   *The Rich Man and the Shoemaker*
The Miller, the Boy and the Donkey

PENGUIN—PICTURE PUFFINS

Captain Pugwash John Ryan
The Happy Lion Louise Fatio / Roger Duvoisin
Paul, the Hero of the Fire Edward Ardizzone
Sam, Bangs and Moonshine Evaline Ness
The Story of the Three Little Pigs illustrated by William Stobbs

SCHOLASTIC PUBLICATIONS (cf. list 'A')

Particularly recommended:
The Man Who Didn't Wash His Dishes Phyllis Krasilovsky, illustrated by Barbara Cooney
The Five Chinese Brothers Claire Hachet Bishop and Kurt Wiese
Six Foolish Fishermen Benjamin Elkin, illustrated by Bernice Myers
The Country Cat written and illustrated by Norman Bridwell
The Three Wishes (retold) M. Jean Craig, illustrated by Rosalind Fry
Mickey's Magnet Franklyn M. Branley and Eleanor K. Vaughan
Little Bear Else Holmelund Minarik, illustrated by Maurice Sendak

Scholastic Publications—*contd.*
  Silly Sam   Leonore Klein, illustrated by Harvey Weiss
  What's Inside (the story of an egg that hatched, with real photographs)
  Mary Garelick, photographs by Rena Jakebsen

SPHERE BOOKS
  The General   Janet Charters/Michael Forman
  Madeline Books   L. Bemelmans
  Ivor the Engine   O. Postgate

TULL GRAPHICS
  (This Company have published the following lively and attractive
  fantasy series. The educational distributors are E. Arnold & Son.)
  Story 1. *Tully Grully Grumble*
  Story 2. *Fluff*
  Story 3. *Hughie Bluey*
  Story 4. *Prickle*
  Story 5. *Dripple*
  (All these stories about 'The Land of Grot' are by C. Rapley).

WARD LOCKE
  Jacky's Trip to the Moon

WARNE & CO.[1]
  The *Peter Rabbit* Books by Beatrix Potter
  * *The Tale of Peter Rabbit*
  The Tale of Squirrel Nutkin
  The Tailor of Gloucester
  * *The Tale of Benjamin Bunny*
  * *The Tale of Two Bad Mice*
  * *The Tale of Mrs Tiggy Winkle*
  * *The Tale of Mr Jeremy Fisher*
  * *The Tale of Tom Kitten*
  * *The Tale of Jemima Puddleduck*
  * *The Tale of the Flopsy Bunnies*
  * *The Tale of Mrs Tittlemouse and others*

WHEATON
  The Little Bi-Plane   *The Blue Bus*   *Said the Hen to the Chick*
  Angelo and Toni
  All by Jane Kriss / Liel Stich

  The Little Night People   August Kopisch, illustrated by Herbert Lentz

  [1] The asterisked titles are also printed in i.t.a.

Susan's Family   Christel Sussman
Breakfast at the Zoo
A Holiday with Henriette
Michael At Work

WORLD'S WORK
I Can Read Books
All suitable for 'B' list children—there are 82 books in this series, all simply written and attractively illustrated:

The *Mother Goose* Library
(All illustrated by Peter Spier (cf. list 'A'). These would also be suitable for list 'B' children)

The Goblin Under the Stairs   Mary Calhouse, illustrated by Janet McCaffery
Hailstones and Halibut Bones   Mary O'Neil, illustrated by Leonard Weisgard
Maurice Goes to Sea   Leon Harris, illustrated by Joseph Schindelman

Science 'I Can Read' Books
There are several Science Books in this series including
The Bug that laid the Golden Eggs (with real photographs)   Millicent Selsam
Where Does the Butterfly Go When It Rains?   Mary Garelick, illustrated by Leonard Weisgard
Terry and the Caterpillars   Millicent Selsam, illustrated by A. Lobel
Greg's Microscope   Millicent Selsam, illustrated by A. Lobel
Potatoes, Potatoes   A. Lobel

World's Work offer a very wide selection of *Picture Story* Books as well as the *I Can Read* Series including
The Cow Who Fell in the Canal   Phyllis Krasilovsky, illustrated by Peter Spier
Amelia Bedelia   Peggy Parish, illustrated by Fritz Siebel
Sad Day, Glad Day   Vivian L. Thompson, illustrated by Lilian Obligado
Sir Kevin of Devon (in verse)   Adelaide Hull, illustrated by Leonard Weisgard
The King Who Was Too Busy   Eugene Fern
When Will My Birthday Be?   Letta Schatz, illustrated by Richard Bergere
Little Toot   Hardie Gramatky
Little Toot by the Grand Canal   Hardie Gramatky
Little Toot on the Thames   Hardie Gramatky
Hide and Seek Fog   Alvin Tresselt, illustrated by Roger Duvoisin
Georgie and the Magician and *Georgie's Halloween*   Robert Bright
(Georgie is a friendly little ghost)

World's work—*contd.*

Wobble the Witch Cat   Mary Calhoun, illustrated by Roger Duvoisin
The Goblin Under the Stairs   Mary Calhoun, illustrated by Janet McCaffey
Spring Snow   written and illustrated by Roger Duvoisin
Where in the World Do You Live?   Al Hine, illustrated by John Allcorn
The Sorely Trying Day   Russell Hoban, illustrated by Lillian Hoban
Too Much Noise   Ann McGovern, illustrated by Simmo Taback
Kiki Dances   written and illustrated by Charlott Steiner (there are five other Kiki Books)
Someday   Gene Zion, illustrated by Arnold Lobel

References[1]

Anderson, I. H. and Dearborn, W. F. (1952) *The Psychology of Teaching Reading* The Ronald Press, New York

Ashton-Warner, S. (1963) *Teacher* Secker & Warburg; Penguin Books 1966

Bereiter, C. E. (1965) 'Academic Instruction for Pre-school Children' in *Language Programs for the Disadvantaged* ed. J. Corbin, NCTE pp. 195–203

Bereiter, C. E. and Englemann, S. (1966) *Teaching Disadvantaged Children in the Pre-school* Prentice-Hall, Englewood Cliffs, New Jersey

Bernstein, B. B. (1958) 'Some Sociological Determinants of Perception' *British Journal of Sociology* vol. 9, 159–74

Bernstein, B. B. (1959) 'A Public Language: Some Sociological Implications of Linguistic Form' *British Journal of Sociology* vol. 10, 311–26

Bernstein, B. B. (1960) 'Language and Social Class' *British Journal of Sociology* vol. 11, 271–6

Bernstein, B. B. (1961) 'Social Structure: Language and Learning' *Educational Research* vol. 3, 163–76

Bernstein, B. B. (1962a) 'Linguistic Codes, Hesitation Phenomena and Intelligence' *Language and Speech* vol. 5, 31–46

Bernstein, B. B. (1962b) 'Social Class, Linguistic Codes and Grammatical Elements' *Language and Speech* vol. 5, 221–40

Bernstein, B. B. (1964) 'Family role systems, socialisation and communication' Paper given at the Conference on Cross-cultural Research into Childhood and Adolescence, Chicago

Bernstein, B, B. (1965) 'A Socio-Linguistic Approach to Social Learning' *Penguin Survey of the Social Sciences*, ed. J. Gould, Penguin Books, pp. 144–68

Bowlby, J. (1953) *Child Care and the Growth of Love* Penguin Books

Brimer, M. A. (1967) 'An Experimental Evaluation of Coded Scripts in Initial Reading' *New Research in Education* vol. 1, 124–30

Britton, J. (1970) *Language and Learning* Allen Lane The Penguin Press; Penguin Books, 1972

Brown, Amy L. (ed.) (1967) *Reading: Current Research and Practice* vol. 1 Chambers for United Kingdom Reading Association

Burt, C. (1931) *The Backward Child* University of London Press (rev. edn 1961)

---

[1] Also included are some titles not mentioned in the text which have been published since this survey was written.

Cane, B. S. (1966) 'A Review of Recent Research on Reading and Related Topics with a Select Bibliography' Appendix E in Joyce M. Morris *Standards and Progress in Reading* NFER

Cass, Joan (1967) *Literature and the Young Child* Longman

Chall, Jeanne S. (1967) *Learning to Read: the great debate; an inquiry into the science, art and ideology of old and new methods of teaching children to read, 1910–1965* McGraw-Hill, New York

Chazan, M. (1962) 'School Phobia' *British Journal of Educational Psychology* vol. 32, 209–17

Colwell, E. (1964) *A Guide to Reading for the Under Fives* Kenneth Mason, Havant

Corbin, R. K. ed. (1965) *Language Programs for the Disadvantaged* NCTE

Creber, J. W. P. (1972) *Lost for Words* Penguin Books

Daniels, J. C. and Diack, H. (1956) *Progress in Reading* University of Nottingham Institute of Education

Dean, J. (1966) 'Words in Colour' in *Second International Reading Symposium* ed. J. Downing and A. L. Brown, Cassell

Denver Public Schools (1962) *Report on the effectiveness of parents in helping their pre-school children to begin to read* Denver Public Schools, Denver, Colorado

Diack, H. (1960) *Reading and the Psychology of Perception* Ray Palmer, Nottingham

Dixon, J. (1969) *Growth Through English* Oxford University Press for NATE (2nd rev. edn)

Downing, J. (1963) 'Is a Mental Age of Six Essential for Reading Readiness?' *Educational Research* vol. 6, 16–28

Downing, J. (1967) *The i.t.a. Symposium—Research Report on the British Experiment with i.t.a.* NFER

Downing, J. (1967) *Evaluating the Initial Teaching Alphabet* Cassell

Downing, J. (1968a) 'Should Today's Children Start Reading Earlier?' *Third International Reading Symposium*, ed. J. Downing and A. L. Brown, Cassell

Downing, J. (1968b) 'Today's Major Problem Group—Socially Disadvantaged Children' in *Third International Reading Symposium*, ed. J. Downing and A. L. Brown, Cassell

Downing, J. and Thackray, D. V. (1971) *Reading Readiness* University of London Press

Douglas, J. W. B. (1964) *The Home and the School* MacGibbon & Kee

Durkin, D. (1961) 'Children who Learned to Read at Home' *Elementary School Journal* vol. 62, 15–18

Durkin, D. (1963) 'Children who read before grade 1: a second study' *Elementary School Journal* vol. 64, 143–8

Fisher, Margery (1961) *Intent upon Reading* Brockhampton Press

Fisher, Margery (1965) *Open the Door* Brockhampton Press

Fisher, Margery *Growing Point*—a review of books for children (9 issues a year)

Flesch, R. (1955) *Why Johnny Can't Read* Harper, New York

Floud, J. N., Halsey, A. H. and Martin, F. M. (1956) *Social Class and Educational Opportunity* Heinemann

France, N. (1964) 'The Use of Group Tests of Ability and Attainment' *British Journal of Educational Psychology* vol. 34, 19–33

Friedlander, Kate (1958) 'Children's Books and their Function in Latency and Pre-puberty' *New Era* vol. 39, 77–83

Frost, J. L. and Hawkes, G. R. (1962) *The Disadvantaged Child* Houghton Mifflin, Boston

Fry, E. (1967) 'The Diacritical Marking System and a Preliminary Comparison with i.t.a.' *Second International Reading Symposium*, ed. J. Downing and A. L. Brown, Cassell

Gardner, K. (1966–7) 'Early Reading—Some Personal Thoughts' *United Kingdom Reading Association* vol. 1, 71–5

Gardner, K. (1966) *Towards Literacy: an Introduction to the Teaching of Reading* Blackwell, Oxford

Gattegno, C. (1962a) *Words in Colour: Background and Principles* Educational Explorers, Reading

Gattegno, C. (1962b) *Words in Colour: Teacher's Guide* Educational Explorers, Reading

Gattegno, C. (1969) *Reading with Words in Colour: A Scientific Study of the Problems of Reading* Educational Explorers, Reading

Georgiades, N. (1968) 'The Testing of Reading Today' *Third International Reading Symposium*, ed. J. Downing and A. L. Brown, Cassell

Gill, W. S. and K. (1952) *The Phonic Side of Reading* Cassell

Goddard, N. L. (1964) *Reading in the Modern Infants' School* University of London Press

Goldman-Eisler, F. (1954) 'On the variability of the speed of talking and on its relation to the length of utterance in conversations' *British Journal of Psychology* vol. 45, 94–107

Goldman-Eisler, F. (1961) 'Hesitation and Information in Speech' *Proceedings of the Fourth London Symposium on Information Theory, 1960* Butterworth

Goodacre, E. (1967) *Reading in Infant Classes* NFER

Goodacre, E. (1968) *Teachers and their Pupils' Home Background* NFER

Gray, W. A. (1956) *The Teaching of Reading and Writing—An International Survey* (UNESCO) Evans

Greenwood, G. (1969) 'Wolverhampton Remedial Teaching Service' in *Aspects of Educational Technology*, vol. 2, ed. W. R. Dunn and C. Holroyd, Methuen

Griffiths, Ruth (1935) *A Study of Imagination in Early Childhood* Kegan Paul

Halliday, M. A. K. (1967) 'Linguistics and the Teaching of English' *Talking and Writing*, ed. James Britton, Methuen

Harris, A. J. (1959) 'Visual and Auditory Perception in Learning to Read' *Optometric Weekly* October 2115–21

Hermelin, B. and O'Connor, N. (1960) 'Reading ability and severely subnormal children' *Journal of Mental Deficiency Research* vol. 4, part 2, 144–7

Hess, R. D. and Shipman, V. (1965) 'Early Blocks to Children's Learning, *Children* vol. 12, 189–94

Hillman, H. (1956) 'The Effect of Laterality upon Reading Ability' *Durham Research Review* no. 7, 86–96

Holbrook, D. (1967) *The Exploring Word* Cambridge University Press

Holmes, J. A. C. (1962) 'When should and could Johnny learn to read?' in *Challenge and Experiment in Reading* Scholastic Magazines, New York

Holt, J. (1964) *How Children Fail* Pitman; Penguin Books 1969

Holt, J. (1967) *How Children Learn* Pitman

Huey, E. B. (1968) *Psychology and Pedagogy of Reading* MIT Press, Cambridge, Mass.

Isaacs, Susan (1932) *The Children We Teach* University of London Press

Jensen, A. C. (1967–8) 'The Culturally Disadvantaged: Psychological and Educational Aspects' *Educational Research* vol. 10, 4–20

Jones, A. and Mulford, J. eds (1972) *Children Using Language* Oxford University Press for NATE

Jones, J. K. (1967) *The Nineteen Stories* (Colour Story Reading) Nelson

Jones, J. K. (1967) *Colour Story Reading Research Report* Nelson

Kelley, M. L. (1965) 'Reading in the Kindergarten', in *Reading and Inquiry* International Reading Association, Newark, Delaware

Kemp, L. C. D. (1955) 'Environmental and other characteristics determining attainment in primary schools' *British Journal of Educational Psychology* vol. 25, 67–77

Kirk, S. A. (1965) 'Language, Intelligence and the Educability of the Disadvantaged' *Language Programs for the Disadvantaged*, ed. R. K. Corbin, NCTE, pp. 250–67

Labov, W. (1972) 'The Logic of Nonstandard English' in *Language and Social Context* ed. P. P. Giglioli, Penguin Books

Latham, W. (1968) 'Are today's teachers adequately trained for the teaching of reading?' *The Third International Reading Symposium*, ed. J. Downing and A. L. Brown, Cassell

Lawton, D. (1968) *Social Class, Language and Education* (International Library of Sociology and Social Reconstruction) Routledge & Kegan Paul

Lee, W. R. (1960) *Spelling Irregularity and Reading Difficulty in English*, NFER

Lewis, Naomi (1965–9) *The Best Children's Books of 1964, 1965, 1966, 1967* Hamish Hamilton

Lines, K. M. (1956) *Four to Fourteen: A Library of Books for Children* National Book League

Loban, W. (1963) *The Language of Elementary School Children* (Research Report 1) NCTE, Champaign, Illinois

Lovell, K. *et al.* (1964) 'A study of some cognitive and other disabilities in backward readers of average intelligence as assessed by a non-verbal test' *British Journal of Educational Psychology* vol. 34, 58–64

Luria, A. R. (1959) *Speech and the Development of Mental Processes in the Child* Staples Press

Lynn, R. (1963) 'Reading Readiness and the Perceptual Abilities of Young Children' *Educational Research*, vol. 6, 10–15

Mackay, D. and Thompson, B. (1968) *The Initial Teaching of Reading and Writing* (Programme in Linguistics and English Teaching, Paper 3) Longman

Mackay, D., Thompson, B. and Schaub, P. (1970) *Breakthrough to Literacy* Longman for Schools Council

Malmquist, E. (1958) *Factors relating to reading disabilities in the first grade of the Elementary School* Almqvist & Wiksell, Stockholm, see also *Educational Research* vol. 1, 1958, 68–79

Martin, J. H. *Freeport Public Schools Experiment on Early Reading Using the Edison Responsive Environment Instrument* Englewood Cliffs, New Jersey (REC reprint)

Mason, G. E. and Prater, N. J. (1966) 'Early Reading and Reading Instruction' *Elementary English* vol. 43, 483–8 and 527

Merei, F. (1949) 'Group Leadership and Institutionalization' *Human Relations* vol. 2, 22–39

Merrit, J. ed. (1970) *Reading and the Curriculum* United Kingdom Reading Association

Ministry of Education (1957) *Standards of Reading 1948–56* Pamphlet No. 32, HMSO

Moore, O. K. (1963) *Auto-Responsive Environments and Exceptional Children* Responsive Environments Foundation, Connecticut

Morris, Joyce M. (1958) 'Teaching children to read: The relative effectiveness of different methods of teaching reading (A) The place and value of phonics (B) The place and value of whole word methods' *Educational Research* vol. 1, 38–49 and 61–75

Morris, Joyce M. (1959) *Reading in the Primary School* NFER

Morris, Joyce M. (1966) *Standards and Progress in Reading* NFER

Morris, Ronald (1963) *Success and Failure in Learning to Read* Oldbourne

Morris, Ronald (1968) 'Today's Children' *The Third International Reading Symposium*, ed. J. Downing and A. L. Brown, Cassell

Moseley, D. V. (1970) *English Colour Code Programmed Reading Course* The National Society for Mentally Handicapped Children

Moyle, D. (1968) *The Teaching of Reading* Ward Lock Educational

Moyle D. and L. M. (1971) *Modern Innovations in the Teaching of Reading* University of London Press

National Book League (1971) *Background to Children's Books: A Book List* NBL

Olson, W. C. (1940) 'Reading as a function of the total growth of the child' *Reading and Pupil Development* Suppl. Educ. Monographs no. 51 Cambridge University Press

Olson, W. C. (1959) *Child Development* D. C. Heath, Boston, Mass. (2nd edn)

Piaget, Jean (1959) *The Language and Thought of the Child* Routledge & Kegan Paul (3rd edn)

Pickard, P. M. (1961) *I Could a Tale Unfold*, Tavistock Publications

Pidgeon, D. A. and Yates, A. (1959) 'Social background and educational progress—a longitudinal study of a nationally representative sample of children' Paper given at the Annual Conference of the British Psychological Society Cambridge

Pfau, D. W. (1967) 'The Effects of Planned Recreational Reading Programmes' *The Reading Teacher* vol. 21, 34–9

Pringle, L. Kellmer and Bossio, V. (1965) 'Language development and reading attainment of deprived children' *Deprivation and Education*, ed. L. Kellmer Pringle, Longman

Rambusch, N. McCormick (1962) *Learning How to Learn—An American Approach to Montessori* Helican Press

Reeves, Ruth (1966) *The Teaching of Reading in Our Schools* (sponsored by NCTE) Macmillan, New York

Robinson, Helen (1964) 'The Role of Auditory Perception in Reading' in *The First International Reading Symposium*, ed. J. Downing, Cassell

Rosenheim, E. W. (1967) 'Children's Reading and Adults' Values' in *A Critical Approach to Children's Literature* University of Chicago Press, Chicago and London

Russell, David H. (1949) *Children Learn to Read* Ginn, Boston and London

Sanders, Jacquelyn (1967) 'The Psychological significance of Children's Literature' in *A Critical Approach to Children's Literature* ed. S. I. Fenwick University of Chicago Press, Chicago and London

Sanderson, A. E. (1963) 'The Idea of Reading Readiness—A Re-examination' *Educational Research* vol. 6, 3–9

Sceats, J. (1967) *i.t.a. and the Teaching of Literacy* Bodley Head

Schonell, F. J. and Schonell, P. E. (1950) *Diagnostic and Attainment Testing* Oliver & Boyd, Edinburgh

Schonell, F. J. (1945) *The Psychology and Teaching of Reading* Oliver & Boyd, Edinburgh (revised 1961)

Schools Council (1965) *English: A Programme for Research and Development in English Teaching* (Working Paper No. 3) HMSO

School Library Association (1962) *Using Books in the Primary School* School Library Association

School Librarian and *School Library Review* Published three times a year School Library Association

Shaw, J. H. (1964) 'Vision and seeing skills of pre-school children' *Reading Teacher* vol. 18, 33–6

Sheldon, W. D. and Carrillo, L. (1952) 'The relation of parents, home and certain developmental characteristics to children's reading ability' *Elementary School Journal* vol. 52, 262–70

Skeels, H. M. *et al.* (1938) 'A study of environmental stimulation: an orphan-age pre-school project' *Studies in Child Welfare* vol. 15, no. 4 University of Iowa

Smith, Nila Banton (1963) *Reading Instruction for Today's Children*, Prentice-Hall, Englewood Cliffs, New Jersey

Southgate, Vera (1965) 'Approaching i.t.a. results with caution' *Educational Research* vol. 7, 83–96

Southgate, Vera (1967) 'Early Reading' in *Reading: Current Research and Practice*, ed. A. L. Brown, W. & R. Chambers

Southgate, Vera (1967) 'The Problem of Selecting an Approach to the Teaching of Reading' in *The Second International Reading Symposium*, ed. J. Downing and A. L. Brown, Cassell

Southgate, Vera (1968) 'Formulae for Beginning Reading Tuition' *Educational Research* vol. 11, 23–30

Southgate, Vera (1972) *Beginning Reading* University of London Press

Southgate, V. and Roberts, G. R. (1970) *Reading—Which Approach?* University of London Press

Spencer, Doris U. (1967) 'An Individualised v. a Basal Reader Program in Rural Communities' *Reading Teacher* vol. 21, 11–17

Standish, E. J. (1959) 'Teaching Children to read, Part II: Readiness to Read' *Educational Research* vol. 2, 29–38

Stern, Catherine and Gould, Toni S. (1965) *Children Discover Reading—An Introduction to Structural Reading* Random House/Singer

Stott, D. H. (1957) 'Physical and Mental Handicaps Following a Disturbed Pregnancy' *Lancet* vol. 1, 1006–11

Stott, D. H. (1959) 'Infantile Illness and Subsequent Mental and Emotional Development' *Journal of Genetic Psychology* vol. 94

Stott, D. H. (1962) *Programmed Reading Kit* Holmes McDougall, Edinburgh

Stott, D. H. (1964) *Roads to Literacy* Holmes McDougall, Edinburgh

Strickland, Ruth (1962) 'The Language of Elementary School Children' *Bulletin of the School of Education* University of Indiana

Sutton, M. H. (1966) 'First Grade Children who Learned to Read in Kinder-garten, *Reading Teacher* vol. 19, 192–6

Thompson, B. B. (1963) 'A Longitudinal Study of Auditory Discrimination' *Educational Research* vol. 6, 376–8

Tucker, Nicholas (1968) 'Books that Frighten' *Where?*, Supplement 15

Tudor Hart, Beatrix (1964) 'Reading and the Acquisition of Speech' in *The First International Reading Symposium* ed. J. Downing, Cassell

Vernon, M. D. (1957) *Backwardness in Reading* Cambridge University Press

Vygotsky, L. S. (1962) *Thought and Language* MIT Press Cambridge, Mass.

Warburton, F. W. and Southgate, V. (1969) *i.t.a.: An Independent Evaluation* John Murray W. & R. Chambers

Weber, Robert E. (1966) 'Early Learning and Language Arts Proficiency in Contemporary Society' Responsive Environment Corporation Englewood Cliffs, New Jersey (REC reprint)

Wepman, J. M. (1960) 'Auditory Discrimination, Speech and Reading' *Elementary School Journal* vol. 60, 325–33

White, Dorothy M. (1956) *Books Before Five* Cambridge University Press for New Zealand Council for Educational Research

Whitehead, F. (1954) 'Rival Reading Methods: A Question of Timing' *Times Educational Supplement* 21 May

Wilkinson, Andrew (1961–2) 'Trends in English Teaching' *Educational Review* vol. 14, 198–214

Wilkinson, Andrew (1965) *Spoken English* Birmingham School of Education

Wisemann, S. (1964) *Education and Environment* Manchester University Press

Wundheiler, L. (1967) 'A psychological basis for judging children's literature' in *A Critical Approach to Children's Literature* ed. S. I. Fenwick University of Chicago Press, Chicago and London

Index

018380

book is to be returned on or before
last stamped below.